Hip Hop Can Save America!

Hip Hop Studies and Activism

Anthony J. Nocella II, Daniel White Hodge, Don C. Sawyer III,
Ahmad R. Washington, and Arash Daneshzadeh

Series Editors

Vol. 5

Michael "Manny Faces" Conforti

Hip Hop Can Save America!

Inspiration For The Nation From A Culture of Innovation

PETER LANG

New York - Berlin - Bruxelles - Chennai - Lausanne - Oxford

Library of Congress Cataloging-in-Publication Data

Names: Conforti, Michael, 1972- author.
Title: Hip hop can save America! : inspiration for the nation from a
  culture of innovation / Michael "Manny Faces" Conforti.
Description: New York, NY : Peter Lang, [2025] | Series: Hip hop studies
  and activism, 2690-6872 ; Volume 5 | Includes bibliographical
  references.
Identifiers: LCCN 2025002091 (print) | LCCN 2025002092 (ebook) | ISBN
  9783034352147 (paperback) | ISBN 9783034352123 (pdf) | ISBN
  9783034352130 (epub)
Subjects: LCSH: Rap (Music)—Social aspects—United States. | Rap
  (Music)—Political aspects—United States. | Hip-hop—Influence—United
  States. | Hip-hop—Political aspects—United States. | Hip-hop—Social
  aspects—United States.
Classification: LCC ML3918.R37 C65 2025 (print) | LCC ML3918.R37 (ebook)
  | DDC 306.4/84249—dc23/eng/20250303
LC record available at https://lccn.loc.gov/2025002091
LC ebook record available at https://lccn.loc.gov/2025002092

Bibliographic information published by the Deutsche Nationalbibliothek.
The German National Library lists this publication in the German
National Bibliography; detailed bibliographic data is available
on the Internet at http://dnb.d-nb.de.

Cover design by Michael "Manny Faces" Conforti

ISSN 2690-6872 (print) ISSN 2690-6880 (online)
ISBN 9783034352147 (paperback)
ISBN 9783034352123 (ebook)
ISBN 9783034352130 (epub)
DOI 10.3726/b22732

© 2025 Peter Lang Group AG, Lausanne
Published by Peter Lang Publishing Inc., New York, USA
info@peterlang.com - www.peterlang.com

This publication has been peer reviewed.

DEDICATION

This one's for you Pops.
With eternal love and gratitude to Ma, Eve, Ta, Porsh, Ki, Miles,
Bree, and Aria.

CONTENTS

· 0 ·

INTRODUCTION

I suppose with such an audacious book title, it might make sense to start by providing some context.

Hip Hop Can Save America! is a podcast series that I launched in 2018, emerging as the latest in a series of journalistic properties I had personally developed, joining several others in which I was deeply involved. This project was intensely personal—my newest creation, entirely my own. I conceived it, developed it, booked the guests, conducted the interviews, wrote the intros, edited the audio, produced the theme song, and created the artwork—everything.

While I openly acknowledge my tendency to pontificate endlessly about Hip Hop's transformative power, this podcast was not about me. Its core mission was to illuminate the groundbreaking work of interdisciplinary innovators who masterfully incorporated Hip Hop music and culture into traditionally unrelated fields. These boundary-crossing practitioners engineered remarkable fusions of knowledge production, creating hybridized approaches that challenge conventional wisdom. Through their work, they demonstrate how Hip Hop's principles can catalyze tangible improvements in lives, livelihoods, and communities, effectively translating cultural wisdom into practical solutions that resonate far beyond traditional disciplinary confines.

We examine fundamental areas of society—education, health and well-ness, science and technology, politics and social justice, business and entre-preneurship, the fine arts, and more. What emerged through this exploration was remarkable: the purposeful, thoughtful integration of Hip Hop into these legacy fields was creating unprecedented opportunities for people to excel and thrive. Even more significantly, this transformative work remained largely unknown to the broader public.

To some readers, this entire premise might seem extraordinarily foreign, and while I believe the chapters to follow will tell the story as clearly as pos-sible, I should establish several fundamental concepts that will help guide our exploration of this book's ultimate purpose: to inspire educators, students, community leaders, parents, changemakers, businesspeople, well-meaning politicians, activists, and any member of the general citizenry seeking inno-vative approaches to address, alleviate, and potentially eliminate our most pressing societal challenges.

While my journey has evolved to encompass substantial independent scholarship, I approach these topics not as a traditional academic, but as a devoted student and chronicler of Hip Hop's transformative power. The theo-ries and background I present might appear revolutionary to some, yet merely introductory to others—and that's precisely where my role as an advocate journalist finds its purpose. Rather than providing the most rigorous academic analysis, I aim to serve as a bridge, introducing ideas that many might recog-nize anecdotally and, where possible, connecting them to traditional canon-ical frameworks.

In this endeavor, I've been privileged to collaborate with brilliant scholars and thought leaders who lend their expertise throughout this book, enriching these connections with their deep insights, gleaned from their on-the-ground experience. Yet this is Hip Hop we're discussing—a cultural force that often defies conventional academic categorization. Not everything here gets tied up neatly with a perfect academic bow, nor should it. Some scholarly lenien-cies will be required, as I frequently lead with a journalist's passionate pursuit of truth rather than the measured restraint typically expected of academic researchers. This approach allows us to explore these innovations with both the rigor they deserve and the authentic energy that Hip Hop demands.

Overall, my hope is that these preliminary insights will inspire deeper exploration. The field of Hip Hop Studies isn't theoretical or brand new—it's an established field of inquiry. Similarly, the capacity of Hip Hop to posi-tively influence academia, healthcare, technology, commerce, and human interaction has been demonstrated repeatedly, to varying degrees. There are plenty of receipts. I've worked diligently to ensure that each focus area within this book can be supported by substantial literature, enabling readers to pursue deeper understanding of their particular interests.

But as previously noted, a major impediment to looking toward these examples for inspiration, is that many remain unaware that this type of work even exists in the first place. So we should start here, by providing some of the background that readers should consider as they approach this book and its larger America-saving thesis. Again, to some, this may be preaching to the choir. To others, these concepts might be epiphanies.

The first one is the big one: Hip Hop is a culture of innovation.

#ForTheCulture

The Merriam-Webster dictionary defines "culture" as "the customary beliefs, social forms, and material traits of a racial, religious, or social group." It further adds that "culture" represents "the set of values, conventions, or social practices associated with a particular field, activity, or societal characteristic."

To many, Hip Hop is simply a genre of music, often referred to simply as "rap." While Hip Hop—the genre—is indeed synonymous with rap music, rap music is but one aspect of Hip Hop—the culture. To wit, Merriam-Webster defines "Hip Hop" as "a cultural movement associated especially with rap music," which makes sense, as people who consider themselves connected to Hip Hop do, in fact, adhere to a set of beliefs, social forms, and material traits. A main throughline of this book, however, is that the general public has a very limited understanding of what those actually are, and might be surprised to learn that, in their entirety, they represent a full-fledged culture, just as worthy of study, dissection, critique, praise, and advocacy as any other social or cultural movement throughout history.

This sentiment is echoed by institutions of higher education who also denote Hip Hop as a culture and have incorporated Hip Hop coursework, fellowships, and archives into their hallowed halls—institutions including Yale University, Harvard University, Cornell University, Howard University, The Ohio State University, Georgia State University, The University of Wisconsin, and many more. Loyola University in New Orleans offers a Bachelor of Science in Hip Hop and R&B. The Peabody Conservatory at Johns Hopkins University offers a Bachelor of Music in Hip Hop. Long-standing cultural institutions recognize Hip Hop's significance as well, including The Smithsonian

Institution, The John F. Kennedy Center for the Performing Arts, Carnegie Hall, and the American Museum of Natural History. This understanding is global, evidenced by the existence of venues such as La Place: Centre Culturel hip-hop de la Ville de Paris, initiatives like the Heal The Hood project in South Africa, and Die Urbane: Eine HipHop Partei, a German political party based on Hip Hop values.

Perhaps most importantly, Hip Hop is considered a culture by its cultural participants. The very essence of Hip Hop's cultural legitimacy manifests in the profound sense of belonging expressed by those who claim it as their own philosophical, spiritual, or social identity, regardless of their connection to any form of artistic output. Just as one need not be a ceremonial dancer to be part of Indigenous cultures or a master chef to claim Italian heritage, Hip Hop's cultural authenticity is validated through the lived experiences and conscious identification of its adherents. What we witness in Hip Hop is the embodiment of what anthropologists term "cultural self-determination"— where the act of claiming cultural membership, understanding its values, and living within its philosophical framework constitutes legitimate participation. This truth resonates deeply with my own journey of cultural understanding, as well as countless other individuals who embody Hip Hop's core principles in their daily lives.

This brings to mind what Dr. Toby Jenkins has called a "Hip Hop mindset,"[1] a uniquely radical lens through which one sees the world, consistently challenging established realities while embracing the art of resourceful reinvention. Drawing from the culture's oft-lauded principle of "making something from nothing," those who internalize Hip Hop's worldview often develop an extraordinary capacity to perceive unconventional solutions that others might overlook. This perspective, born from the culture's legacy which produced turntables as instruments, public parks as concert halls, and street corners as universities, cultivates a distinctive problem-solving methodology that thrives on creative recontextualization.

When applied to fields ranging from education to healthcare to technology to entrepreneurship, this Hip Hop-informed mindset manifests as a powerful tool for innovative thought. The culture's emphasis on "remixing" doesn't just suggest alternative solutions—it fundamentally restructures how problems themselves are perceived and approached.

We're going to explore several examples of what this looks like in practice throughout this book, across several disciplines. Most will focus on direct, interdisciplinary integrations of Hip Hop music, culture, and spirit into fields and institutions that have often been quite resistant to change or modern-ization. We will hear directly from practitioners who have incorporated Hip Hop into their work, their testimonies documenting how these innovations have directly impacted and improved lives, particularly, but not exclusively, the lives of young people from communities that have been historically under-served, under-resourced, and under-loved by the proverbial powers that be.

All of which leads to the second big concept I would ask that you keep in mind as you allow me to lead you on this journey, one which closely mirrors the one I myself took to arrive at this place of optimism and advocacy: Hip Hop really can help save America.

This Is America

Back to the audacious book title. Suggesting that something can "save America" implies many things. First, it implies that America needs saving. Considering the messaging of the 2024 U.S. presidential election cycle, and the extraordinary focus, from both major party lines, on the need to "protect our democracy," it can certainly be argued that regardless of your political affiliation, you probably felt as if the country needs saving.

Many still do.

Still, the podcast, and by extension, this book, aren't necessarily partisan. The question really becomes, "Well, what does America need saving from?"

To me, and therefore what the premise of the podcast became, was pri-marily to examine areas in which the application of Hip Hop music, culture, and spirit was showing promise in saving America from its own legacy set of deep-rooted disparities, namely racial and class divides across areas such as education, healthcare, the economy, and interpersonal relationships, and how reducing or removing those disparities could help lift the country toward its storied, yet still wholly unrealized potential.

This book will demonstrate ways in which the vast social and cultural movement known as Hip Hop can indeed inspire inclusive, loving, caring, innovative ways of correcting those long-standing chasms of inequity—even as we grapple with the thought that this isn't necessarily what everyone in America wants.

For those that do, the third and final point to consider throughout this journey is that saving America through Hip Hop won't look (or sound) any-thing like what most people think.

They Reminisce Over You

In October 2016, a 35-year-old man died in Las Vegas.

A week later, a memorial event at an iconic New York City performance venue overflowed with people paying tribute to this man.

He was, among other things, a musician, songwriter, recording artist, and activist. Those who spoke in his honor included fellow activists who had worked alongside him to combat human rights violations in places like Cuba and Palestine. Others were members of Justice League NYC and Copwatch, organizations he had partnered with to help address police brutality and discriminatory law enforcement practices. Many in attendance were his musical comrades, including a collective of rap artists who pledged to continue the public performance series he founded—one that entertains tens of thousands of people annually at no cost.

This man's disdain for injustice manifested not only through his music but through his actions. He invited criminal justice reform organizations to staff information tables at album release parties. He marched through New York streets, standing arm in arm with other artists and protesters in response to the death of Eric Garner, the Staten Island man who died while being forcibly apprehended by members of the New York Police Department. He contacted organizations on the ground in Ferguson, Missouri, to coordinate New York-based protests in response to the police killing of eighteen-year-old Michael Brown.

At his memorial, friends and collaborators spoke of his unwavering optimism and inspirational energy. "He saved my life," said one. "He helped me find my purpose," said another. Dozens of people from various disciplines and walks of life spoke emotionally about the positive impact this man had made in their personal and professional lives.

The man's name is Daniel "Majesty" Sanchez, and he touched these lives through Hip Hop.

Majesty's is one of countless significant Hip Hop-related stories from around the world that remain untold. No major media outlets covered his memorial—Hip Hop or otherwise. No mainstream rap superstars paid homage. There were no radio station tributes, despite him residing in the city where once-influential station Hot 97 purported to be "Where Hip-Hop Lives."

Yet, to the hundreds directly affected and the thousands throughout the world who collectively mourned this notable man's loss, Majesty *personified* Hip Hop.

He is among the first people I think of when I hear critics decry the substance, lack of talent, authenticity, or activism in "today's Hip Hop." He quickly comes to mind when those unfamiliar with the genre's depth degrade it, dismissing any notion that it could contain more than misogynistic, vice-riddled, self-destructive, talentless drivel.

These elements do exist in Hip Hop. Yet knowing what Majesty and countless others across multiple disciplines have accomplished utilizing Hip Hop music, culture, and spirit in ways far removed from the corporate-controlled rap music industrial complex, we must consider: Inasmuch as it has influenced music, radio, popular culture, fashion, and advertising to create industries and benefit commerce, can we afford to ignore Hip Hop's potential to positively influence other areas such as education, healthcare, technology, politics, entrepreneurship, fine arts, and spirituality in ways that benefit the citizens of the nation that birthed it?

As I've already hinted, I found the answer to be a resounding, "No!"

I came to this realization many years ago during my time as founder and editor-in-chief of *Birthplace Magazine*, an online publication I launched to document Hip Hop music and culture in and around the New York Metropolitan area.

While other media outlets chased flash-in-the-pan trends like the lucrative but creatively stifling rise of "ringtone rap," or gravitated to areas capitalizing on the economic ecosystems between regional radio and strip clubs, I was chronicling the in-depth, New York-area Hip Hop narrative by highlighting artists and movements that I believed truly represented Hip Hop's creative ingenuity, challenging naysayers who doubted the ongoing importance of the genre's spiritual epicenter.

While covering local musicians, lyricists, DJs, and producers, however, I would also discover people and organizations applying Hip Hop in innovative, sometimes unexpected ways. I encountered nonprofit directors touting their Hip Hop-friendly programming such as Urban Word, which "elevates young voices through literary arts and civic engagement,"[2] and other community leaders and artistic practitioners, many who had been connecting the music and culture to fields like education, social work, counseling, community organizing, and the fine arts, for years.

New York City teemed with these innovators. I met teaching artists and youth mentors like Mikal Amin (who we'll hear from in this book), Sam Sellers (formerly known as Rabbi Darkside), and Toni Blackman. I witnessed international collaborations being forged by Farbeon Saucedo and The

Bronx-Berlin Connection, "a year-round cross-cultural exchange program that uses the mediums of spoken word and music—particularly, rap and hip hop—to explore and express the unique experiences of urban youth around the world, the critical challenges they face and the solutions necessary to enact change in their communities."[3] I was introduced to the dynamic Martha Diaz, a beloved, film-producing member of the Hip Hop community, and a champion of Hip Hop education and archival work through her Hip-Hop Education Center at New York University. I found out about educational technology companies like Flocabulary. I witnessed Hip Hop theater orchestrated by Kamilah Forbes at the Hip-Hop Theater Festival and through Baba Brinkman's one-man shows (long before *Hamilton* was a thing). I covered graffiti artist Meres One and advocate Marie Flaguel leading the legal battle to protect 5 Pointz, the unofficial but undisputed graffiti headquarters of the world, from illegal destruction.[4] I wrote about Crazy Legs and the B-Boy and B-Girl dancers of the famed Rock Steady Crew. I interviewed Christie Z about her involvement with the Tools of War old-school Hip Hop park jams and the DJ turntablism competition, the DMC World Championships.

I met Hip Hop educators, Hip Hop authors, Hip Hop filmmakers, Hip Hop activists...

My man Majesty.

While Hip Hop's influence on the business of music entertainment and popular culture was nothing new, and no big secret, it became increasingly apparent to me how influential Hip Hop was becoming in these other fields. It was also striking how the general public was so unaware of this innovative work. Even those who considered themselves connected to Hip Hop seemed largely oblivious as to how much their beloved music and culture were being used to improve lives, livelihoods, and communities.

Thinking back to education, the specifics were inspiring. In one case, after being introduced to Hip Hop-based learning methodology, students were passing previously failed exams at an astounding rate of success—upwards of 80%—according to Fresh Prep, a New York City-based test preparation program.[5] School counselors were reporting how young people were opening up about their personal struggles in unprecedented ways through Hip Hop-based counseling and therapy.[6] Edtech companies were rolling out Hip Hop-based products to thousands of schools across the country.

I began to seriously wonder: Since Hip Hop's appeal reaches across ethnic, religious, racial, cultural, ideological, and regional boundaries, could the work of these passionate, inventive practitioners I was becoming familiar with collectively help balance some of the country's social, economic, and cultural inequities through this powerful social and artistic movement?

Can't Knock the Hustle

Hip Hop has been a uniquely powerful force for innovation since its humble beginnings. From its genesis, Hip Hop has birthed entire industries while significantly transforming many others. An electronic music-making and manipulating industry exploded after the turntable wizardry of audio engineering pioneers like Grandmaster Flash became folklore in the 1970s. Run-DMC's million-dollar Adidas sneaker endorsement in 1986—the first ever for a non-athlete—ushered in a multi-billion-dollar streetwear industry. In the 1990s, the mainstream advertising industry would fully fall under the spell of the "tanning of America," a Hip Hop-fueled phenomenon that "rewrote the rules of the new economy".[7]

Hip Hop has always found ways to make money—and lots of it.

Of course, it wasn't always the creators and innovators themselves who reaped the rewards. Often, and especially in Hip Hop's early days, it was the savvy, resource-heavy, opportunist outsider who saw a good, co-optable thing and capitalized on it, reaping the lion's share of profit in the process.

Nevertheless, those who know Hip Hop, know its penchant for innovation. Whether it was the hijacking of electricity from street lamps to fuel park jam sound systems, street-pharmacists-turned-music-execs, mixtape hustling DJs turned radio and TV personalities, local designers turned fashion moguls, bedroom rappers turned world-touring independent artists, or near-billionaire, headphone-slanging producers, Hip Hop heads—often people of color—have found a multitude of improbable ways to infiltrate and invigorate capitalist systems that, in many cases, were literally designed to keep them out.

If necessity is the mother of invention, Hip Hop has proven to be its cool ass auntie.

While dissecting the complications, machinations, and shortcomings of the U.S. economy falls way outside of my expertise, I kept coming back to my original premise: to improve the overall economy we need to decrease disparities. In a landscape riddled with systems set up to support those disparities, and despite occasional rises in economic indicators or dips in unemployment rates, clear racial and class divides continue, along with a seemingly ever-increasing wealth gap. For America to compete globally, we must continually craft new innovations that transcend traditional boundaries. This demands a bold reimagining of education to spark creative thinking, a renewed focus on holistic well-being that unlocks human potential, and dynamic approaches to career development that anticipate tomorrow's challenges. Only by breaking down systemic barriers and creating truly inclusive opportunities can we transform the promise of American possibility from an abstract ideal into a concrete reality for every person who calls this nation home.

If only there were a group of people with a mentality to match those directives, one with demonstrated success in creating "innovations that transcend traditional boundaries." A group of people with an inherent knack for making something out of nothing—or, more fittingly, making something completely new out of everything that came before it. A group of organic intellectuals that literally invented entire industries out of burned out buildings, rubble, and despair, against all odds, and all-too-often, against insidious opposition.

A group that knows how to make a dollar out of fifteen cents. . .

Hold up... Wait a Minute...

OK, let's pause.

I hope it's already becoming intriguingly clear that I believe Hip Hop-inspired solutions to societal ills won't mean we're going to rap our way out of our problems. It's important to note that when I think about Hip Hop, *music* is one of the *last* things I'm thinking about. Because of my experiences, and the conversations I'm going to share in this book, my first thought when looking at any crisis is, "What is a Hip Hop way of solving this problem?"

It is the Hip Hop *way of thinking* that is the key.

Everything in this book is based on the concept that "Hip Hop" is more than a genre—that rap music on the radio is merely a subsection of this larger way of life. A mentality. A philosophy. A worldview.

A culture.

Veteran recording artist, author, and lecturer KRS-One perhaps said it best: "Rap is something you *do*. Hip-hop is something you *live*."

You don't have to be a rapper to be Hip Hop. You don't have to be African-American to be Hip Hop. You don't have to live in the "inner city" to be Hip Hop. You don't have to be from New York to be "real" Hip Hop.

Across this country, across all regions and demographics, most American youth are a part of, or to some degree influenced by, Hip Hop culture. Many adults are as well, as Hip Hop enters its sixth decade of existence. Members of the Hip Hop community at large come from all walks of life, all levels of financial standing, all neighborhoods, all ethnicities, all political leanings, and all religions. They are artists, educators, students, valedictorians, dropouts, media personalities, businesspeople, laborers, politicians, scientists, civil servants, athletes, parents...

A connection to the music unites them, sure, but also the language, the mannerisms, and the philosophy that present as a collective consciousness. A cultural je ne sais quoi that cannot be contained by any border or by strict definition. Much of it derived from people of color working hard to survive and excel in a society designed to oppress them.

This ability to resonate with and reflect human experiences of marginalization and misunderstanding helps explain Hip Hop's remarkable capacity to cross borders and barriers, speaking to hearts and minds across vastly different cultural landscapes. The culture's essence invites anyone who has felt pushed to society's edges, seeking both voice and validation.

Yet with this power and potential comes extraordinary responsibility. Hip Hop naturally intertwines with youth culture precisely because young minds possess an innate courage to question established norms and push against artificial boundaries—a characteristic that carries both promise and risk. In communities where Hip Hop took root and continues to flourish, young people often navigate worlds of limited resources and constrained opportunities. Their innovative spirit frequently emerges raw and forcefully, taking form as street-level intelligence and aggression that outsiders might misinterpret amid surrounding turbulence. What has become clear, however, through countless conversations with community leaders and educators and members of those communities themselves, is that the same behaviors that society often dismisses as ignorant rebellion, actually contain sparks of brilliance. When guided away from the destructive pathways that threaten to entrap young minds in cycles of institutional and economic struggle, this raw creative energy can transform into groundbreaking innovation and problem-solving capabilities that can benefit, and even unify, entire communities.

U.N.I.T.Y.

The common refrain from politicians and community leaders during times of crisis—as well as in an age of endlessly divisive political views, ideologies, and racial tensions—is a call for unity, urging the populace to "come together."

We rarely do. It is rarely that simple.

However, this is another area where a Hip Hop mentality can help. After all, at its core, Hip Hop culture is based on collaboration and community. From early days when the budding music, dance, and visual arts scenes coalesced to lead once-violent, gang-affiliated youth to unimaginable creative heights, to the age-old power of the cypher—a circular, communal exhibition of expression—to the original rap formula of one DJ, one emcee, Hip Hop absolutely knows how to collaborate.

Again, it is important that skeptics resist the temptation to view these theories through a narrow-minded understanding of rap music and its audiences. Despite its often-derided characteristics, Hip Hop possesses a uniquely powerful ability to unite, a point that KRS-One articulated well, proclaiming, "Nowhere in the world do you see [Dr. King's 'I Have a Dream Speech,']... This part... 'My children will grow up in a nation where they will not be judged by the color of their skin, but by the content of the character'... That's nowhere on the globe. Nowhere." He continued, "The only place you see that actually happening, actually going on culturally—is in Hip Hop."[8]

Consider the profound implications of this phenomenon: A human being connected to Hip Hop through social, cultural, or artistic channels can travel anywhere on Earth and locate a Hip Hop space where they will be welcomed. There will be shared understanding, mannerisms, references, and way of seeing the world, a transcendent social and emotional connection that requires no shared language, no common complexion, no unified religion, nor even practical experience in Hip Hop's artistic elements. This is a genuinely global citizenry, liberated from the constraints of descriptors, tribalism, or artificially constructed borders.

Where else can this truly be found, but in Hip Hop?

With so many humans alive today who are touched in some way by Hip Hop music or culture, I argue that there exists a built-in starting point for empathy and perspective between groups of people who might never otherwise cross paths, but share at least this small common denominator.

To be clear, I'm not so naïve as to believe that Hip Hop alone represents some miracle panacea that can end problematic divides within our borders. Solving race relations in America, for example, is obviously far outside the scope of what this book can promise, but I must state this: Around this country and throughout the world, there are few, if any, social groups that unite people with such diverse cultural, ethnic, geographic, linguistic, ideological, or religious backgrounds like Hip Hop does. In this regard, Hip Hop represents an incredible, largely untapped potential, and later in this book, we'll explore specific examples which may help convince skeptics just how powerful Hip Hop can be in bridging even the most ideologically fraught divides.

Before we begin, let's look at the last foundational concept that readers should consider as they approach the rest of this book. It's a recurring theme we've touched on, but one I want to point out with some degree of data analysis and rigor, so that it's abundantly clear to Hip Hop detractors and supporters alike: Hip Hop is very much more than meets the ear, and for it to have the positive effect on our nation that we are advocating for, we must all recognize just how much media and societal bias have been clouding our collective view when it comes to what Hip Hop actually is, and how looking past these narratives is essential for it to be fully viable as a force for good.

The Message

Don't let my unabashed cheerleading belie the fact that I thoroughly approve of a healthy critique of Hip Hop. In fact, Hip Hop's cultural participants do this constantly. Discussions abound regarding the impact of rap music content that mainstream outlets deliver to the masses—whether it truly reflects the tastes and lifestyles of the communities from where many artists emerge, or whether there exists some form of conspiracy to purposefully indoctrinate young people, particularly Black and brown youth, with detrimental imagery through music.

The quizzical nature of exactly which material the corporations in charge choose to promote certainly warrants deeper interrogation, especially for those who advocate for the types of interdisciplinary use of Hip Hop that we're examining. After all, to casual or infrequent listeners, overly negative lyrical content will likely shape their perception, and that negative perception severely damages Hip Hop's chances of being accepted as a complex, respectable culture with immense value to humanity.

So again, the heart of the matter is that when many people think "Hip Hop," they tend to envision only rap music, and all too often, only a small sliver of the genre's full spectrum.

There are many reasons for this, not the least of which is that this massive cultural phenomenon has largely ceded control of its own narrative, allowing misconceptions and misrepresentation to run rampant. To help illustrate this, consider some interesting "facts" that have been disseminated to the public about "Hip Hop":

1. Hip Hop is run by a white, blonde Australian woman
2. Hip Hop prevents Black and brown people in America from succeeding in the world, even more so than racism
3. Frank Sinatra is the Godfather of Hip Hop

Even those with little to no Hip Hop experience or interest should recognize a level of absurdity in these statements.

However, to the tens of millions of visitors per month to Forbes.com, the nearly 2 million people who might have watched an episode of Fox News' *The Five*, or the millions who listen to NPR, these are, almost word for word, messages they would have received.

The portrayal of Hip Hop by mainstream media has long been rife with such mischaracterizations. To the chagrin of many within the culture, the output from Hip Hop's own media hardly fares better. At best, these journalistic practices are simply signs of the times, the result of a decimated industry forced to stay alive by prioritizing salaciousness and controversy. At their worst, and in the case of Hip Hop, they become tools of cultural genocide.

This must change if our country is going to reap the rewards that forward-thinking Hip Hop and its progressive artistic, pedagogical, social, and cultural contributions can deliver.

There was a time when Hip Hop had diverse and respectable media representation. In their heyday, print magazines like *The Source* and *XXL Magazine* presented a wide breadth of Hip Hop coverage, including long-form features and interviews detailing various aspects of Hip Hop's wider cultural landscape. In fact, *The Source*'s tagline was once "The magazine of Hip Hop music, culture and politics," demonstrating the early ideals that while music was surely the most visible and lucrative aspect of this explosively expanding American youth culture, the "culture" part was not insignificant.

Initially, mainstream media was also friendly to aspects of rap music, even if somewhat late to the party. In 1981, two years after the breakout success of "Rapper's Delight," ABC News program *20/20* aired a segment shedding fairly positive light on the "new phenomenon" of rap music, touching on its potential to influence beyond pure entertainment.[9]

The segment noted that rap was "likely to influence popular music for years to come," observing that "it has tremendous staying power because it lets ordinary people express ideas they care about, in language they can relate to, put to music they can dance to." It described programs incorporating Hip Hop into educational settings, some 30 years before the burgeoning "#HipHopEd" movement we witness today.[10]

Rap was portrayed as a community-building phenomenon. The program highlighted park jams and large, festival-sized concerts while noting how rap was being incorporated into other genres of music. *20/20* recognized how rap was beginning to appear in advertising and observed its emerging role as a tool to encourage involvement in the political process.

Coverage was, to borrow a particular media entity's former tagline, somewhat fair and balanced.

However, as rap exploded through the 1980s into public consciousness, the content would evolve, often increasingly bold, brash, and explicitly descriptive of harsh conditions and lifestyles.

As a result, public opinion would turn.

Prominent examples included the law enforcement backlash against 1989s "Fuck The Police" by L.A.-based N.W.A, coverage of the 1990 obscenity case against the perennially sexually explicit 2 Live Crew, or the uproar over the pseudo-rap of Ice-T's song, "Cop Killer" in 1992.

As these cases drew national attention, Middle America was being told, loudly and convincingly, that rap wasn't so great anymore.

Ironically, rap was becoming greater. In 2013, NPR created a series called "Hip Hop's Golden Year: Stories About The Game Changing Albums of 1993."[11] The inaugural story, "'The Chronic': 20 Years Later—An Audio Document Of The L.A. Riots," began with: "Our series about rap's greatest year begins with the album that drew directly on cultural and social upheaval to make one of the most popular rap albums of all time."

From NPR to *New York Magazine*[12] to many profound thinkpieces, 1993 is widely regarded as a highly transformational year for Hip Hop music.

In hindsight.

At the time, however, stories about rap or Hip Hop were almost exclusively focused on negativity surrounding the genre. An archive search of *The New York Times*, the nation's newspaper of record, shows that during the year that came to be so highly regarded in the pantheon of rap music history, the outlet primarily delivered stories like "Harlem Protest Of Rap Lyrics Draws Debate And Steamroller,"[13] "Rap Star And 2 Others Accused Of Murder,"[14] "Radio Station Bans Harmful Music,"[15] and "Rap Star And 2 Friends Indicted In Sexual Assault."[16]

A November 28, 1993 piece titled "Gangster Rappers: The Lives, The Lyrics"[17] firmly painted the genre in a dismal, obscene light, ignoring anything other than the most unsavory examples of the rapidly evolving artform. The piece overflowed with commentary from individuals far removed from the environments actually producing rap music. Weighing in were legislators, sociology professors and, with a jaw-droppingly invidious response, music critic Stanley Crouch. Crouch, responding to the argument that gangster rap was an acceptable extension of Black America's youthful, rebellious energy, asked, "What is rebellious about a bunch of Negroes going around murdering people, raping people and sitting around a table playing cards and drinking 40-ounce bottles of beers?"

Even purported rap supporters such as journalist Kevin Powell, writing for *Vibe Magazine* at the time,[18] and record label owner Russell Simmons,[19] expressed measured distaste over rap's "hard-core" side, though both were actively making their living writing about or selling records from some of the genre's best-known practitioners of such expression.

In articles *The New York Times* relayed to its readers that year, there was little to no mention of the plethora of artists and albums being released which were balancing the rough, rugged, and lewd sounds of Snoop Dogg and others. Nothing about the musical evolution and positive vibes at work in A Tribe Called Quest's *Midnight Marauders*, an eventual platinum seller which reached the top spot on Billboard's R&B/Rap charts the day before the "Gangster Rappers" piece went to print. Nothing regarding the acclaimed poetry and jazz-influenced styles of *Reachin' (A New Refutation of Time and Space)* by nouveaux beatnik crew Digable Planets. No sign of the eclectic brilliance of De La Soul's third studio album, *Buhloone Mindstate*, or the lyrical prowess displayed on *Inner City Griots* by L.A.'s Freestyle Fellowship, which delivered an impressive and accessible alternative to the gang- and violence-infused rap of their city's brethren.

There was no mention of the intelligent, self-affirming *Black Reign* by Queen Latifah. No one noticed *Organix*, the independently distributed album by a groundbreaking Hip Hop band from Philadelphia named The Roots, who some 21 years later would become a household name across America as the house band for the iconic late night talk show, *The Tonight Show*.

The wealth of creativity emerging within Hip Hop music in 1993 was staggering. Yet, so-called thought leaders like Mr. Crouch were publicly describing rappers as "a bunch of opportunists who are appealing to an appetite that America has for vulgarity, violence and anarchy inside Afro America." Ironically, this sort of tendentious critique perfectly exemplifies the problem, as the very newspaper quoting him was appealing to that same appetite by covering at great length the salacious moral and legal issues surrounding some of the genre's brightest stars while shunning others equally fit to print.

Though mainstream media has become somewhat more aware and respectful of Hip Hop music and culture's nuances in recent years, examples of Hip Hop prejudice continue to abound. In an HuffPost.com interview[20] and again on FOX News' roundtable news talk program *The Five*, Geraldo Rivera's unsubstantiated assertion that "Hip Hop has done more damage to Black and Brown people than racism" demonstrates that many still embrace deep-rooted connections between rap, Hip Hop, negativity, and violence.[21]

This reductionist view of Hip Hop as nothing but violent and criminal-istic is not the only misconception perpetrated by mainstream media. This was evidenced by the cultural insensitivity in the title of a Forbes.com article anointing recording artist Iggy Azalea, exclaiming that "Hip Hop Is Run By A White, Blonde, Australian Woman."[22] The headline (which Forbes subse-quently changed after massive online backlash), equated Azalea's short-lived dominance on music charts with her Top 40 pop-rap hit "Fancy" as dom-inance over an entire genre, and by extension, its associated culture. This was inaccurate and disrespectful across many levels—racial, cultural, and historical—representing another callous example of American media's long record of hoisting a white artist to the top of a traditionally African-American genre and declaring them to be its sovereign king.

Or in this case, queen.

This carelessness in reporting on the Hip Hop genre, coupled with wide-spread misunderstanding of Hip Hop culture, is evidenced in part by the results of the *Reputation of Rap and Hip-Hop* research study that I co-authored and published through The Center for Hip-Hop Advocacy, along with Dr. Joy Sever, Ph.D.[23]

The study, designed to gauge public perception about rap and Hip Hop, reported that 67% of Americans who don't even listen to rap music believe that rap music is "negative."

This is telling.

Are these people aware that Ivy league universities have curriculum, departments, fellowships, and archives dedicated to rap music and Hip Hop culture?

Have they heard that Broadway has been revolutionized by the rap-infused *Hamilton*, perhaps the most heralded production of its time?

Do they know that rap artists, Hip Hop-influenced activists, and organiza-tions continuously work on the frontlines of the fight for social justice, youth empowerment, and women's rights?

Are they familiar with Kendrick Lamar, one of rap's biggest breakout stars in recent years, and how he expounded on critical societal issues through complex, poetic, self-affirming lyrics with an avant-garde musical approach, producing *To Pimp A Butterfly*, one of the most critically acclaimed albums ever, from any genre, later winning a Pulitzer Prize for his subsequent album, *DAMN.*?[24]

Well, no. The research suggests that many are simply not aware of these things.

At one time, Hip Hop magazines helped balance some of the uninformed scales, but "pay-for-print" and the downturn of the journalism industry as a whole helped silence much of whatever quality Hip Hop journalism existed before the onslaught of bloggers and clickbait farms.

The lackluster and often dangerously inept writers and outlets that remain compound the issues with mainstream media's coverage, leaving the task of documenting this vast, expansive cultural and artistic phenomenon largely to the unqualified or uninterested.

While some individual journalists and scholars continue to represent Hip Hop adequately enough through the written word, podcasts, and video punditry, a large portion of America receives content pushed out by multi-million dollar radio, cable, and online corporations. They have become the entities dictating the narrative, controlling the imagery, and directly affecting what history will likely say about Hip Hop.

The full, frightening significance of this may not be totally clear, even to those who enjoy Hip Hop music or consider themselves part of Hip Hop culture. Often, Hip Hop's anti-establishment DNA leads its supporters to shrug off whatever perceptions others may have of them. But despite Hip Hop's success, it is crucial to recognize that those in positions of authority regarding Hip Hop's placement in society are still not necessarily highly versed in Hip Hop.

These people might be executives at record labels, radio stations, and streaming platforms. They might be the ones booking entertainment venues. They might be magazine, newspaper, and website editors. They could be the ones who greenlight film projects or sign book deals. They might control the incorporation of Hip Hop into educational programs.

It is quite likely that gatekeepers and decision-makers in industries that could achieve great innovation and inspiration from Hip Hop-minded citizens and Hip Hop-oriented viewpoints harbor a negative perception of what

Hip Hop actually is, and therefore, would never entertain the notion of incorporating Hip Hop into their operations.

As this book will show, this could be a costly mistake. And while Hip Hop practitioners often dismiss these people as insignificant outsiders, I would contend that it is those outsiders who need to be educated to understand that they have likely been misled in ways that not only perpetuate negative stereotypes about the genre and its participants but hinder the advancement of these beneficial intersections.

Otherwise, we will continue to watch yet another creation which emerged from Black American culture, one that has now become ubiquitous throughout the world, become co-opted, misappropriated, and skewed by those with greater voice, reach, and power, often with vastly unhealthy ulterior motives.

The general public will continue to be miseducated by stories like the one broadcast on NPR, where an *All Things Considered* segment crowned Frank Sinatra as "the Godfather of Hip Hop."[25]

Not A godfather. *THE* Godfather.

His something-from-nothing rise to fame and fortune, his run-ins with the law, and the fact that he was name-checked by a couple of big rappers were somehow enough credentials for this venerable, respectable media outlet to anoint Sinatra a rightful position atop an entire social and creative community.

This, despite the fact that Hip Hop had already collectively anointed a "Godfather"—Afrika Bambaataa.[26]

Not to mention DJ Kool Herc, who has been collectively anointed as the "Father" of Hip Hop.

Then there is Grandmaster Flash, The Last Poets, Gil Scott-Heron, James Brown, Cab Calloway—*Africa!* All ancestors of Hip Hop that are infinitely more viable than Ol' Blue Eyes.

These examples of Hip Hop's portrayal in the media demonstrate why this book and the various efforts by individuals and organizations profiled herein are so crucial. Public perception can no longer be allowed to be skewed by racial bias, artistic ignorance, or cultural insensitivity. The damaging misrepresentation of Hip Hop's value to society—past, present, and future, artistic and cultural—must be countered with more accurate accountings of the depth of artistry which actually exists, as well as what this book is highlighting, the work being done by those who are leading groundbreaking integrations of Hip Hop into fields not typically associated with rap music.

Sky's The Limit

So again, as we move on to the meat of this book, I ask you to consider that the content of rap music must not be judged merely on what might appear on radio, award shows, or popular sections of the internet. No matter your experience, knowledge, or connection to rap music, I ask that you trust that an inventory of quality, inspiring rap music exists, that not all rappers create music rife with less-than-desirable imagery, language, or style, and that even when they do, those works should not be discounted without first taking time to understand the artistic, cultural, and societal influences that help create that material.

Second, consider that Hip Hop as a culture is extremely vast and, as such, is as worthy of respectful exploration and documentation as any other social group or movement. No matter your experience, knowledge, or connection to Hip Hop culture, I ask that you consider that many industries and disciplines are already being inspired in positive ways by Hip Hop's touch.

In the pages to follow, I will detail real-life examples that I believe will handily prove these points.

There is a great amount of Hip Hop music today that is replete with positive attributes. Inventive artistry, self-love, intelligence, musicality, feminism, lyricism, activism, honesty, vulnerability, storytelling, philosophy, spirituality, fear, and hope abound.

And as we'll now begin to explore, areas where Hip Hop music and culture are influencing society in positive ways continue to expand, in fields such as education, healthcare, entrepreneurship, social justice, fine arts, and more.

Those who embrace and respect these artforms, this culture, these communities, and their innovations hold a vital responsibility. They must seek out and share these stories with both authenticity and impact, strengthening the work of pioneering changemakers while protecting these narratives from those who would distort or diminish their profound significance. In doing so, they honor the full complexity of these social movements and their tremendous potential to transform our shared human experience.

Those who might be reading, for whom this is all new and intriguing information, also share in this responsibility. If "saving America" means doing all that we can which is morally and ethically right to live up to the ideals of our founding documents (and their necessary amendments) we must all be willing to examine and embrace ideas that emphasize inclusivity, modern thinking, and unexpected intersectionality.

These characteristics have spread Hip Hop—a culture which lives by a creed of "peace, love, unity, and having fun"—throughout the world. Now, decades later, it is creating interdisciplinary ecosystems that are changing the way we care for our citizens, young and old, across all demographics, in ways that are improving quality of life across multiple aspects of their existence.

Through these innovations, I contend we are finding inspiration as to how we can become a nation continuously improved by progressive artistic and cultural creativity. A country where communication through the arts is always expanding, where innovation thrives through collaboration, and where technological advancement rises from fearless experimentation. A society where disconnected communities can intertwine through common interests to expand each other's perspectives. An educational landscape where teaching and learning are not forced to follow strict, unbending, uninformed, outdated practices, but allowed to welcome in a generation of young people through personal, culturally affirming connections. An America where Hip Hop sensibilities and nuances among youth culture are respected, nurtured, praised, and protected, where culture is as popular as popular culture, and where Hip Hop can be equally effective in turning out the vote as it is at turning up the club.

By spotlighting and uplifting those elements in Hip Hop that are already being used to positively impact society, I am hopeful that this book will demonstrate how other communities and industries can benefit in the same manner, which in turn can help increase the number of individuals and organizations doing this sort of work across the board.

It is this balance that can help Hip Hop help us.

To help substantiate all of these claims, I have carefully selected illuminating interviews from the podcast series which offer foundational insights to underscore the arguments presented so far. Through thoughtful dialogue with practitioners, scholars, and thought leaders, these interviews reveal the profound ways in which marginalized voices can contribute to our collective understanding and growth—if we have the collective courage to welcome it.

While these conversations have been judiciously edited for clarity and coherence, I invite you to journey alongside me as I reconstruct the path that led to my current position as an optimistic advocate for these transformative possibilities. This intellectual and personal evolution reflects not just my own trajectory, but it is my hope that it will help inspire a societal awakening to the power of overlooked cultural wisdom.

Let's go.

Notes

1 Jenkins, T. S., & Kimbrough, W. M. (2023a). *The hip-hop mindset: Success strategies for educators and other professionals*. Teachers College Press.

2 urbanwordnyc. (2024, September 12). *Youth Development | Youth Poetry | Critical Literacy | Urban Word NYC*. Urban Word. https://www.urbanword.org/

3 *The Hip Hop Re:Education Project*. (2024). Reeducate.org. http://www.reeducate.org/BronxBerlinConnection.html

4 Cramer, M. (2020, October 6). Artists have final victory in a case of destroyed Graffiti. Nytimes.com; *The New York Times*. https://www.nytimes.com/2020/10/06/nyregion/graffiti-artists-5pointz.html

5 Otterman, S. (2011, August 12). With fresh prep, mixing regents test material with Hip-Hop. Nytimes.com; *The New York Times*. https://www.nytimes.com/2011/08/12/nyregion/with-fresh-prep-mixing-regents-test-material-with-hip-hop.html

6 Hu, W. (2016, January 19). Bronx School embraces a new tool in counseling: Hip-Hop. Nytimes.com; *The New York Times*. https://www.nytimes.com/2016/01/20/nyregion/bronx-school-embraces-a-new-tool-in-counseling-hip-hop.html

7 Stoute, S. (2011). *The tanning of America: How hip-hop created a culture that rewrote the rules of the new economy*. Gotham Books.

8 Amsterdam, in. (2013, June 26). *Hiphopcore Special: Hiphop lecture by KRS-ONE in Amsterdam part two*. YouTube. https://www.youtube.com/watch?v=qEzSEbv7FH8

9 Coplan, C. (2014, September 6). *Watch this surreal ABC News special on hip-hop music from 1981*. Consequence. https://consequence.net/2014/09/watch-this-watch-this-surreal-abc-news-special-on-hip-hop-music-from-1981-abc-news-special-on-hip-hop-music-from-1981/

10 The Hip Hop Ed movement, often identified by its hashtag #HipHopEd, is a loose collective of educators, professionals, advocates, activists, Hip Hop fans, practitioners, and others who support Hip Hop as a valuable educational tool.

11 *Hip-Hop's Golden Year*. (2014, February 6). NPR. https://www.npr.org/series/172716049/hip-hops-golden-year

12 *Did 1993 Change Everything?—New York Magazine—Nymag*. (2013, February 2). *New York Magazine*; Nymag. https://nymag.com/arts/all/features/1993-culture-events/

13 Levy, C. J. (1993, June 6). Harlem protest of Rap Lyrics draws debate and steamroller. Nytimes.com; *The New York Times*. https://www.nytimes.com/1993/06/06/nyregion/harlem-protest-of-rap-lyrics-draws-debate-and-steamroller.html

14 Press, T. A. (1993, September 8). Rap Star and 2 others accused of murder. Nytimes.com; *The New York Times*. https://www.nytimes.com/1993/09/08/us/rap-star-and-2-others-accused-of-murder.html

15 Sims, C. (1993, November 13). Radio Station Bans "Harmful" Music. Nytimes.com; *The New York Times*. https://www.nytimes.com/1993/11/13/us/radio-station-bans-harmful-music.html

16 The. (1993, November 25). Rap Star and 2 friends indicted in sexual attack. Nytimes.com; *The New York Times*. https://www.nytimes.com/1993/11/25/nyregion/rap-star-and-2-friends-indicted-in-sexual-attack.html

17 Sims, C. (1993, November 28). THE NATION; Gangster Rappers: The Lives, The Lyrics. Nytimes.com; *The New York Times*. https://www.nytimes.com/1993/11/28/weekinreview/the-nation-gangster-rappers-the-lives-the-lyrics.html

18 Powell, K. (2019, July 7). *Snoop Dogg: "Hot Dogg" Cover Story, Sept 1993*. VIBE.com. https://www.vibe.com/features/editorial/snoop-dogg-sept-1993-cover-story-hot-dogg-655530/

19 *Rap Roundtable—Charlie Rose*. (2024). Charlie Rose. https://charlierose.com/videos/20113

20 Buxton, R. (2015, February 17). Geraldo Rivera: "Hip-Hop has done more damage to Black and Brown People than Racism in the last 10 years." *HuffPost*. https://www.huffpost.com/entry/geraldo-rivera-hip-hop-racism_n_6701628

21 News, P. (2017, April 14). Why Kendrick Lamar's new album is preoccupied with Fox News. *PBS News*. https://www.pbs.org/newshour/arts/kendrick-lamars-new-album-preoccupied-fox-news

22 McIntyre, H. (2014, May 19). Hip-Hop's unlikely new star: A White, Blonde, Australian Woman. *Forbes*. https://www.forbes.com/sites/hughmcintyre/2014/05/19/hip-hop-is-run-by-a-white-blonde-australian-blonde-woman/?utm_campaign=forbestwittersf&utm_source=twitter&utm_medium=social

23 The. (2015, November 17). Nearly 3 in 10 U.S. Adults Say Hip-Hop Should Be Taught in Schools. The Center for Hip-Hop Advocacy. https://www.hiphopadvocacy.org/hip-hop-education-research/

24 https://www.pulitzer.org/winners/kendrick-lamar

25 Glinton, S. (2015, December 11). *On his 100th birthday, Why Sinatra is the Godfather of Hip-Hop*. NPR. https://www.npr.org/2015/12/11/459392805/on-his-100th-birthday-why-sinatra-is-the-godfather-of-hip-hop

26 A pivotal DJ and founder of the Universal Zulu Nation who helped establish Hip Hop culture's foundations, though his legacy was later tarnished by allegations of sexual abuse.

· 1 ·

THE FOUNDATION | DR. BETTINA LOVE

My journey from independent music journalist to Hip Hop cultural documentarian and advocate was gradual. I can't recall any singular "aha moment" that started me on this path. However, I do know for sure that there was a tipping point, a moment when I understood how important this work was. It was a moment that shaped everything I've done since, and therefore, a perfect place to start this journey of discovery and inspiration.

As I began exploring Hip Hop beyond entertainment, and focused on its ability to affect societal change, education was the first link to capture my attention.

Generally speaking, Hip Hop in education appears in two main forms: Hip Hop as a subject to study and Hip Hop as an educational tool. (We'll discuss a third later.) By the time I started connecting with pioneers and innovators in this field, the pedagogical approach known as "Hip Hop Based Education" (HHBE) had been flourishing for a while. Back in 1991, Howard University had emerged as an early adopter of this juxtaposition, offering a Hip Hop course and hosting the first major conference exploring its cultural and educational importance.[1] By the 2000s, HHBE had expanded beyond theory into literature, including research projects and books such as Marc Lamont Hill's, *Beats, rhymes, and classroom life: Hip Hop pedagogy and the politics of identity.*[2] By the late 2010s, as I began covering the phenomenon, papers, books, curricula, conferences, fellowships, and Hip Hop minor[3] programs had emerged.

My initial research was less formal, though no less informed, as I was speaking directly with people like those you'll hear from in this book—teachers, school counselors, teaching artists, and more—about how they were incorporating Hip Hop into their work, informally at first, and then as time progressed, in more structured ways.

There are numerous ways to integrate Hip Hop into K-12 and college-level classrooms. They could include test prep programs using fact-filled rap songs to help students remember important material, such as a now-defunct New York City program called Fresh Prep,[4] to comprehensive programs like Science Genius,[5] where teaching artists collaborate with science teachers to help students master scientific concepts, create songs about them, and perform for peers, faculty, family, and their community.

I began to recognize that despite varying pedagogical methods, certain key threads explained their shared potential for success. The effectiveness stemmed not from the *content* but from the *culture*—less about *appearing* cool and more about *being* authentic. Most importantly, these progressive educators demonstrated that success came from fully and unapologetically recognizing young people's value in ways that traditional educational institutions consistently fail to do.

For me, I had seen no one explain this more concisely, passionately, and with true Hip Hop flair, than Dr. Bettina Love.

A former elementary school teacher, Dr. Love was, at the time, Associate Professor of Educational Theory and Practice at the University of Georgia. Her research focused on how urban youth engage with Hip Hop music and culture to form social, cultural, and political identities, creating new and sustainable ways of thinking about urban education and intersectional social justice.

Those juxtapositions were exactly what I was trying to better understand, so after hearing her name mentioned multiple times, I sat and watched her 2014 TEDx Talk, *Hip Hop, grit, and academic success.*[6]

Immediately, everything I was yearning to better comprehend made so much more sense.

As I developed the concept of the *Hip Hop Can Save America!* podcast, I felt there could be no better way to kick it off than with Dr. Love. We had never previously met or spoken, yet she was gracious enough to be the show's inaugural guest. As you might be able to tell as we proceed through this book, Dr. Love set the tone—and the bar—for every episode that came after.

The Interview

Manny Faces: Dr. Love, thank you again for taking the time to speak with me today. Truly a pleasure for me to be able to speak to you. I'm sort of a fan. . .

Dr. Bettina Love: Aww, thank you.

Manny Faces: So, along with your many titles, I imagine you also wear many hats, as many of us do. How do you currently define who you are today from a professional standpoint?

Dr. Bettina Love: It's really hard as a person of color to define yourself just in a professional standpoint, because when you're a person of color and you come from so many different groups that are marginalized and that are oppressed and they intersect, those identities make who you are as a person. So, when I think about who I am as a professional, so much of that is about just who I am as a kid growing up in Rochester, New York. And here I am a professor at the University of Georgia. Me being a scholar and a researcher and a writer and trying to be a radical educator, all those titles come from me as a little kid trying to understand Hip Hop, trying to understand what it means to be queer, trying to understand what it means to be working class, almost going into poverty. So, who I am as a professional is just driven by who I am as a black person in this world.

Manny Faces: I hear you. You are you.

Dr. Bettina Love: Mm-hmm! [LAUGHS]

Manny Faces: . . .I definitely want to talk about some of your prior work, the connection between Hip Hop and education. And then I want to hear more about how that work extends out to civics and civic education. I think that's where we want to end up.

I've covered Hip Hop music and culture as an independent journalist in the New York area for many years. A lot of it was covering the artistry, but obviously delving into the cultural aspects. In New York City, we still have the

O.G.s[7] walking around. We still have people that are doing every aspect of Hip Hop—all the elements[8]—old school stuff, new school stuff, it's all here. It was really exciting for me to poke around where Hip Hop is being used in some nontraditional spaces. Of course, I start running into people like Dr. [Chris] Emdin[9] and the folks at Teachers College and Martha Diaz[10] and some of these folks who are working in the education field.

So when I started being more interested in this, I found your TED Talk and some of your other talks. And what I love about your work and your talks is that you really do emphasize the concept that I try to help translate to people who aren't as *Inside Baseball* when to comes to Hip Hop. The idea that Hip Hop is more than just a genre of music, it's a full-fledged culture with a lifestyle that contains specific and unique characteristics, which, contrary to what most people in the public space think, are valuable characteristics, as opposed to being ignorant or wasteful or just youthful nonsense. You've spoken about it eloquently in the past. Can you speak to some of the characteristics that you feel that Hip Hop-minded young people bring to the table of society?

Dr. Bettina Love: Yeah, I think we're watching it right now. We're in a moment right now where young folks are rebelling and speaking up against the system. And I think Hip Hop has a huge role to play in that. But I want to back up to where I see Hip Hop playing in all of this, because as a person of color, as a Black person in this country, we don't get anywhere without our voice. That's just the bottom line. It's ahistorical to think about narratives where we have had some type of justice without our voice. It's ahistorical to think that we can actually live without oppression by just simply asking, and then [they respond], "Hey, why didn't you ask before? I mean, we been waiting on y'all..."

Manny Faces: [LAUGHS] That's all it was going to take!

Dr. Bettina Love: Right? That was all it was gonna take? So I think if you look at history and you understand how Black folks and indigenous folks and folks of color in this country have been able to get oppression off our necks—not fully, but some—it's been through our voice, it's been through our protest, it's been through putting our bodies on the line. If you understand that, the trajectory of that, of course you get Hip Hop, right? Hip Hop doesn't just come out of anywhere. Even though I'm from New York, I'm from upstate New York. I like to get into arguments all the time because Hip Hop doesn't start in the Bronx. Hip Hop doesn't start in New York. Hip Hop has been something that was breathing and living and on the cusp of something. And it just so happened that all those things came together in New York at that time, but the very foundation that it was on, has always been there.

Manny Faces: I think you said somewhere it's the *most recent iteration* of these traditions, right?

Dr. Bettina Love: Right! We're in that iteration of it. From slave songs to narratives to James Baldwin to Audre Lorde. All of these iterations are us using our voice and our bodies and our talents and our gifts to try to speak back to something, and [now] Hip Hop, because it's in our DNA, right? Our sensibilities to improvise... People think you improvise because you don't know. You improvise because you *do* know, right? That's why you improvise. You understand the structure of the system is so tightly wound and that you're not going to be a part of it, so you understand how to improvise. So, when you talk about Hip Hop having this element of improvisation, it's a cultural thing of course, because we've been having to improvise in this country for 400 years.

Manny Faces: I like how they build those business models just trying to recreate that natural thing, right?

Dr. Bettina Love: Right. Or saying, "Kids got to have grit." Grit?! I'm African-American. What do you mean, "I got to have grit?" I ain't never had a problem with grit. This country is based on, and a product of, my grit. So, what I really try to do is use Hip Hop and take the sensibilities, the ways of being, our ways of knowing, and our cultural productions as folks who are deeply embedded in this culture—because it is a culture. And then try to help individuals understand that the things that are deeply embedded within Hip Hop culture, like creativity, like improvisation, like grit, like social and emotional intelligence—all these things you say you want kids to have—their culture actually provides that. You just don't know how to tap into it. Or when you see it, you don't know what you're seeing. So you label it deficient. But [you're] actually not understanding that our kids have it. It's in our culture. It's in our DNA. I think we have to grapple with that.

And that's not to say that all kids love Hip Hop and that all Black people can dance. That's not what I'm saying. What I'm saying is that there is tradition, right? And there are mindsets and sensibilities. And every culture has traditions. Every culture has sensibilities. Every culture has things they pass down. That's a culture. And everybody doesn't do the culture well. Everybody doesn't subscribe to the culture 100%, but it is a culture. And so I think we have to get teachers and individuals who say they love Black children to really understand this and understand how we relate to each other, how we talk to each other, how we love on each other. Those are ways that we show our humanity. And Hip Hop is one of those ways.

Manny Faces: Obviously, this isn't just talking points. You've done this work. You've seen the success. You've taught young children and had the evidence. You got the receipts.

Dr. Bettina Love: Yeah. And you got to keep receipts!

Manny Faces: Right. Let me ask you about that now. First of all, almost all the *Hip Hop Ed*[11] folks probably have had this kind of problem to deal with—the hindrances or the hesitations by the institutions, the schools, the boards of education or where you're trying to bring this to fruition, when you try to put this into practice. What have been the hindrances or hesitations that you've had to grapple with or that you've heard other people grappling with, and how do you overcome them?

Dr. Bettina Love: I think one thing we have to really help folks in the field of education with is learning how to use the words that education loves to throw around, and throw them back in their face.

For me, when I'm talking to a principal or I'm talking to teachers, I'm going to use the words that schools love to use. "Critical thinking." "Social and emotional intelligence." We have to speak their language. So when I go in and I feel like folks are being resistant, I just simply say, "Well, I'm here to talk about students' social and emotional intelligence."

"Oh, OK. I thought this was just about Hip Hop?"

"No, I'm here to talk about students increasing their critical thinking and problem solving skills."

"Ohhhhh!"

And so I think we have to be able to use the language that educators know. Oftentimes what happens is that folks in the Hip Hop world are not necessarily in the education world. They know instinctively that Hip Hop is an educative tool, but they don't have the language to go into schools and put those things together. So how do we get these artists in residence that can be doing amazing work in schools but can't get their foot in the door because they want to talk about—rightfully so—Hip Hop and cyphers.[12] But cyphers are social and emotional intelligence. Cyphers are places of peer evaluation and self-evaluation. So [it's about] making sure that folks who know how to do this work and can be authentic in this work can actually do it, and making sure they understand that you need the language so that educators can say, "Oh, OK, that's exactly what I've been trying to talk about."

Both of you are having a conversation, but since you don't have the same language, you're not actually hearing each other. I think the very first thing is to get folks speaking the same language and then making a space and finding that time. You know, teachers and principals and school administrators, they feel like they can't let any of their time go. I do believe that every second with children is precious. However, you do have time. So [it's about] coming up with creative ways—either after school or in school.

Then I think the last thing, if possible, is to document. Can you videotape? Can you audit? Can you—like we're doing—record voices? Because I think people do need to see documentation that this works. Sometimes, the teacher or the artist in residence just saying that it works is not enough. We also have this language that we have to worry about because folks are coming in on grants and folks are coming in on monies that are very temporary without proof and documentation. We live in that world, so I think we have to be able to do some of those things really well. That's where researchers and practitioners and educators like myself come in and team up with folks who have the amazing skill set, but need that entry into the classroom.

Manny Faces: Since this work has gained some steam in the past few years, is the road easier? Are you finding that the doors are opening a little?

Dr. Bettina Love: No, not at all. Not at all. I mean, schools are resistant. Schools are places that are just naturally resistant to change, even though what they've been doing is not working. You would think if you've been doing something for 200 years and it's not working, you would be so open to change. But in schools you have a ton of teachers who truly don't understand Hip Hop culture, so there is a lot of back work that you need to do. For instance, I teach a class at University of Georgia called Hip Hop Education for Social Justice, and my students get really mad at me because the first five weeks is just readings, and they're like, "We want to do Hip Hop."

Manny Faces: [Imitating students] "Where's the Hip Hop?"

Dr. Bettina Love: It's like, you don't know anything about the culture! But they want to jump in and start building Hip Hop curriculum because it's flashy, it's fun. But I'm like, do you know Jeff Chang's work?[13] Have you read Trisha Rose?[14] Do you understand where this stuff comes from and why it's important?

Manny Faces: How do you explain that to them? They may be surprised [to hear] that Hip Hop is more than just what they have in their mind.

Dr. Bettina Love: Right. Because if Hip Hop is based on just solely what you have in your mind... For many of my students that is basically a lot of stereotypes. The music that they know is only the 10–15 songs that Clear Channel[15] plays anyway. . .

Manny Faces: If you're lucky, ten. . .

Dr. Bettina Love: If you're lucky, ten, right. You are going to create curriculum based on stereotypes, based on misconceptions, based on the myth-making machine that we call America. For it to be something that students will actually say, "Yeah, I'm going to ride with you with this lesson," then you have to be authentic and know where they come from. So [educators] can't create curriculum that's ahistorical of people, because, again, that's whiteness washing out Black folks. And then you insert yourself into the culture as if now *you* are the authority, because you are the teacher. And here we go again, doing things that are gimmicky and have no real impact on students.

Manny Faces: That's important. I've spoken to people about this and I've seen some people outside of the education space—but in the Hip Hop community—looking sideways at Hip Hop-minded educators to make sure that they're actually coming from an authentic place...

Dr. Bettina Love: That's right. . .

Manny Faces: Like, "Oh, Hip Hop is the thing of the moment. Let's use it to *hook* these students," but then not really teach them the real value of those characteristics that may be innate in them. Or you may be introducing them to it for the first time, but without that cultural background, without the real soul of it.

Dr. Bettina Love: Right. This is not a gimmick. This is a way of life. I need you to look at the world through this lens. I need you to be able to say, "OK, when do I improvise? When do I not improvise? When do I have to understand these skills? When can I be critical? How do I have a critical voice in this world? How do I frame things in this very Hip Hop critical way?" All of those things are important. This is not just a gimmick to get kids in the seat. It's to try to get them to understand that you already have the tools that you need. I'm trying to enhance them. That's not a gimmick.

Manny Faces: That's good teaching, right?

Dr. Bettina Love: That's good teaching! That's what you call good teaching. You sit your butt in that seat and we're going to go at it. And you're gonna say, "Oh, I didn't know I was this smart! Oh, you mean to tell me the things that I've been doing and talking about and rapping about, if I put it on paper... Or the movements and the dance styles or those beats. . ."

[It's about] trying to get young kids and young folks to realize that you don't have to change for education, education has to change for you. And that your culture is beautiful, and who you are is beautiful. And you're not only beautiful, and it's not only fun, it's not only creative, but it's also what you need to be successful in this world. I think that's the key part.

There's a beautiful part in the Nas[16] documentary *Illmatic*[17] where he talks about his dad telling him to quit school. And his dad says, "They're going to kill the creativity of my boy."

Manny Faces: Mmm. He recognized that. . .

Dr. Bettina Love: Right! He recognized that. I think for Black folks, we have to understand that art education is more than just art. It's Black folks civics. It's Black folks being. It's the way we respond to this world. So, when you take art out of schools, you're taking the ways in which we like to respond. All of that is very important to a holistic way of thinking about educating Black children and children of color.

Manny Faces: That's very interesting. You've spoken about when creativity is blocked at the door—your great example of "banging on the table" as opposed to *drumming*...[18]

Dr. Bettina Love: Right!

Manny Faces: When you block that sort of thing, you're creating an uncomfortable space in the classroom. That's one thing. But now you're also saying, it's not just the music they listen to or the songs they dance to. [It's their] perspective [. . .]

Dr. Bettina Love: Right. Right.

Manny Faces: And you're going to block their perspective and not take it into consideration. Why would that be a thing anyone would want to do?

Dr. Bettina Love: Right. And by perspective you're really saying, "That's my culture!" You're devaluing who I am as a person. But it's a tricky thing—and that's why the first five weeks of my class is readings and conversations—because Hip Hop is a tricky subject to talk about, because you can't not address the homophobia. . .

Manny Faces: Right, the problematic aspects...

Dr. Bettina Love: Right. You all want to jump into pedagogy and lesson planning, but we haven't got to these very tricky issues that have to be teased out and that we have to talk about. But it's one of the most right places to do this type of work because it gives you so much content to talk about, and so many avenues. That's what makes it such a really fruitful place to have these conversations and ideas.

Manny Faces: Yeah, that's what I hear from a lot of teachers that use Hip Hop in the classroom. "Oh, OK. You don't like the content? Good. Let's talk about why that content exists," or "What's the root cause of this person, this artist, feeling this way. Where does it come from?"

Dr. Bettina Love: Or you *do* like the content, right?

Manny Faces: [LAUGHS] And why that's a problem...

Dr. Bettina Love: Why is that, like, OK. . . You *do* like Migos. OK, why? Tell me why. So we get to have those conversations. And I think there's conversations we don't really get to have in schools, where we can have conversations about Black masculinity, toxic Black masculinity. . . We can have conversations about capitalism and sexism and homophobia and transphobia. We can really have those conversations. And that's what education should be.

Another reason why my Hip Hop class starts out very boring is because our job is not to necessarily critique students' music to a point where we're doing all the critiquing...

Manny Faces: Right. You don't wanna be a "stuck in the 90s" professor...

Dr. Bettina Love: Right. The kids are like, "Who? Common? Who? KRS-One? Who? MC Lyte? Who?" They may know who Lauryn Hill is, just because of the gossip, but they [just] don't know [some of these older artists]. So you have to really try to meet them where they are with their music. And some of this stuff I just really don't like, but I want them to become critical consumers. Not just consumers—we're all consumers—but how do you become a *critical* consumer? How do you think about what you consume? How do you consume it and still be critical about it and understand that this doesn't have to be a personality or persona that you take on.

And then also understanding the circumstances around you. Kids don't consume Hip Hop in a bubble. They consume it in gentrified urban spaces that are collapsing in front of all of our eyes. So that's something we have to take into account. They don't consume it in a bubble and then go out in the world and say, "Oh, what's this thing called 'the world?'" No. They're consuming it in conjunction. It's like a beautiful dance. [They] listen to it, then [they] see it. So, how do we have conversations with kids that really help them understand their day to day lived experiences and what that means? But that's not ahistorical right. I don't want you to think this started today.

Manny Faces: Right, or in 1973...[19]

Dr. Bettina Love: Right, right! That's why you have to understand the culture. You have to understand Black culture, Black music. Black history. And then move into Hip Hop. But we can't pick this thing up at 1960 or 1979 and just keep rolling.

Manny Faces: You speak in one of your talks about Hip Hop *characteristics*, Hip Hop *sensibilities* being predictors of success and all these good characteristics that students and young people have that should be amplified and encouraged. You say that it's not enough, and that society continues to present enormous systemic, racist-driven challenges for people in those communities. So that sentiment, I think, dovetails into your more recent endeavors with the

Get Free initiative. Can you speak to what you're doing with a civics-minded mindset?

Dr. Bettina Love: I really feel that we are trying to make the best strides we can in education, but education is not the fix to everything. Education can help, but it's not the fix. And we put too much on teachers and the field of education, like education is supposed to fix homelessness, poverty...

Manny Faces: Mental health issues...

Dr. Bettina Love: ...mental health issues. Y'all don't even want to pay nobody! For me, it's always about how we can support teachers, number one. And then, how we can think about justice and liberation in ways that are not ahistorical. What I mean by that is, if we say, "Just wait, everything will [happen], we just have to give it time," that's ahistorical. That's never how it's happened.

So for me, I see civics. And civics for people of color is totally different than civics for white folks. Civics for white folks could mean voting, participating in an election, maybe running for office, maybe doing community service. That's this very general sense of civics. But I think for people of color, for Indigenous folks, for Black folks in this country, civics means my survival. I have to participate. It's not just about an election. It's about... I have to find community. I have to think about ways that I can fight towards justice.

And that's not my work. I don't want anybody to ever think that the life work of Black folks and brown folks and Indigenous folks is fighting racism. That's racist itself. But that is our work if we're going to survive here. So, we are automatically doing civics just when we wake up in the morning. We're doing civics because we are in a place that is constantly saying that we are disposable. We are trying to live here, we are trying to find community, we are trying to be whole, we are trying to get it right, we are trying to love. That is what civics means for people of color.

If we extend that to think about Hip Hop, Hip Hop is this new iteration of our art and our ways to express through a very civic minded place. Because civics also is about critique. It is about social commentary. It is about exposing what is wrong with the world and thinking about the ways in which together we can heal, and be together, and resist, and have this place of protest [with] our bodies and direct action. All of those things that we do to try to survive in this place and hopefully thrive, is civics. Hip Hop is this place where we can do that.

In 2016, I had an opportunity to get a [Nasir Jones HipHop fellowship] at Harvard.[20] I took that time at Harvard to work on a website called "Get Free: Hip Hop Civics." It takes the elements of Hip Hop, of Afrofuturism, and of activism. If you talk to an activist for about 20 minutes, an activist will never tell you what happened today. An activist will give you a 20, 30, maybe a 100 year description of how you got to today. So I went around the country for about a year interviewing activists. I wanted to get their stories on tape and [document] what they thought about the movement that we were in, this Black Lives Matter movement, and what that meant for their actual city. Because I think civics also should be very local. We ask people to be globally minded, but I need to know what's going on in my hood first, before we become globally minded. Then I also think that Hip Hop is global, but it's also very local...

Manny Faces: Community...

Dr. Bettina Love: It's very community, but it's also driven by the community. For instance, a rapper like Big Freedia[21] comes out of New Orleans. Freedia's popularity has to start in a place like New Orleans because it's such a gender bending space, right? Could Freedia pop off in the Bronx? I don't know. Maybe now, but not ten years ago.

Manny Faces: Right. For sure.

Dr. Bettina Love: Hip Hop also has its locale. The slang that they use out in Oakland we don't use in New York, we don't use in the South.

Manny Faces: You hella right! [LAUGHS]

Dr. Bettina Love: Right. You hella right! Like, it's hella hot, right? So it's local because you are dealing with the local issues, the local slang, but you're all under the umbrella of Hip Hop. Civics needs to be like that too. This idea that you understand your community, you understand what's going on in your community, how to speak to the folks in your community, how to research your community. That's what civics should be about.

That's why the curriculum is about a particular city and understanding that city and what's going on in that city. Because Hip Hop has this idea of locality.

It's not that we don't want you to be globally minded, but we first want you to know what's going on at home.

And then the idea of Afrofuturism... I think kids need places to dream. I think we all need to dream, to dream about what is possible. We always ask, "What would we do if there was no racism? What would we do?" I don't even know what that would look like. So we got to dream it. We got to think about it. We got to work from a place of justice, then try and get there. Afrofuturism allows us to see ourselves in very powerful ways. I mean, that's why *Black Panther* makes $1 billion in four weeks. It's not just about a superhero movie. It's about Black folks seeing themselves in powerful ways, in ways that we can't even think of. When they say in the movie, "Welcome home," and it's Wakanda, I think every Black person raised up in their seat like, "Let me see what home looking like over there! I want to see home!"

So, for me, civics and this idea of freedom is about Hip Hop inspiring us to take charge in our local communities and to use our imaginations and to get involved, but not to be ahistorical. To understand that there is a playbook. Our ancestors have left us a playbook. They didn't leave us with nothing. So draw on that playbook and draw on the work of Black women and queer folks. That's another thing that's intentional about the website. We're going to look up folks like Ella Baker.[22] We're going to make sure you understand folks like Audre Lorde.[23] The [Get Free] website has a reading list for ages zero to 80, right? Books for babies to talk about activism. A is for activism, B is for boycott, C is for cooperation. Or you can read *The New Jim Crow*.[24] We got PDFs on the website of actual books, articles, videos, trying to get people to understand there is a knowledge that you need to have to go out here and fight.

Manny Faces: You bring up a good point. You talk about starting really early. I read an article[25] about the Parkland, Florida students.[26] They were speaking out against gun [violence]. For what it's worth, I think they're doing great stuff. One of the things that the article pointed out was that in Florida there's some kind of curriculum mandate that civics is actually taught—because right now you might not find a civics class at all in most high schools...

Dr. Bettina Love: No, you won't.

Manny Faces: They actually get taught as early as 7th grade. So part of the reason why they're so well versed with the topics, so well-spoken and ready to go out there and do all the things, is because they've been taught civics...

Dr. Bettina Love: That's right.

Manny Faces: . . .at an early age. And you are amplifying that by saying, "Yeah. It has to be done when they're young."

Dr. Bettina Love: Yeah. I think oftentimes kids come to college—and I'm a college professor—they come to school. . .

Manny Faces: It's the first time they're having this. . .

Dr. Bettina Love: . . .it's the first time they're having this. You're like, "Oh, where you been?" And it's beautiful to see the eyes light up, and they want to get involved, but there's so many things that they're still pushing up against. . .

Manny Faces: Or that they could have done earlier...

Dr. Bettina Love: . . .or they could have done earlier. And the older you get, the more resistant you get to change. And we don't think [about] 18-year-olds and 19-year-olds. They're coming into who they're going to be, and not everybody's going to take a class on diversity.

Manny Faces: Right.

Dr. Bettina Love: When you can get kids started in fourth grade and fifth grade thinking about these things, that's a powerful thing, because now you're going to change humanity. You're going to change the way we look at each other. These kids are going to be different, and I think these kids are going to do amazing things, with or without [that] shooting. The shooting amplifies who they are. But I don't think they were just docile kids walking around playing video games all day.

Manny Faces: A switch didn't get flipped. They were ready. . .

Dr. Bettina Love: Right. They were ready. And I think with all movements that are always youth led, these youth are ready. We got to give youth more credit. I don't know what happens to us. I don't know if it's like at 31 [years old], but—where's our switch? Because we *forget* all of a sudden. We used to be those kids. I think that supporting them, with teachers feeling as though they can implement and feel safe implementing a type of radical civic education, is important.

That's why for me, this was more about having something where teachers feel like they're comfortable using it, parents want to use it, and folks just feel engaged. That's why it's music, there's videos, there's comic books, all types of stuff, trying to get folks saying, "Oh, civics just doesn't have to be about us doing a community project or us registering to vote." All those things are important. I'm not saying stop those things, but the idea is, "Do you understand how liberation works?" "Do you know that there's a playbook there?" "Do you know that folks have done this work and they're passing the baton to you?"

Manny Faces: And you could flip it. You could remix it if you have to, right?

Dr. Bettina Love: Right!

Manny Faces: This is Hip Hop. You could take it and flip it and remix it and make something new out of it, but keep it going.

Dr. Bettina Love: Keep it going. Moving forward. So that's what the curriculum really came out of. I also go around the country doing talks—and I love doing talks. I love talking to teachers. I do an hour-long talk and teachers are hyped and excited, and then they're all like, "Well, what are we going to do when you leave?"

Manny Faces: Right? "What's next?"

Dr. Bettina Love: So I really wanted to create something that I could leave and say, "Well, this is next."

Manny Faces: Right. Go here.

Dr. Bettina Love: Go here. Here's the curriculum. That was my thinking. But I really want Black folks to know—particularly Black youth to know—how beautiful they are in the ideas of social change. I think one thing we don't talk about enough in schools is. . .

You know, we tell them that Black folks were slaves. We tell them about the Trail of Tears. We tell them all of these things, these historical events, but we don't tell them that we resisted. There's no talk about how we resisted. The civil rights [movement] is the only time we resisted, and that was only because Martin gave a speech. . .

Manny Faces: . . .and only *one* speech.

Dr. Bettina Love: . . .and only *one* speech. No, there were tactics. There were strategies. There were ways in which they went about this. And they argued. They didn't always agree. But there was a playbook, and we resisted. And don't get me wrong, I think it has to be hard for a white person to sit up in a classroom full of Black kids to talk about how Black folks resisted. The conversation about slavery is an *easy* conversation. It's one that we've had over and over and over again. But we haven't told kids that, "No. No. We didn't just chill. We resisted. And we resisted in multiple ways."

That conversation needs to happen so they know that there's a history here that is about resistance. Still about love and joy and care for each other, but we did resist. And this is what it looks like, because the story of resistance is actually the story of how we get free.

Manny Faces: And that's civics.

Dr. Bettina Love: And that's civics.

Manny Faces: I've always said with Hip Hop influencing these other areas of society, Hip Hop's gotten *community* down pat. But what Hip Hop still has trouble doing is turning that community into *constituency*.

Dr. Bettina Love: Yeah. . .

Manny Faces: Some of that is saying, "OK, we can join together as a community, as communities, that have like-minded ideals and work with those playbooks." But it's that networking, that like-mindedness that Hip Hop has. It just has to be channeled.

Dr. Bettina Love: Yeah. And I think that's what young people today are really doing. If you look at the strategies of Black Lives Matter or United We Dream,[27] they're really trying to be local. They're trying to be as grassroots as possible because they understand that grassroots is how we will work a national agenda.

Black folks ain't never going to agree. We're just not going to agree. You can't take everybody everywhere. But community, and community sovereignty, is what this is about. I think you're seeing young folk today who are pushing back on, "Here's our leader. Here's the person who's in charge of all of us," and really saying, "No. This is a leader. And this is a leader. And a leader looks different. And we can have a leader-full movement."

You're seeing young folk push back on that narrative because they have studied and they have learned from our mistakes of the past, and are trying to say, "This is how we get free. Freedom doesn't have to look like the one man that gives the speech, and then after the speech, we all somehow get freedom." It didn't work like that. I think you're watching young folk who are very civically minded, but civically minded in the ways in which Black folks have to take up civics. They're remixing the narrative and the tactics, and we're watching that right now.

Manny Faces: Well, good luck!

Dr. Bettina Love: Ayyy, ayyy. They need it!

Manny Faces: We all need it. That's a great way to take us out because I've ambitiously named this podcast *Hip Hop Can Save America!* It may be a lofty theory, but in your experience and from your point of view, what are the best reasons to consider Hip Hop music and culture when looking for ways to truly improve lives and livelihoods and communities in this country?

Dr. Bettina Love: I think about Hip Hop and the power of Hip Hop and what Hip Hop can do for us to even save lives or be a country that's truly focused on justice… And when I say justice, I mean intersectional justice. That's housing justice, that's health justice, that's immigration justice, that's queer justice. If we're going to be a country that really strives for that—and I'm hopeful, you caught me on a hopeful day. Some days I'm not—But I think Hip Hop has the power because Hip Hop is about humanity. And humanity doesn't mean that you have to be clean cut and you deserve rights because you are a profound great speaker and you look good in a suit. That's not humanity. Hip Hop is about love and compassion and grace and anger and voice and temperament. Everything it means to be human. That's what Hip Hop does. I think about Hip Hop on any given day. I can listen to something that is just filthy, then I can listen to something that is just righteous. Then I can listen to something that puts me in a mellow mood, a chill out mood. Then it could be some lovemaking. In a matter of 24 hours. I can go through all of those emotions with Hip Hop. That's humanity at its finest.

And I think Hip Hop has the space where people get to voice who they are as human beings, good, bad and the ugly. And if we're ever going to move to a place where this country is about the work of healing, it has to be about the work of healing for all. And if it's about the work of healing for all, then it has to take people as they are and it has to embrace their humanity with the full-fledged dignity of humanity. And I think Hip Hop—Black culture in general—is always this complex space of juggling our humanity and what it means to be a full-fledged person with all the quirks and the complications and the complexities of what it means to be human. Hip Hop just truly takes that on—and it's such a complex thing—but it just takes it on and it lays it on the table flat. Like, "What!? You either take it or you don't." And I think that's the beauty of Hip Hop and that's the beauty of the humanity that we are trying to create.

Hip Hop is that complex place that opens the door to all of that. So if we're truly going to be in a place where we all can be free and live our lives freely, then it has to be a place that we see ourselves and we see that our humanity is raised up. And I think Hip Hop is a space to try to have those conversations and think about that holistically.

Manny Faces: Well, that's what's up. Dr. Love, thank you very much for your time and your insight and your perspective and for your work and for your. . . did I say inspiration?

Dr. Bettina Love: Aww, thank you so much.

Manny Faces: And I hope to do my little part in this to share this talk and let people hear from you—these very important and insightful things.

Dr. Bettina Love: I appreciate that with all my heart. Thank you so much for having me.

Afterthoughts

In her TEDx talk, writings, teaching, and throughout our conversation, Dr. Love offered profound insights into the intersections of race, class, gender, and culture—particularly in relationship to legacy systems and institutions. Her perspective illuminates critical considerations for anyone seeking to radically reimagine these spaces. Dr. Love's analysis of how Hip Hop and Black culture intersect with education, youth empowerment, intersectional justice, and civic engagement has fundamentally shaped my work—and represents essential knowledge for any adult entering spaces where they may hold author-ity over young people, across all demographics.

For me, and for this book, this starting point was crucial. Dr. Love established essential mandates for anyone exploring these interdisciplinary connections: This work transcends mere engagement metrics or superficial implementation. It is about equality, freedom, and survival.

Our conversation crystallized another vital truth: engaging with Hip Hop Based Education is inherently an act of social justice. Creating a Hip Hop-influenced civics education program *is* activism. It reinforced my core belief that Hip Hop's changemaking potential extends far beyond music, media, and celebrity. The true revolutionary spirit of Hip Hop can only reach its full power through the mindsets of those pushing for transformative change *outside* of commercial and capitalistic endeavors. After all, Hip Hop is, at its essence, more than music, more than culture even—it represents a unique form of revolutionary thought.

In an age where government-controlled institutions face mounting threats of becoming pawns in extremist partisan warfare, Dr. Love's work creating an adaptable initiative that can exist *outside* these systems represents another Hip Hop-flavored style of remixing traditional practices—a necessity that may grow even more urgent as time goes on.

While the emphasis of this first episode began with education, Dr. Love's work applying the same concepts to civic engagement helped foreshadow the throughline of the show, this book, and my work: that through authentic, nuanced, and holistic approaches, the use of these ancestral-driven, diasporic-influenced elements in Hip Hop's DNA hold immense power to uplift lives, livelihoods, communities, and industries in unparalleled ways, increasing equity, fairness, and opportunity across all sorts of fields and disciplines.

With her powerful philosophy illuminating the path, so began my journey—and now begins ours—to better understand Hip Hop's transfor-mative potential to help save the country that birthed it and improve all of humanity.[28]

Key Takeaways

1. Hip Hop is more than just music; it's a full-fledged culture with valu-able characteristics that can be applied to education and society at large.

2. Culturally relevant, responsive, and affirming pedagogy should aim to incorporate youth culture, including Hip Hop, to better engage and educate students.
3. Hip Hop embodies important skills like creativity, improvisation, and social-emotional intelligence, which are valuable in education and beyond.
4. Educators need to understand Hip Hop culture deeply to effectively incorporate it into their teaching, avoiding gimmicks or superficial and culturally insensitive use.
5. Hip Hop can be a powerful tool for addressing complex social issues and fostering critical thinking in students.
6. Civics education for people of color is intrinsically linked to survival and community engagement, and Hip Hop can play a crucial role in this.
7. The Get Free initiative combines Hip Hop, Afrofuturism, and activism to create a comprehensive civics education curriculum.
8. Early exposure to civics education and activism can empower youth to become more engaged citizens and leaders.
9. Hip Hop's local and global nature makes it an effective tool for understanding both community-specific and broader social issues.
10. Hip Hop represents the full spectrum of human experiences and emotions, making it a powerful medium for exploring and expressing humanity.

Discussion Questions

1. How can we integrate Hip Hop culture into our curriculum in a way that respects its complexity and avoids superficial or gimmicky approaches?
2. What strategies can we employ to help teachers who are unfamiliar with Hip Hop culture become more comfortable and proficient in using it as an educational tool?
3. How might we redesign our civics education programs to incorporate Hip Hop and address the specific needs of students of color?

4. In what ways can businesses and organizations outside of education use Hip Hop's principles of creativity and improvisation to foster innovation and problem-solving?

5. How might healthcare professionals incorporate Hip Hop culture to improve patient engagement and health education, particularly in underserved communities?

6. How can civic leaders and policymakers use Hip Hop's local-global dynamic to create more effective community engagement strategies?

7. In what ways can the principles of Hip Hop education be applied to professional development and training programs in various industries?

8. How might the entertainment industry leverage Hip Hop's ability to express the full spectrum of human experiences to create more diverse and inclusive content?

9. How can social justice organizations and well-meaning politicians use Hip Hop's history of resistance and community-building to inform and enhance their activism strategies?

10. In what ways can tech companies incorporate Hip Hop culture and its principles to create more culturally relevant and engaging digital products and services?

This podcast episode was originally released on June 4, 2018.

Notes

1 1990s: Tha Golden Era | Howard Magazine. (2023). Howard.edu. https://magazine.howard.edu/stories/1990s-tha-golden-era

2 Marc Lamont Hill. (2009). *Beats, rhymes, and classroom life*. Teachers College Press.

3 Several educational institutions have introduced Hip Hop-related minor programs, including Columbia University, Bowie State University, Columbia College Chicago, SUNY Brockport, and as of Spring, 2025, Howard University.

4 Otterman, S. (2011, August 12). With Fresh Prep, mixing regents test material with Hip Hop. *The New York Times*. https://www.nytimes.com/2011/08/12/nyregion/with-fresh-prep-mixing-regents-test-material-with-hip-hop.html

5 Science Genius—HipHopEd. (n.d.). HipHopEd. https://hiphoped.com/science-genius/

6 Love, B. (2014, April 8). Hip hop, grit, and academic success: Bettina Love at TEDxUGA. YouTube. https://www.youtube.com/watch?v=tkZqPMzgvzg

7 The term O.G.—originating in 1970s Los Angeles gang culture and later popularized through film and Hip Hop—refers to an originator or pioneer, derived from "original gangster."

8 Hip Hop comprises four primary artistic "elements" or pillars, with a fifth element acknowledging its broader cultural significance: DJing, emceeing (rapping), graffiti art, breaking (dance), and knowledge (of self). While some organizations recognize additional elements, these five remain the most widely accepted foundations of Hip Hop culture.

9 Dr. Christopher Emdin, a leading figure in the Hip Hop education movement, focuses on science education. He co-founded the online community #HipHopEd and its related conference series, and has authored several books exploring the connections between Hip Hop and education.

10 Martha Diaz, a renowned figure in Hip Hop Based Education and media, founded both the Hip Hop Education Center and the Hip Hop Odyssey (H2O) International Film Festival.

11 The Hip Hop Ed movement, often identified by its hashtag #HipHopEd, is a loose collective of educators, professionals, advocates, activists, Hip Hop fans, practitioners, and others who support Hip Hop as a valuable educational tool.

12 A cypher is an informal, performative gathering where practitioners—typically emcees or dancers—assemble in a circle and take turns as featured performers.

13 Jeff Chang authored *Can't Stop, Won't Stop: A History of the Hip Hop Generation* (2005), a seminal text exploring the origins of Hip Hop music and culture.

14 Tricia Rose is an acclaimed scholar who has authored foundational texts in Hip Hop studies, including *Black Noise: Rap Music and Black Culture in Contemporary America* (1994) and *The Hip Hop Wars: What We Talk About When We Talk About Hip Hop—And Why It Matters* (2008).

15 iHeartMedia (formerly Clear Channel) is a media conglomerate that owns numerous radio stations nationwide. Their standardized approach to radio programming has been criticized as another step in the increasing corporatization of musical art.

16 Nasir "Nas" Jones debuted in 1994 with the acclaimed album *Illmatic* and has since established himself as a prolific Hip Hop artist, businessman, and venture capitalist.

17 The documentary *Time Is Illmatic* (2014) chronicles the creation and cultural impact of Nas's landmark debut album *Illmatic* through intimate interviews and archival footage.

18 Dr. Love argues that perceived classroom disruptions like "banging on a desk" may instead represent forms of musical expression such as drumming and pen-tapping.

19 While no single moment marks the creation of Hip Hop's diverse culture, August 11, 1973, is widely recognized as its symbolic birthdate—when Bronx, NY resident Cindy Campbell and her brother DJ Kool Herc hosted a party that featured musical and cultural innovations that would come to define Hip Hop.

20 The Nasir Jones Hiphop Fellowship, established at Harvard University in 2013 through the Hiphop Archive and Research Institute, supports scholars and artists who demonstrate exceptional creativity and scholarship in areas related to Hip Hop. The fellowship is named after the rapper Nas.

21 Big Freedia, the "Queen of Bounce," emerged from New Orleans in the late 1990s and has established bounce music's presence in mainstream culture through high-profile collaborations and dynamic performances.

22 Ella Baker was a civil rights activist and organizer who helped establish the Student Nonviolent Coordinating Committee (SNCC) in 1960.

23 Audre Lorde was a Black feminist writer, poet, and activist known for her groundbreaking work addressing intersectionality, particularly concerning race, gender, sexuality, and class.

24 In *The New Jim Crow* (2010), legal scholar Michelle Alexander demonstrates how mass incarceration serves as a modern system of legal segregation.

25 https://washingtonmonthly.com/2018/03/05/the-civic-education-program-that-trained-the-parkland-student-activists/

26 This refers to survivors of a February 14, 2018 school shooting at Marjory Stoneman Douglas High School in Parkland, Florida

27 United We Dream is a nonprofit immigrant advocacy organization.

28 In the years since our first podcast interview, Dr. Love has continued to be a renowned expert voice on these matters and has published several acclaimed books, including *We Want to Do More Than Survive: Abolitionist Teaching and the Pursuit of Educational Freedom* (2021) and the *New York Times* bestseller *Punished for Dreaming: How School Reform Harms Black Children and How We Heal* (2023).

· 2 ·

THE EMPATH | DR. IAN LEVY

As I continued to explore examples of practitioners across various fields and disciplines who incorporate Hip Hop music, culture, and sensibilities into their respective practices, one common throughline emerged: a focus on youth. While youth development and empowerment were the expected end goals in many of these cases, what proved more interesting was the emphasis on connection and empathy as the means to achieve them.

Hip Hop and youth culture are inseparable, as Dr. Bettina Love and other educators we'll explore in later chapters explain. What's unique now is that for the first time, adults responsible for young people are often products of Hip Hop culture themselves. As Hip Hop moves into its sixth decade, this confluence of culture offers a powerful, cross-generational connection, if utilized effectively and authentically.

As Dr. Love emphasized, teachers are well-suited to take advantage of this in a one-to-many approach. However, in educational settings, there are those perhaps even better positioned for one-on-one interactions: school counselors.

Dr. Ian P. Levy was named School Counselor of the Year in 2016 by the New York State School Counselor Association (NYSSCA),[1] recognized for his development, implementation, and evaluation of a Hip Hop-based counseling framework in an urban school setting. Dr. Levy has also evaluated mental health practices in these schools, interrogating the role of school counselors and other staff to ensure the emotional lives of young people are adequately addressed. His work has been featured on CNN's *Great Big Story*[2] and in *The New York Times*,[3] but most importantly, he has used Hip Hop to directly impact the lives of his students in inspiring ways.

At the time of this interview, Dr. Levy had evolved from practitioner to instructor, teaching up-and-coming counselors about the approaches he had successfully implemented with his groundbreaking, in-school recording studio that had emerged as a uniquely effective vehicle for youth development, empowerment, and catharsis.

This exploration felt like the next logical step in my journey of discovering and documenting innovative ways in which experts in established fields were incorporating Hip Hop to reach young people through previously untapped methods. It also provided an early example of the added perspective that can emerge when someone in such a position is a participant in Hip Hop arts. As a rapper himself,[4] Dr. Levy was perhaps uniquely qualified to champion Hip Hop songwriting as a therapeutic approach for middle and high school students.

Once he was able to secure institutional buy-in, the results would speak—and rap—for themselves.

The Interview

Manny Faces: Dr. Levy, when it comes to education, counseling, and all the various things that you do, how do you currently define who you are from a professional standpoint?

Dr. Ian P. Levy: Right now, I consider myself a counselor educator. I've taken this plunge into this new role where I've shifted from being a direct practitioner of counseling services—I worked for upwards of five years in New York City schools as a school counselor—and now I work training school counselors to go into schools and deploy culturally relevant counseling services and learn how to advocate for both themselves and students in schools.

Manny Faces: *Culturally relevant* is such an interesting angle, obviously, as we talk about Hip Hop and education and bringing cultural relevance into schools and into counseling environments.

How do you describe the state of this field, this counseling? What are you trying to get across as you begin this journey of instructing other counselors and other people in this field? What are some of the key takeaways or bullet points that you're really focused on?

Dr. Ian P. Levy: It's multifaceted. Our role as school counselors has developed significantly over time, originating from being a person in the school who helps students make sure that they're on point academically and focused on what they need to be focused on. Over time, we've learned the importance of addressing socio-emotional concerns of students' learning as well. Now, our field exists in this place where we're ideally supposed to be able to address the personal, social, academic, and career interests and points of development for young people in schools. This multifaceted role of the school counselor is really what I'm trying to push forward to my students as they enter schools that will most definitely have very different understandings of what their role is.

Because our profession has dramatically transformed over the last 60 years, a lot of schools don't know what a school counselor is. Our roles will be differently defined depending on what district you're in, what city you're in, what school you're in. Being prepared to advocate for your role is a huge component of what it means to be a school counselor in today's world. Ultimately, if we're not able to advocate for our role, then we're never going to be able to provide adequate services. We might be viewed as bureaucratic pawns who are just filling out paperwork and getting stuff done and not supposed to be running group counseling services with young people or engaging in in-depth individual counseling services with young people, if that's what we need to do in our school. So, it really is important that school counselors are able to individually define and advocate for their work in schools which will not, when they enter them, understand what they're supposed to actually be doing.

Manny Faces: Interesting. I'm not a counselor. I'm not a social worker. I'm not into this field. But doesn't that make sense, being very specific towards the environment or the students and how they see the world, and putting that focus on how you counsel them and how you deal with them?

Dr. Ian P. Levy: From a counseling standpoint, absolutely. In sessions and in groups, I'm always going to make sure—which is why Hip Hop is so beautiful—that I can use different approaches to counseling that allow young people to lead that process and for us to adapt our work to respond directly to the lives of young people. There are folks that are going in and are ready, prepared, and have the skills to do excellent, really hands-on counseling work—individual or group. But their school might say, "OK, well, in our school, school counselors don't do that. In our school, counselors have to help with getting tests ready and administrating tests in the school. We need you to manage really big pieces of data and look at grade point averages for your cohort and be able to report that out to other people in the school." That should be, in some way, part of our role, but not all of it. Oftentimes because our roles aren't understood, even if we have these great tools, we're not able to use them. And so that's what I mean by a need to be able to advocate for your role the way that you see it.

We want to be able to utilize counseling modalities that are youth-driven and go where young people need to go and can be adapted and tailored to the specific needs of the young people we're working with. But we face this larger, systemic concern around what our role is in schools.

Manny Faces: Got it. Let's talk about Hip Hop in your field or how you've incorporated Hip Hop into your work. Just give a 50,000-foot view of how Hip Hop has been one of the methods that you've been using with success.

Dr. Ian P. Levy: For me, Hip Hop has been a platform through which I've delivered direct, individual, or group counseling services to young people in schools. I've taken this idea of lyric writing and performing and look at those as naturally cathartic processes for any artist. It's a space for folks to condense thoughts and feelings and relay them to an audience, and oftentimes, we use that process to talk about thoughts and feelings that we've never talked about before. I've seen that in personal experiences as an emcee, but also from interacting with friends who are emcees, that Hip Hop culture allowed people to open up in ways that they would not in other settings, and that it was the perfect medium to bring into counseling services in schools.

So, I worked hard to develop a [recording] studio space in the school, in my actual counseling office. It took a while to really get it going and have it fully fleshed out, but [in time] I had a full recording studio in my office. And I worked with students to create emotionally themed mixtapes[5] every year—at least one, sometimes more. We would have group counseling processes where we would discuss various topics, if it was self-doubt or if it was police brutality or if it was fear or stress. Any of those themes could be discussed because the young people knew that once they discussed them, they'd be able to write lyrics, record songs, perform songs, put songs online, that were about those emotional concerns.

It allowed me this pathway into their worlds and allowed me to help them sort through these thoughts and feelings. And oftentimes when you write a song, you want it to be really concise. You want your concept to be on point. You want the audience to understand what you're talking about, which means that you can't write a really good song about fear unless you really understand what fear means to you. This allowed me this perfect platform to say, "Well, where does this fear come from for you?" and engage in that traditional talk therapy that you would engage in, but for the sole purpose of then helping them craft better lyrics that could engage an audience. And then, we would work on performances. How do you move on a stage in a way that represents the content of your song? If you're talking about fear in a verse or you're talking about perseverance in a verse, how does your performance look different? How do your vocal inflections sound different, to really relay those messages? On the surface, it's helping young people just make fire tracks. But at this deeper level, it's helping them refine their own understanding of their emotional experiences and their ability to communicate these emotional experiences to the world in ways that they might not have been comfortable doing prior.

Manny Faces: Right. I think that when we talk about Hip Hop being used in these settings, to those who are relatively unfamiliar or haven't seen this in practice or hadn't really thought much of it, there's that perception of what rap and rap music are to the general public. Very often when you say the words "Hip Hop" and you merge it with education, they often think that it's not compatible.

What was it like when you first started doing this and saw how students were able to take this medium that they're familiar with in the entertainment world and use it in this way? How surprised were you?

Dr. Ian P. Levy: I don't even know if *surprised* is what I would say, because for me, this is what a cypher[6] looked like. You know Legendary Cyphers[7], right? Massive, amazing [public, outdoor, freestyle rap] cypher [that happens at] Union Square Park [in New York City]. I'm there at Legendary Cyphers and I hear one person randomly start spitting[8] a bar about issues with his father. And immediately, this domino effect, this cascade of bars follows from other participants about issues with their family—instantaneously! This is something that's happening already in Hip Hop...

Manny Faces: ...and organically...

Dr. Ian P. Levy: ...and organically! And it's what Hip Hop is about. Hip Hop literally was created to push back against larger systemic issues and forms of oppression. It was about people putting tensions aside and coming together to talk and build and push back against stressors and struggles in their lives. Naturally, I've made this argument, as have others in the field of Hip Hop therapy, that Hip Hop in and of itself is cathartic, we could say.

When we transfer this cathartic process to a traditional counseling space, I can now start building on that natural catharsis. Like, if I say, "Write a song about stress," young people already are down to do that because they might, (A) have already done that, or (B) of course, I can find Jay-Z songs where he writes about stress. It's not uncommon to address emotional concerns in Hip Hop. That's a very normal thing to do, culturally. But now, because that's happening, we as counselors are able to then build skills on top of that. I'm then allowed to say, "OK, cool, this bar where you're talking about a struggle with your father... What is that like? What are those struggles?" I can then engage in more direct conversations with the individual as they're emoting through this natural community-defined catharsis—this songwriting process. I can build on top of that.

What surprised me wasn't necessarily their willingness to engage in the work, but how the work naturally developed in our schools. One of the things we talk about in the field of mental health in general when working with young people, particularly young people of color, i developing *help seeking behavior*.[9] If something is going on with [a young person], knowing who they can talk to about that thing. There're a lot of reasons, like stigmas, why that doesn't happen. The fear of being perceived as weak or vulnerable is a reason why folks are not willing to just open up to other people. But this process, this studio space within the school, quickly became known naturally in the school community as the place to go to talk about things without me even having to push that.

I'll share a quick little story. I had been running my program for a year. It went really well, and my students put out this really dope mixtape which paid homage to Trayvon Martin.[10] But it was also the year that we had lost Eric Garner[11] and Mike Brown,[12] and because the media was really flooded with these images, the group sessions that we were running naturally were focused on that. So we wrote a lot of songs that were centered around social justice issues concerning police brutality. And they called the album *Hoodies Up*, and it was awesome.

So this was a really great process with this group of young men and women in my first year at this school. Summer came. The next year started. It was the first week of school. I worked with 9th graders, so I had 150 new 9th graders, and I didn't know all of them yet. It was literally the first week of school and this one student comes up to me in the hallway and he's like, "I heard that I could come record a song with you. My cousin just passed away, and I want to work on a track with you about it."

I don't know who this kid is. It's the first week of school. So I said, "Yes, please come to me at lunch." So he came to me at lunch, and I was like, "How'd you find out about the space?" And he shouted one of my students from the year before, "Oh, A.J. told me." He had been somewhere in the school and had been talking to another student who said, "Oh, you're going through something? Go to the studio."

I'm not even pushing this at this point. It's become entrenched in the community where now this is the place to go. And at that point A.J. was a 10th grader, so we have 10th graders being the model for help seeking behavior, right? Like, "Oh, let me talk to A.J. about what I should do about this emotional struggle, because he has been able to deal with that." And this is a new 9th grader. It's the first week. But he knows that this album came out the year before because the kids have it online, and it's the talk around school, and they know that the focus of the album is this emotional stuff. So it becomes natural. It became this built-in part of the experience in the school for students.

So this student came. We wrote this awesome track. He had lost a cousin whose name was Nana, and so he chose Kanye's "Hey Mama" beat and he wrote a song called "Hey Nana." And it was really tough for him, but really amazing. He wound up asking me if his sister could come after school—his sister was older and went to a different school—if she could come after school and record the hook. So him and I wrote this track. His sister pulled up after school and recorded the hook.

They played the song at the memorial service that weekend. He came back and told me all about it. His family had heard the song, and it was just like… this moment where… all I did was create a space, you know what I mean?

And the students knew that they could make it their own and take it where it needed to be taken, and they used it how it needed to be used in their lives.

It wasn't me doing anything there other than being available, and there are so many other moments like that. So I think if there's any surprise, it's not about the effectiveness of it, but it's about what this can morph into and how this can really shift school culture and change the way that young people interact with schooling, but also interact with difficult emotions and not be scared to address them and actively seek pathways to talk through difficult thoughts and feelings.

Manny Faces: A student talking to another student about this may have never happened before. For them to even go to another student as a mentor or somebody who is familiar with your program is a great side effect as well, because now you have interpersonal relationships being built.

Dr. Ian P. Levy: Actually, now that we're thinking about this, this is amazing... You know how XXL Magazine has the Freshman Class every year[13]—[in school] there's a freshman class of folks every year, so I took this idea and said "You guys are the 10th graders. You have literal freshmen coming into school. I need you to find me the freshman class for the club this year." What I meant by that was to find out who can spit or is interested in spitting and bring them to the studio. That was what I meant.

But I think because they were given this responsibility of, "OK, you were the inaugural group, and you need to find who the next group is," and because the focus of the work was naturally emotional, they also found students who were dealing with significant emotional concerns beyond just if somebody could spit or not. Which is awesome.

Manny Faces: What I love—and this is sort of a side note—but what you're doing is obviously great for the students and the counseling aspect of all of this, but it's also good for Hip Hop. Because it's letting young people know, "Hey, listen, there's the partying, there's the radio songs, there's the entertainment value. . . But this thing of ours, this thing of yours, can still be used this way." I think that every bit of that helps.

Now, your school might have been very open to these ideas, but I'm sure you might have had some hurdles along the way. Maybe you've heard from peers and colleagues about some hindrances to incorporating Hip Hop into these fields? Administrators in institutions sometimes just don't *get it*, generally speaking. What do you think are some of the problems with being able to start these programs and keep these programs going?

Dr. Ian P. Levy: I had this studio up and running fully in the last three years, but I did this work for almost five, really six years, before I was even working full-time in the school. When I first started doing this work, I did an after-school program where I would pull up to this school and bring my studio equipment with me. I had a portable mic, and I was on the subway with a mic stand and laptop in my backpack.

The only time that this principal was giving me was after school. Which is normal. If you're bringing something innovative, they're like, "Cool, great, you can do it during lunch or after school." But what student wants to sacrifice their lunch block? What student wants to stay after school? These are not ideal times at all to run something. So that's what happened initially.

At another school I did a Hip Hop lesson one day that was so amazing. It was so good. And the class was, like, bouncing off the walls. We were loud, but not loud in the distracting kind of a way, loud in a super engaged Hip Hop kind of way. I came out of the class and my administrator was like, "That was really loud. You guys need to be quiet. You need to calm it down next time," and almost had assumed that it didn't go well just based on volume. So there's always this lack of understanding of what expression looks like through Hip Hop and how it can be perceived as, "Oh, these individuals are engaging in Hip Hop. That's dangerous or that's loud or that's disorderly."

So there's a lot of these negative connotations, particularly from folks who are not part of Hip Hop culture, and that can be a hindrance as well.

At my previous school in the Bronx, the program ran after school, which started around like 4:30, and it could run until 6:00. They literally would have to kick us out of the building at 6:00. And I'm talking like 20 kids deep. It was so popular and so powerful—and this is why I say school counselors have to be able to advocate for their roles—that I eventually was able to say to my principal, "Listen, I have this interest, I need this during the day." And I figured out how to finagle it based on my experience with music—and the fact that I was in a charter school—to actually start a music elective class.

So I had a scheduled class called Hip Hop Lyricism, which was on student schedules for the next two years, and they were able to enroll in these classes. I had a block period during the day where I could do this work, but I was not able to do that until I basically proved its worth through these other spaces, like after school.

I think one of the challenging things I realized through doing this work is that schools—generally speaking, and urban schools in particular—are radically uncomfortable places for young people because they're not designed to meet them where they are. So you have young people walking into schools and they don't feel like they belong. They might be forced to walk through metal detectors when they walk into the school, so they might be feeling like they're labeled as threats or criminals. There's a bunch of different negative thoughts and feelings that go through an individual's head when they're walking into a school that doesn't understand them or appreciate them or value them or honor them.

When you create a space like a really awesome Hip Hop studio in a counselor's office, it flips that whole thing on its head. Students in my room were so connected to the work, they were so comfortable, they were so authentic, that when they left that room and had to go back to a math class that didn't engage them in the same capacity, they were just not having it, right? They would start trying to flex in those spaces in the way they could in my room— and that was not going over well with teachers. Eventually word would get back to administration. And of course, when this is heard, admin has to step up and protect their teachers—or at least that's what they perceive they have to do. What that means is that "Mr. Levy really isn't doing the work he's supposed to be doing with students. He's just making Hip Hop music. He's not teaching them how to really work on behaviors and bring them to our classroom spaces," when the reality was, I was teaching them how to be themselves, in school.

But, there was still an area of growth for me there—whether it's code switching[14] or whatever it is—but to say "OK, yes, you can be yourself in my room. But when you get to this other room, even if you can't be yourself, you need to figure out how to put on whatever face you have to put on just to get through it." We have to figure out what that looks like. Right? That's open to debate. I don't even like that approach of just settling and dealing. I'm not really even a huge advocate of that. But the fact is this was and still is an area of growth for me as well, and something that I didn't expect.

I just wanted to go into school and create amazing spaces for young people. But I didn't realize that when you do that, it shines a light even stronger on all the other spaces in school where they *can't* be themselves. They were so comfortable in *my* room that they were like, "Yo, school is B.S..."

Manny Faces: [LAUGHS]

Dr. Ian P. Levy: You know what I mean? "Why can't it always be like this?" "Why is there only one period where I can feel this way?" And that was such an important moment.

Manny Faces: OK. On another note. Thinking about how these ideas can not only apply in the counseling setting or in the behavioral work, but in other fields...

Dr. Ian P. Levy: Absolutely.

Manny Faces: ...it can apply in math and science, as we know...

Dr. Ian P. Levy: Yes, absolutely. My mentor, Dr. Christopher Emdin,[15] is doing ridiculously awesome work in the world of science education using Hip Hop. And that's what #HipHopEd as a group and as an entity is focused on,[16] bringing Hip Hop culture into every aspect of schooling. That's why the work is so important.

From a school counseling standpoint, it makes me think of this modern understanding of what a school counselor is supposed to be. We're supposed to be able to deliver school-wide interventions and collaborate with educators. So there's work I can do in training my school counseling students—if they're doing something effective, collaborating to see how they can assist teachers in implementing different types of strategies in their classrooms that allow students to feel the same way they feel in these counseling spaces.

But that has to be something that's championed by administration, and there generally has to be a really strong understanding and appreciation for Hip Hop culture, for youth culture—which I would say is Hip Hop culture. If at the core the school is not trying to do that, then you're consistently going to run into barriers everywhere you are.

So school-wide approaches are key. And I think that is something that becomes really apparent for anybody doing great work in an isolated classroom or counseling office. You start to see how students react to other aspects of schooling when you just have this *one* dope space, and it shows us that we need school wide approaches.

Manny Faces: I think that a lot of people may find value in what you're doing in [schools within communities of color]. How much do you think that this kind of mentality, this Hip Hop incorporation, can help in communities that aren't typically associated with Hip Hop, that aren't "inner city" or "urban" or "Black and brown"—is there a more universal potential for what you're working with?

Dr. Ian P. Levy: Absolutely. I think that if you don't come from Hip Hop, if you don't understand Hip Hop, and you go and try to look up what Hip Hop is and you look on television or in certain spaces, you're only going to see a sliver of what Hip Hop is. You're only going to gather certain perceptions of Hip Hop—the guns, the violence, the drugs. These are components of Hip Hop culture, and that's fine, but it's not all of Hip Hop culture. What this work has the potential to do for non-Hip Hop spaces is to allow folks to understand the complexities of Hip Hop culture at a deeper level and then subsequently understand the complexities of youth culture and urban communities at a deeper level.

I think it really becomes this workaround helping folks cultivate an appreciation for and an empathetic understanding of the different circumstances, situations, and experiences that [other] folks in this world face. I think Hip Hop is the best way to communicate experiences for anyone, so I think that you can engage in a lot of that work in traditionally white or non-Hip Hop schools.

I also think that there's vast potential for really critical race related work using Hip Hop as the medium. I'm in planning stages of considering how to help white folks in particular look at their white racial identities in some capacity related to Hip Hop or analyzing what stereotypes they hold or prejudices they hold to other communities, using Hip Hop as an anchor for that discussion.

Manny Faces: Yeah. First of all, white kids listen to rap. They rap, they know all the things. And to let them use the same songwriting techniques, I think that's universal and can be applied everywhere.

Dr. Ian P. Levy: Absolutely. I think the content is different. And that's why I think race becomes important. I've gone into predominantly white schools, to engage in work like this, and heard young people start talking about all the stereotypical things, like being on a block or doing certain types of drugs or engaging in certain types of behaviors that I know, or I have a pretty good feeling, that they're not [actually] engaging in. But that then becomes a critical entry point, like, "Why do you feel like that's what you have to talk about and what does that mean?" There are so many ways to engage in the work. That's why I think race and understanding perceptions of other individuals in this world, via Hip Hop as that medium, is really important.

Manny Faces: I think that's one of the overarching themes that I'm trying to get at with this podcast is to try to amplify that message. Because I think we know that to save America, to save our society, what we do need is better understanding, empathy, and perspectives. I think that could help, generally. I know that, as you might agree, Hip Hop is a great vehicle for doing that across all demographics.

I want to ask you one thing, to piggyback off of that. You tweeted, "Hip Hop is Vibranium. Colonizers will try and steal it and create fake versions of innovative work in schools. We owe it to students to help them harness their brilliance and protect their hip hopness as they grow."

When we talk about Hip Hop in education, when we talk about Hip Hop in fine arts, with the explosion of *Hamilton*, with all of the ways that Hip Hop might be becoming, for lack of a better term, a buzzword in some of these nontraditional spaces, what's the concern there? How do we continue to have an authentic approach to merging Hip Hop with education and counseling in some of these other fields?

Dr. Ian P. Levy: Well, the concern is that it's about youth experience, right? It's about the experience of urban communities. That's what Hip Hop has always been. And every time it's been commercialized, whether it's the B-Boy, whether it's the emcee, you see folks starting to engage in it for money. You see a lot of different reasons why folks try to commercialize it. But ultimately what you see is that the work starts to move further away from being focused on the direct and real experiences of the creators of the work.

In urban education and in using Hip Hop in educational spaces, it's about students and their experiences, and them being able to express their experiences authentically. The more we try to concretize and create curriculum or just think it's cool to spit a rap here and there as a teacher in a classroom, the further we get from understanding that this is a culture and a form of expression. This is a way that young people can show us how to fix our schools.

Young people can take this work in whatever direction they want to take this work. The fear is that we lose out on that organic process of Hip Hop growing authentically if we try to commercialize it.

It's the same sort of commercialization process that we've seen happen historically. In my opinion and in the opinion of others as well, Hip Hop education is just another element of that. It's just this new lane that is in this authentic place but is also being threatened by inauthentic versions of it.

It's about helping young people harness the fact that they *are* Hip Hop and what they have to say is valued and is original. We have to let this be a process that's guided by youth and it has to be authentic and rooted in their experiences. And I think that the more we commercialize it, the further we get away from that.

Afterthoughts

Through my conversation with Dr. Levy, I began to recognize that Hip Hop and other culturally responsive and affirming approaches could not only help young people feel seen and empowered but could potentially *save lives* through mental health intervention and hybridized counseling methods. His case-study presentation reinforced Dr. Love's foundation: the effectiveness of these approaches depends heavily on authority figures being unapologetic in their advocacy while stepping back to allow what many might view as *student-led* initiatives. As both guests so far demonstrated, while these authentic, progressive ideas may challenge administrators in legacy institutions, they remain essential for program success.

Dr. Levy expanded on a theme we explore throughout this book: how Hip Hop mindsets and innovative thinking can be applied across various fields. He also offered a crucial warning, one we'll revisit, about protecting these authentic ecosystems from commercial, capitalistic interests.

The interview also reinforced another crucial element in advocating for Hip Hop-inspired innovations—one that Dr. Love emphasized—the need for "receipts." Dr. Levy has contributed significant scholarship through research projects, papers, chapter contributions, and books, including *Hip Hop and Spoken Word Therapy in School Counseling: Developing Culturally Responsive Approaches* (2023), works which help document the effectiveness of Hip Hop-incorporated efforts by mental health professionals in various settings, providing advocates with crucial academic support for expanding these inspiring initiatives.

You'll notice I ask many interviewees about the potential impact of incorporating Hip Hop into fields serving young people from communities not typically associated with Hip Hop. To be clear, I believe the primary emphasis must be on improving educational and emotional outcomes for youth within traditionally Hip Hop-connected communities, as they have been historically underserved, under-resourced, and undervalued. The aforementioned "receipts" help demonstrate that these approaches work *precisely* because they are more culturally aligned with these students than typical pedagogical approaches. However, as Dr. Levy points out, overall youth culture and Hip Hop culture share significant overlap, so it shouldn't be too far of a stretch to see how these kinds of Hip Hop integrations can be effective across all kinds of communities.

A more interesting thought avenue emerges as we listen to Dr. Levy reflecting on Hip Hop's capacity to serve as a "workaround helping folks cultivate an appreciation for and an empathetic understanding of the different circumstances, situations, and experiences that [other] folks in this world face." Despite being a CIS-gendered white man, I grew up highly immersed in Hip Hop culture—and, by extension, Black American culture. While white people today don't need such immersion to be influenced by Hip Hop or Black American culture—those influences are ubiquitous, though full understanding and respect of them are often only superficial—I have no doubt that my deep engagement with these cultures served as a powerful window into the lives, thoughts, fears, and dreams of people from demographics different from my own.

As Dr. Love stated, those within Hip Hop have an inherent understanding of its community building qualities, its ability to bring together people from all walks of life. Through that close connection forged by a common factor, relationships and understanding can emerge that might not have otherwise. What Dr. Levy suggests goes beyond helping white kids who love rap music stay engaged in school or build trust in counseling sessions. The thought emerges—could some of what happened organically for non-Black or Latino folks like us—Hip Hop as a bridge-builder—be applied in an intentional manner to help invite cross-cultural dialog and understanding?

I would go on to explore this idea with later guests, some of whom we'll hear from in later chapters.

Key Takeaways

1. Hip Hop can be an effective tool for delivering direct, individual, or group counseling services to young people in schools.
2. Lyric writing and performing in Hip Hop can serve as naturally cathartic processes, allowing students and young people in similar settings to express thoughts and feelings they might not otherwise share.
3. Hip Hop-based counseling can help young people refine their understanding of their emotional experiences and communicate them effectively.
4. This approach can foster "help-seeking behavior" among young people, especially those of color, who might otherwise be reluctant to seek emotional support.
5. Hip Hop counseling can create a space where students feel comfortable addressing difficult emotions and actively seek pathways to discuss their thoughts and feelings.
6. The method can shift school culture and change how young people interact with schooling and difficult emotions.
7. Hip Hop counseling can create peer mentorship opportunities, with older students guiding younger ones to seek help.
8. There can be challenges in implementing Hip Hop counseling, including misconceptions about Hip Hop culture and resistance from school administration.
9. Creating a Hip Hop-friendly space in schools can highlight the disconnect between this engaging environment and traditional classroom settings.
10. Hip Hop counseling has potential beyond urban or minority communities and can be used to cultivate empathy and understanding across different cultural groups.

Discussion Questions

1. How might the principles of Hip Hop therapy be adapted for virtual or remote counseling settings to reach more young people?
2. What innovative ways could schools create safe spaces for emotional expression similar to Dr. Levy's recording studio model?

3. How could Hip Hop-based counseling approaches be integrated into workplace wellness programs or corporate mental health initiatives?
4. What role could Hip Hop therapy play in intergenerational family counseling or parent-child relationship building?
5. How might the principles of Hip Hop counseling be adapted for crisis intervention or emergency mental health response?
6. In what ways could Hip Hop therapy techniques be incorporated into group therapy settings for adults dealing with workplace stress or career transitions?
7. How could the success of Hip Hop counseling inform the development of new therapeutic approaches for other creative forms of expression?
8. What possibilities exist for integrating Hip Hop therapy approaches into rehabilitation programs or recovery settings?
9. How might Hip Hop counseling techniques be adapted for working with elderly populations or in memory care settings?
10. What role could Hip Hop therapy play in community healing and reconciliation programs following social or civil unrest?

This podcast episode was originally released on June 13, 2018.

Notes

1 *TC's Ian Levy Named NY State School Counselor of the Year.* (2017, January). Teachers College—Columbia University. https://www.tc.columbia.edu/articles/2017/january/ian-levy-named-ny-state-school-counselor-of-the-year/
2 Finding Yourself Through Hip-Hop. (2016, March). *Finding Yourself Through Hip-Hop.* YouTube. https://www.youtube.com/watch?v=iL82x-diQAY
3 Hu, W. (2016, January 19). Bronx School Embraces a New Tool in Counseling: Hip-Hop. *The New York Times.* https://www.nytimes.com/2016/01/20/nyregion/bronx-school-embraces-a-new-tool-in-counseling-hip-hop.html
4 As of this writing, Dr. Ian Levy's latest release was the album *Sometimes I Forget Where I've Been* (2023).
5 Mixtapes, popularized by Hip Hop DJs in the 1980s and 1990s, began as custom compilation albums on cassette before evolving through CD and digital formats. The term now can refer to any curated music collection resembling a traditional album, regardless of artist count or medium.
6 A cypher is an informal, performative gathering where practitioners—typically emcees or dancers—assemble in a circle and take turns as featured performers.
7 Legendary Cyphers, founded by the late Daniel "Majesty" Sanchez, is a public performance series where core emcees lead rap cyphers and invite public participation. The group

performs outside New York City's Union Square subway station on Friday nights, 8 p.m. to midnight, May through November, as well as other pop-up locations and commissioned events.

8 Spitting, in this context, is a colloquial term for rapping.

9 Help-seeking behavior describes actions individuals take to obtain mental health support, whether through informal networks or professional mental health services.

10 Trayvon Martin was a 17-year-old Black youth killed by a neighborhood watch volunteer in Sanford, Florida, in 2012. His death and the subsequent acquittal of his killer sparked national protests and helped catalyze the Black Lives Matter movement.

11 Eric Garner was a 43-year-old Black man killed by New York City police in 2014. His death by chokehold during an arrest for allegedly selling loose cigarettes, and his repeated plea of "I can't breathe," became powerful symbols in protests against police violence.

12 Michael Brown was an unarmed 18-year-old Black man killed by police in Ferguson, Missouri, in August 2014. His death and the subsequent lack of indictment of the officer sparked protests and drew national attention to police violence and militarized responses to community protests.

13 The "Freshman Class," launched by XXL Magazine in 2007, is an annual showcase of Hip Hop's rising artists considered most likely to impact the industry.

14 Code-switching refers to alternating between different languages, dialects, or communication styles based on social context, particularly common in communities navigating between vernacular and institutional speech.

15 Dr. Christopher Emdin, a leading figure in the Hip Hop Based Education movement, focuses on science education. He co-founded the online community #HipHopEd and its related conference series, and has authored several books exploring the connections between Hip Hop and education.

16 The Hip Hop Ed movement, often identified by its hashtag #HipHopEd, is a loose collective of educators, professionals, advocates, activists, Hip Hop fans, practitioners, and others who support Hip Hop as a valuable educational tool.

· 3 ·

THE TEACHING ARTIST |
MIKAL AMIN LEE

During my time as an independent journalist covering New York-area Hip Hop music and culture, the so-called "Mecca" of Hip Hop had lost some of its luster. What had been, for quite some time, essentially a New York/Los Angeles bi-coastal monopoly on the genre had fractured, and other major American cities and regions had begun asserting their influence. The South, in particular, was thriving, with cities like Houston flourishing and Atlanta rising to become the genre's universally accepted modern day epicenter.

Back in New York, mainstream artists such as A$AP Rocky and French Montana would eschew any allegiance to the "boom bap"[1] roots of the Big Apple, adapting their style to better emulate Hip Hop's twang du jour.

It wasn't necessarily the best time for traditional New York rap.

However, my focus was never much on the "industry" per se. I enjoyed covering the independent and underground scenes, which were still very much alive and well. More than half a dozen regular event series were continuing to deliver innovative and often inspiring displays of artistic prowess on any given day of the week, in any given borough of the city.

One such staple was Freestyle Mondays.

Led and hosted by lyrical impresario Corey James Gray, f.k.a., Illspokinn, Freestyle Mondays had been a weekly showcase series for more than ten years by the time I started poking my nose around the scene, and when I discovered it, I was transfixed.

The premise was simple enough. This was, in essence, a live game show. Typically, eight emcee "contestants" would sign up to compete. Each round would pair two contestants at random. A game show-esque wheel would be spun, each pie-like slice of the circle representing a category, like one might find in a trivia game: Current events, science, food chain, Hip Hop, history, and so on.

The wheel would stop on a category, and the host would call out a corresponding challenge—one that the contestants were hearing for the very first time.

"OK. Food chain. Contestant one, you're a shark; contestant two, you're plankton. Go!"

Each verbal warrior would then, for the duration of the timed round, perform unprepared, impromptu raps—completely off the top of their heads—representing whatever random concept had just been assigned to them. They would attempt to out-rap, out-style, and out-wit their competitor, staying on beat and on theme, hoping to garner enough crowd support to win the audience-driven vote of applause at the end of each round, until a champion was crowned at the end of the night.

The level of skill, imagination, and intelligence needed to take a random topic, rap about it for several minutes with no rehearsal, no practice, and no previous knowledge, performing with extraordinary articulation, charisma, and flair, was simply astounding. These were, quite literally, some of the smartest, most talented rap artists—in fact, some of the smartest *people*—that I had ever encountered.

Oh. Did I mention the live band?

Backing these brilliant spontaneous wordsmiths were some of the city's funkiest musicians, the pizazz of live instrumentation creating captivating crescendos to accompany the verbal brilliance on display.

To this day I contend that Freestyle Mondays is one of the best live events ever created by humankind, period.

In fact, I often noted that it was one of the only places you could bring a top echelon teacher or scientist, fully removed from Hip Hop culture, along with the most hardcore, gritty, street-savvy rap fan, and they'd both have the time of their lives.

So again, from the first visit, I was amazed at the prowess of these artists. You couldn't just be good at rapping; you had to be good at *thinking*. You had to be mentally sharp, quick on your verbal feet, and you really had to know a lot of *stuff* to be able to compete in this setting without making a fool of yourself. I suppose it was little surprise then, as I began talking to some of the regulars, to find out that they were really smart people, doing really smart things in the world. Some worked in business, some in journalism, some in nonprofits, and some were educators. Many would exemplify a term that I might have been familiar with, but never to its full extent: teaching artist. Someone who was willing and able to take their talent and use it not just for personal gain, but for the greater good.

One of these remarkable individuals is Mikal Amin Lee, artistically known at the time as Hired Gun, later switching to Mikal Amin. Mikal and I would go on to have many conversations about the role of Hip Hop music and culture as a force for education, social justice, and the upliftment of marginalized communities, as well as its potential to inspire national and global unity and foster youth development and empowerment.

A skilled emcee, world traveler, educator, mentor and big brother figure to many, and deep thinker about all that Hip Hop is and could be, I've always found great inspiration and insight in our interactions, and I was thrilled to document some of his thoughts for the podcast. At the time, Mikal had joined the staff at the prestigious Brooklyn Academy of Music and was bringing his varied Hip Hop-flavored experiences to the forefront of that respected institution, adding yet another important angle of exploration, one which touched on the inclusion of Hip Hop music, culture, and sensibilities within the halls of legacy organizations.

The Interview

Manny Faces: Let's talk about your past work a bit, particularly incorporating poetry, spoken word, and Hip Hop into your work with young people. How do you look back on that time?

Mikal Amin Lee: Absolutely. I'm still doing that work. I just did a storytelling workshop with young men between nine and 13, using Hip Hop as a means of storytelling and performance. I feel like what I learned from my own experience as a teenager growing up is that I always wanted to be heard. What drew me to Hip Hop so much was seeing these artists who just didn't really give a damn about what the media was saying, like Chuck D, or what history was saying if it was KRS-One, or what public perception was if it was Nas or Big Daddy Kane or Queen Latifah. It was definitely not just bravado or being cocky. It was, "I got something to say. It's important. You need to hear it. You have been told the wrong story. You haven't been told the full story. You don't really know what's real. I do, because I'm living that. Let me tell you about it. But I'm going to also make you bop your head to it and you're going to groove on it and you're going to feel it."

So whether it was X-Clan, Poor Righteous Teachers, De La Soul—I can go on and on. . . The throughline for all of them has always been this necessity to bring you the reality that wasn't being exposed or shown. First-hand accounts. First person perspectives...

Manny Faces: . . .as I love to say, Hip Hop *as* journalism. . .

Mikal Amin Lee: Exactly. It was a no-brainer to me because, not to date myself, but the idea of teaching artists or the idea of bringing contemporary art into a school where you're going to allow students to create their own work [is relatively new]. Art has always been in schools in some capacity, in terms of the classics, right? You learn how to play an instrument. You do theater. . . And you do traditional theater. You don't do devised theater. You don't do Hip Hop theater. You do Shakespeare or you do some type of Broadway play, and that's great. That's wonderful and it's necessary. It should be there.

But teaching artists and art education kind of diverged for a moment where it was like, "Wait a minute. These individuals, these young people, have amazing imaginations. They have stories to tell. They have a willingness and a desire and a need to tell them. Let's give them the tools. Let's give them the guidance and let's give them the space to do it." That's what excited me about the work and that's what I saw, especially when it came to spoken word poetry and Hip Hop, because the format and the form is so open, it can literally be anything. It's all about an authenticity to the author. It's all about, "Are you talking about something you really understand and know?" And even if you didn't live it, you need to really be able to convey that you have a knowledge or a sense of it. You can't just say stuff to say stuff, because people would check you on it. So even if you're Nas, who wasn't a gangster and he wasn't a killer and he wasn't necessarily a big time drug dealer. But he's from Queensbridge. He was *in* Queensbridge. Homie was on the block. He was in the midst of it. He just wasn't *of* it.

So that is something hugely attractive to a young mind of 13, 14, 15, when you give them the opportunity or you open the way for them to [tell their stories]. Because they're going to take [that opportunity] regardless. The question becomes, can you be a part of the process?

And that's what excited me when I first started getting into the work and what excites me still today. I think that's the uniqueness and the power of rap within the pantheon of Hip Hop for me. Really, all of Hip Hop's artistic forms in some way can and do tell a story, or express a reality, or express truth, whether it's the physical form of dance, through the visual forms of graffiti, the sonics of production and DJing—you're still telling a story.

I love words. I'm a huge, staunch supporter and advocate of the written and the spoken language. I think it gets a lot of unnecessary pushing to the side but I think we all read and speak and write—or at least the goal is for us to aspire to that. That's a primary way we communicate. Why not master that? Why not find the best ways to manipulate it? I think that Hip Hop as a culture has always been so inviting because it's telling you, "Come as you are, speak your reality, say it with force, say it with pride, say it with strength and you're going to get accepted." Just as long as you come real and you come raw. It doesn't really matter if you speak English or you speak Czech or you're a woman or whatever identity you have. And that's not to say that we're not insulated from misogyny and all these other things. We're not, because we're still living in a society that. . .

Manny Faces: . . .breeds that. . .

Mikal Amin Lee: . . .breeds that, and champions those things, as opposed to equality and equity and safeness. But I would contend—and I think you've been witness to this—in certain communities and spaces, the culture's raw tenets [reflect] a code of, "Hey, you got to be nice, you got to spit some realness. . ." Those people that do that, it doesn't really matter where they're from or what they look like. People will be like, "I feel you."

Manny Faces: The potential for inclusivity has always been there, and it's still there. I think that it's perhaps growing and that's good. We have this commodified mainstream entertainment genre that rap and Hip Hop is too often solely affiliated with, right? But you're talking about the balance, all this other stuff that is there and has always been there.

Mikal Amin Lee: Absolutely. And I think even those lines have been blurred a little bit in the mainstream, to a certain degree. You still have individuals that are popular figures that are saying things that are dangerous or not safe like a Rick Ross or some of the things that Migos has alluded to. But I would also say if we peel back the whole picture, you do have a type of reflection of what youth are today. One of the things that's been very great about *this* generation is their willingness to be who they are. Their energy in asserting, "You know what? I'm Queer and I'm not going to hide that." And in fact, even further, "I'm going to check you and I'm going to go at you. . . I'm not going to stand here in the dark and wait for you to accept me. You're going to accept me and I'm going to make you take a look at yourself or I can't even be around you."

I see a lot of energy in that, and that's crossing over to Hip Hop. You look at people like XXXtentacion—who I'm not a fan of. . . Not just because of the music, but he also is problematic. But you see his representation and how he presents himself. Lil Uzi Vert, how he presents himself. Young Thug, how he presents himself. Rich Homie Quan, how he presents himself. Cardi B. . . They're clearly representing more than just what we have expected in terms of, I guess a heteronormative or a more conservative look. You've got bright colors, you've got more flamboyance. You've got all of these things that really kind of speak to how young people say, "I'm going to wear and do and be whatever I'm going to be. And if you don't like it, middle finger to you. I'm not changing. . ."

Manny Faces: . . .which has always been Hip Hop.

Mikal Amin Lee: Right.

Manny Faces: I know it's nails on the chalkboard for purists and traditionalists, musically, sound-wise, what [those artists] are delivering as their product—and even as how they present themselves. But that's what this has always been about. And if we start to see that, that's opening some doors to at least start these conversations, showing young people today that you don't have to be tied to what was considered "normal." I think that's a positive thing.

Mikal Amin Lee: I do too. And I'm one of those people that definitely wrestles with that. You know, I come from the 1990s and the late 1980s generation. I'm a little bit on the younger spectrum of that, but I wrestle with that too, because there's a lot of the music and the creative aspects that I'm not really for. But, I step back [and think about] the things that really have made Hip Hop something that was never going to go away, now going into its fifth decade. Something that's becoming institutionalized right under our noses, that's becoming entrenched in Americana. Its story as a bedrock of a creative expression that defines the United States and the American experience when only three decades before it was being laughed at from the mainstream and the masses as some little ghetto trend fad that only a bunch of little Black kids did.

Now it's in the Smithsonian.[2] Now it's got archives in Cornell University[3] and in Harvard.[4] It's being studied from Stanford to Columbia. The Brooklyn Academy of Music and Lincoln Center are about it. Kennedy Center[5] just got Q-Tip as the artistic director. So, we're not talking about a fad anymore. We're not talking about a trend anymore. We're talking about a cultural creative force that is considered a part of the fabric and the narrative of the American experience. And when you start digging into that, you realize it's really telling us about ourselves.

I say all that to say that I have to look at new artists today and be a little bit more critical of the things that I'm not comfortable with, not from an identity standpoint but from a music standpoint, and go, "OK, I don't necessarily have to rock with that part." But, from a cultural perspective, from a historical perspective, the kids are doing exactly what Hip Hop is designed to do. They're carrying that forward. It's really about us finding the ways—especially the older generation—how we can speak about it in those terms.

I think sometimes what ends up with our generation, is we get into—I'll call it *sports talk radio mode* or the top five debate[6]. I know we've joked about this before, where it's like, "Who's your best five? Who's the G.O.A.T.?"[7] And those are great, those are fun conversations. But for me, even though I have them in jest with my friends and they're fun to have, from a serious, critical, cultural, sociological [point of view], it doesn't really serve a purpose. Because at the end of the day, creativity is subjective. Doesn't mean I'm going to change what I think is dope or not. But if we're talking about the larger conversation, about the culture continuing to grow and about its importance continuing to be manifested and preserved, then we'll die if we just say, "Well, all the dopeness stopped in 1998. All of this [newer] stuff is not [dope]." Then you basically cut off your nose to spite your face, and now you're unmooring all of the work and all of the foundation that's been done, that's just being manifested [differently] by a new generation. I think that's one part of the complexity of the conversation.

I can absolutely be like, "Yeah, I'm not necessarily going to go buy Desiigner's record," but I can defend and understand his musical path and what he's expressing and conveying for the youth and his own community today as being very much Hip Hop. It's just as important. And if we don't allow it to be completely co-opted, we can still use it as a tool to be *anti-*.

I think that's the work outside of the microphone for me and what I'm trying to convey as an educator. For me, it's not about theory. I'm literally in a classroom with these young people, listening to them and talking to them about what they like. I'm at Riker's Island through Cyphers for Justice[8], talking with the young men who are incarcerated and not trying to give them a one-on-one on LL Cool J and Def Jam, but more like, "OK, so you're feeling whoever you're feeling..."

Manny Faces: ...like 21 Savage...

Mikal Amin Lee: Yeah, 21 Savage. Let's work with him. Let's work with that energy, at least. Let's take that and see how we can craft and instead of trying to mimic or emulate whatever the reality he's talking about that you might be able to relate to, you have another reality that you also haven't really talked about that's just as deep and just as powerful. So let's try to have you talk about your whole picture as well, without taking away by saying, "Well, you can't do that. It's not real." [I tell them,] "You've got more real than you know." Let's talk about the whole of that. Let's get into that and then use that power of Hip Hop, that same aggression, that same energy, that same skill and style to bring that out.

That's the reason I think Hip Hop has been co-opted, because Hip Hop makes everybody cool. You know what I'm saying? It makes the most dorkiest dude cool.

Manny Faces: [LAUGHS] Right!

Mikal Amin Lee: That's the other thing people don't realize. Here's the dirty secret: A lot of people in rap are nerds. And not just new rappers, old rappers! Rap is like any other art form. To really be a creative person, you don't got time to smoke a cigarette and just chill out in the back of the lunchroom. You're trying to figure out these tools and knobs and buttons, and you're trying to come pontificate about the universe, and that's nerdy! That's not cool. Cool people sit in the mirror all day and see how coiffed they are. You know what I'm saying?

Manny Faces: They're peacocking!

Mikal Amin Lee: Exactly. And obviously, rap and Hip Hop has always been about being fresh and all. But we never want to talk about Marley Marl figuring out the sampler or [DJ Grandmaster] Flash and [DJ Kool] Herc. . .

Manny Faces: Right. That's engineering.

Mikal Amin Lee: Right! And I am not the biggest [Kanye West] fan by any stretch of the imagination, but what I can't take from him, and what's very clear, is that he's a nerd! He is a geek to the utmost. This dude picks things apart. He deconstructs things. He reconstructs things. He is constantly trying to whittle and tear and peel away and understand and dissect and reattach. Cool people don't got time for all that! That's not what cool people do.

So, there's definitely an inquiry, an imagination, an intelligence that's built into the craft of *trying to figure it out*. Trying to push boundaries and be experimental and do everything that's not on the table, when you really get into the philosophy of the culture, is a clear tenet. "If you did it, then I can't. . . If you did it, I gotta do something that is two leagues different from that because I can't be compared to you." I can't be, "Oh, you're the next Eminem. . ." Nah, that's not going to work. "Oh, you sound like Kanye. . ." That's not going to work.

And I know there's this thing with *type beats,* where [aspiring] producers are actually profiting by creating derivatives of popular producers and leasing those beats [to artists to record over]. That's become a real culture and a real money generator. That complicates things because now that it's mainstream, now that it's in the public consciousness, that means it is now fully in the teeth and the throes of capitalism. So now we're looking at it through this lens where some of what we purists would consider to be the code and the ethic, those traditions become secondary in the face of commerce.

Still, it's very clear that there are multiple strands and multiple dimensions within this whole universe of Hip Hop that can actually live side by side. You just have to make the choice. We can argue that some aspects are more important than others or point to some people that are stopping us from doing it [in a certain way.] Or you can realize there are a lot of people on this planet—myself being one of them, *humble brag*—being flown all around the world on a regular basis, talking and speaking with people in other places outside of my area code about this culture. And I'm never going to be on anybody's magazine front page. I doubt that Charlemagne [Tha God] is going to invite me to *The Breakfast Club* anytime soon[9] and I don't know if I'd even take the invite—but I'm definitely a part of a large discussion of influencers and a lot of us are names that a lot of people don't know.

Manny Faces: When you say you travel around and you do workshops throughout the boroughs, throughout the country, internationally, what's an example? Give some people who aren't familiar with how Hip Hop is being used in some of these ways, what kind of workshops that you put together?

Mikal Amin: Absolutely. One of the programs that I've been a part of and helped to build from the ground up has been Cyphers For Justice, founded by Dr. Limarys Caraballo, and co-founder and director Dr. Jamila Lyiscott, who I worked with also at [youth-oriented nonprofit] Urban Word[10]. I'm one of the site coordinators of our Rikers Island program. What we do is we go into Rikers Island twice a year and do a week-long intensive, guiding and supporting young men, creating content with video, song, and podcasting around their story. And the premise is: The world's been telling us who you are. You're this serial number at Rikers. You're a thug because you're from this place. You're a criminal because you're on Rikers. But that's not your story. That's *their* story. That's their story about you. What's *your* story? What are the things that you have done that matter to you? Who do you see yourself as? Let's talk about that, and then let's put that to a beat or put that on camera, make it look fresh, and you can talk about the things that matter to you.

Manny Faces: Give me something that stood out to you in doing this work that really exemplifies why blending Hip Hop with storytelling and giving folks an opportunity to tell their stories is so powerful.

Mikal Amin Lee: It unearths hidden gems. I kind of stopped saying this only because of how people process things and I never want to be misconstrued— but Hip Hop sets a low bar for invitation. You don't have to have a $100 instrument. You don't have to spend hundreds of dollars to get tutors. You don't need to be in a specific place and get equipment. There's a reason why basketball is such a popular sport in urban areas. It's not just because it's cool. It's because the only thing you need is a ball and there's a hoop already there. It's the same reason why soccer is the world's global game. It's not just because it's fun or it's interesting. It's because a pickup game can just happen on a field.

As opposed to football [for example], where you have to have hundreds of dollars of equipment to keep you safe. Same thing with hockey. . .

Manny Faces: I was going to say, try playing hockey without any equipment. . .

Mikal Amin Lee: Right! And people don't think about these things to that depth. It's about economics. Economics of space, economics of money. It's always beautiful to see these young men's brilliance shown to people who have thought otherwise. There's definitely a private, "I told you so," when they get to do their thing, because you're like, "Yeah, you thought they were just some, *whatever*. . ." But I've had some of the deepest conversations, some of the deepest literary critical theory conversations inside of Rikers Island with 17-year-olds breaking down why they love Kendrick [Lamar], but they also love the drill genre[11] and how both of those are real but they're doing completely two different things, and why that matters. In their own words.

They've actually realized, "Kendrick's not my *turn up*.[12] Kendrick, though, when I need to study the stars and the moon and the earth in the galaxy, I sit down with him. And I sit down with him regularly. But yo, when I'm feeling like I want to punch a wall, I can't listen to him. I'm going to go listen to so and so."

Manny Faces: Right. It shows, really, the breadth, the cultural vastness of Hip Hop and everything associated with it, is never going to be in a box. It's never going to be monolithic. It's going to be complicated. Because it mirrors humanity. It mirrors people.

Mikal Amin Lee: Yeah. You know what it is, Manny? People don't want to say it but the kids have taste. They know what they're listening to, they know why they're listening to it.

Manny Faces: And most importantly, it's a way, as you said, to now give them the opportunity to express themselves in their cultural language, their way of seeing the world, their perspective, and the art form that comes along with it. It's very natural that way. And not just guys that are sitting in Rikers, not just people in Black and brown communities, but young people in general, knowing how Hip Hop and rap has touched everybody. It's that easy way whereas asking them to sit and write an essay about themselves might be a little bit more difficult.

Mikal Amin Lee: Yeah, it's the language in which they speak, for sure.

Manny Faces: I don't know how much you've dealt with this going into Rikers Island, or bringing your curation and your program management to the Brooklyn Academy of Music, but what are some of the hindrances or challenges bringing this stuff into institutions that are traditionally not affiliated with Hip Hop and culture?

Mikal Amin Lee: The biggest challenge is educating them on the power and the value of Hip Hop as a cultural piece as opposed to a trend or an economic commodity.

There's still this lack of understanding that Hip Hop as a philosophy, as an ideology, as a cultural piece that has a high art and a craft to it, that it's connecting and hugely impactful and deeply, deeply rooted in some of the most important aspects of the way in which we critique and define culture and ideas and hold historical narrative. I think that a lot of places are just like, "But wait, I just thought it's a bunch of young kids dancing and going crazy." Or like, "Oh, I thought it's just a bunch of aggression." That [perception] is still here, 40-plus years later. It's still people's first instinct. Like, "Isn't rap just a bunch of people talking about drugs in a strip club?" Well, no, it's actually this other thing and has always been. That [stuff is] around it. That's a part of it. But again, there's more real than is being revealed.

That's the primary challenge for other things—like resources, like support, like advocacy for nontraditional artists. You never would say, "Oh, we don't want this soprano to come in to sing this opera. What is that about?" People are like, "It's opera. It's the most esteemed musical form of human existence." You know what I mean? You don't even blink if [Wynton] Marsalis says, "I want to do a concert in the park." It's like, "Oh, what day do you want?"

Manny Faces: [LAUGHS] Right.

Mikal Amin Lee: And rightfully so. But then, you know what? That should also be the case for Pharoahe Monch. That should also be the case for Nitty Scott. That should also be the case for Omega Cipherella. That should also be the case for Mikal Amin. Because we're doing similar work. We have a similar power and impact. We have now crossed over the threshold of being something that had a shelf life. We are now Americana. We are now the way this country sees itself, expresses itself, and tells its story—the whole story. So you need to actually respect that. And that's still a process.

Manny Faces: So what do you do? Is it just showing and proving? I've heard people say, "We show them. We have research now. We actually have Hip Hop research. We have education. We have proof. We got the receipts!"

Mikal Amin Lee: It's all of that. And then being very much in the spirit of the culture, like, "Guess what? I'm kicking in the door. I'm coming, and there's nothing you can really do about it." I think on the institutional level—be it academic or art or culture—results is really the name of the game. Whether it's filling seats or getting really good press, if when you see the work presented, it's like, "Wow," it becomes a much easier conversation to have.

I think that's what I've been doing, and what drives me. How can I continue to put my music as an artist, the work of my young people, and the people that I bring in as a producer, in the best light? How can I make sure that everything getting put on the table is fresh, hot, flavorful, and you can't get enough of it? That's kind of the challenge that I put forth with myself.

A little insight. There's something that I've learned since I've been at BAM and Urban Word, and in some of these other spaces like Columbia University, and overseas places like Dortmund University. There's this little word that they love called *precedent*. Essentially, "Well, if it worked before, then we're going to stick with that." If it's something that has been created as a norm, it's only because something has happened prior. It's worked, they've tried it again, it worked. Now it's just how they do things. They're very [adverse] to change, and that's another challenge.

Manny Faces: Your work merging Hip Hop into all these spaces and these pro-grams that you've worked with definitely help those who are intimately con-nected to Hip Hop music and culture, or as the rest of the world says, "Black and brown kids… Minority communities, etc." But what's the potential for this, universally? Not just in communities of color, which I think most people think is the only place where this can be effective.

Mikal Amin Lee: I think the potential is infinite, and I think that the best example that I can tell you about that I'm directly involved with is at the University of Dortmund. They've created what's called Hip Hop School, a summer arts youth camp over four days, where students ages eight to about 13 learn two of the Hip Hop arts. They either get an opportunity to do break-dancing, or in my case, we do rap workshops. We create a little crew. We get rap names. We build rapport, and then they learn how to write and perform rap music.

I partner with another emcee in Dortmund. His name is Slack. The last two summers I've gone out there and worked with these young people. They have a summer concert series where they present an artist—which, for the last two years, was me—and we work with the young people and have them perform. They basically open up the show and do their music and their dance performance, and then I'll perform. But I spend the whole week there working with them to create their work.

Manny Faces: My guess is that they're not rapping about drugs and strip clubs.

Mikal Amin Lee: They're not. And they're also coming from what a lot of people would consider definitely non-urban spaces. They're not in the hood. Even though Dortmund has a hood. I've been to it several times.

Manny Faces: Everywhere's got a hood!

Mikal Amin Lee: Everywhere's got a hood. Dortmund definitely has a hood. But the thing about what makes it authentic is we're also not doing, like, cotton candy rap either. They're young, so they're not going to necessarily be super gritty either, but they're saying real things that are happening and real things that they see. They talk about diversity in Dortmund and what they want to see, and they speak back against people that are oppressive in their music and what they're talking about. So, the potential is universal because the tenets of the culture, even though it is a Black music, a Black/brown music traditionally in terms of who created it and who were the originators of it. But the ideas to participate are just the ideas of humanity. Be yourself, be real, come correct. Do things at a high level. Speak your truth. Tell a story. That's just the human experience. Hip Hop just creates a way and an avenue where you don't have as many barriers—be they financial, be they environmental— to be able to do that.

Manny Faces: I want to take it out with one question you've kind of touched on a little bit. The name of this podcast is *Hip Hop Can Save America!* It may be a lofty theory. I didn't say *only* Hip Hop can save America. But in your experience, for people who may not be *of* the culture, and even for us inside, why should we consider Hip Hop music and culture when looking for ways to truly improve lives, livelihoods, and communities in this country.

Mikal Amin Lee: Because at its purest, it invites everyone to tell their story. At its purest, it demands that you tell the whole story and reveal what isn't revealed. And the only way for America to redeem itself for its sins of racism, for its demands of global hoarding of economic resources, or of its war making, is for it to come to terms with those faults, and acknowledge those faults, so that it can figure out the ways that it could be better.

Hip Hop inherently forces you to look in the mirror or puts the microscope squarely on you. If America is going to be saved, it's got to accept and admit to its fault and its deficiencies and stop trying to create this mythical idea that we're the purveyors of freedom and justice and that we are the best economic system just because we have the most. When you look at history, you know it wasn't a fair game. It was definitely a shell game. There was definitely a lot of bullying going on. It wasn't so clean.

Manny Faces: The richest societies that have ever existed no longer exist in their domination. So that's not a guarantee, just having all the stuff.

Mikal Amin Lee: Absolutely. I don't know if America needs saving or I don't know if we *want* to save America, but if Hip Hop is going to have a role in that, it's because when you really get to the actual, pure core tenet of what the culture is about, you have to be real. And I think that's what America really needs a dose of right now. Reality. Its own reality, and not the one that tries to create and pick and choose.

Afterthoughts

I was left with so much to think about from this interview and our many subsequent discussions on the podcast and in person. This conversation feels particularly important to highlight because again, Mikal showed how many of the Hip Hop-infused practices that Dr. Love and Dr. Levy champion can extend beyond educational spaces. As Dr. Love pointed out, educators can't solve all of society's challenges, and as Mikal notes, many who could most benefit from these practices might not even be found in traditional school settings. Given schools' reluctance to introduce some of these concepts and considering complications from increasing political influence in our K-12 systems, Mikal's dedication to working with people inside correctional facilities, for instance, becomes especially vital.

Mikal also powerfully amplifies another core throughline of my work and this book: meeting the next generation where they are is key to Hip Hop's evolution as a force for the greater good. As we heard, Mikal is particularly adept at pushing back against longstanding stereotypes held not only by members of the general public that are typically less connected to Hip Hop culture, but also by those *within* Hip Hop culture who let generational bias cloud their own ability to connect with young people. Having a thorough knowledge of Hip Hop history, but also being willing to challenge his own traditionalist impulses, Mikal strikes a highly effective balance that allows him to reach and work with young people facing even the harshest conditions—providing an essential blueprint for others to do the same.

Another crucial dynamic Mikal highlights that we'll explore several times throughout this book is how Hip Hop-inspired innovations can positively impact young people across all demographics. While Hip Hop-inspired innovations may be particularly well-suited to help uplift communities traditionally underserved by legacy institutions and oppressive systems, Hip Hop's universal appeal allows us to explore similar approaches across many communities, and as Mikal touched on, across national and geographic borders.

We'll explore this last point more deeply in later chapters, examining how an interdisciplinary to Hip Hop studies can help lead to greater cross-racial and cross-cultural understanding, to consider ways that Hip Hop might be uniquely positioned to help *unite* America.

As of this writing, Mikal Amin Lee balances youth development work, journalism, and scholarship across multiple organizations while producing major Hip Hop and spoken word events at institutions like the Brooklyn Academy of Music. He continues recording and performing under the name Mikal Amin and has been a repeat guest on the *Hip Hop Can Save America!* podcast.

Key Takeaways

1. Hip Hop provides a powerful platform for storytelling and self-expression, especially for those whose voices are often marginalized or misunderstood.
2. The culture of Hip Hop inherently demands authenticity and encourages individuals to share their true experiences and perspectives.
3. Hip Hop has low barriers to entry, making it accessible to a wide range of people, particularly youth.

4. There's a need to educate institutions about the cultural value and artistic merit of Hip Hop beyond its commercial aspects.
5. Hip Hop culture is evolving, with newer artists challenging traditional norms and expressing diverse identities.
6. The commercialization of Hip Hop has created tension between maintaining cultural authenticity and pursuing financial success.
7. Hip Hop education and workshops can be powerful tools for engaging youth, including those in challenging environments like correctional facilities.
8. The culture encourages creativity, experimentation, and pushing boundaries in artistic expression.
9. Hip Hop has become a global phenomenon, with the potential to connect diverse communities and foster cross-cultural understanding.
10. The principles of Hip Hop (authenticity, creativity, self-expression) have universal appeal and application beyond just music or art.

Discussion Questions

1. How can Hip Hop be used as a tool for community engagement and social change in your specific context or community?
2. What strategies can be employed to bridge the gap between academic institutions and Hip Hop culture to create more inclusive educational environments?
3. How might Hip Hop-based programs be designed to address specific social issues (e.g., youth empowerment, racial justice, mental health) in various communities?
4. In what ways can Hip Hop culture and its principles be integrated into existing nonprofit programs or community initiatives to increase their effectiveness and appeal?
5. How can teaching artists and educators use Hip Hop to create more culturally responsive and engaging learning experiences for diverse student populations?
6. What are some potential challenges in implementing Hip Hop-based programs in traditional institutions, and how might these be addressed?

7. How can community organizers leverage Hip Hop culture to mobilize youth and create platforms for their voices to be heard on important social and political issues?

8. In what ways can Hip Hop be used to foster intercultural dialogue and understanding in diverse communities?

9. How might nonprofit leaders and community organizers use Hip Hop as a means to challenge negative stereotypes and promote positive narratives about marginalized communities?

10. What role can Hip Hop play in developing critical thinking skills and media literacy among youth, and how can this be incorporated into educational or community programs?

This podcast episode was originally released on June 27, 2018.

Notes

1 "Boom bap" is a Hip Hop production style named for its characteristic combination of heavy kick drums ("boom") and crisp snare hits ("bap"). This raw, sample-based aesthetic defined East Coast Hip Hop's sound throughout the 1990s.

2 From the Smithsonian's National Museum of African American History & Culture website, "With its work rooted in collections, research, and exhibitions, and building on the release of the *Smithsonian Anthology of Hip-Hop and Rap* in 2021, the museum is continuing its commitment to presenting the voices, memories, and belongings of the fans, critics, and communities that create and challenge this ever-growing musical form."

3 The Cornell Hip Hop Collection, established in 2007, is housed at Cornell University's library, preserving thousands of recordings, photographs, flyers, and other artifacts from Hip Hop's formative years, particularly focusing on the 1970s and 1980s. Its assistant curator, Ben Ortiz, is featured later in this book.

4 The Harvard Hiphop Archive and Research Institute, founded in 2002, supports academic research and archival work in Hip Hop culture. The institute houses the Nasir Jones Hiphop Fellowship.

5 The John F. Kennedy Center for the Performing Arts, America's national cultural center, has formally recognized Hip Hop as a vital art form through performances, educational programs, and its prestigious Kennedy Center Honors.

6 A hallmark of Hip Hop discourse is the debate over one's "top five, dead or alive," referring to a personal ranking of greatest rap artists.

7 G.O.A.T. (Greatest Of All Time) refers to one's personal declaration of rapper considered the most influential or skilled of all time.

8 Cyphers for Justice is a youth and educator development program that "apprentices NYC high school youth and educators as critical researchers through the use of hip hop, spoken word, digital literacy, and critical social research methods"

9 The Breakfast Club, launched in 2010, is a nationally syndicated radio show known for interviews and cultural commentary, hosted by radio personalities Charlamagne Tha God, Angela Yee (until 2022), and DJ Envy.

10 According to their website, "Urban Word champions youth voice by providing platforms for literacy, self-expression, civic engagement, and leadership through free creative writing, college prep workshops, and performance opportunities."

11 The drill sub-genre of rap emerged from Chicago in the early 2010s, and is typically characterized by dark, often violent lyrics, trap-influenced beats, and local storytelling. The style has spawned regional variations, particularly in New York and London.

12 "Turn up" is a colloquial term referring to high-energy social situations, particularly parties or dancing.

· 4 ·

THE TECHNOLOGIST | RICHARD ACHEE

Growing up, I had a buddy—a "brother from another mother" kind of deal—whom I knew since I was seven. His family was religious, and so between his private school, worshipping community, family, and friends, he lived in a bit of a social bubble.

These were the 1980s. Hip Hop hadn't reached the masses like it would in later decades, and so his bubble was pretty far removed from the music and culture emerging in the streets and on radios in New York City which was rapidly spreading to other communities in our nearby Long Island suburbs.

For that, I served as something of a conduit. Hip Hop was becoming a big part of my life. Like many kids my age in more demographically diverse communities, I was becoming an avid listener of rap music. My fashion sense mirrored the growing streetwear phenomenon, and I was adopting the same cultural influences from my circle of mostly African American and Caribbean American friends and classmates that they were adopting from their older siblings.

My friend would never become a huge Hip Hop head, though to this day he can still recite a couple of songs that I forced him to listen to at the time. Through the years, as I delved deeper into the music and culture, I would keep him updated on my various Hip Hop-related endeavors, from DJing, to pursuing—and failing to achieve—a career as a rapper and producer, to my work as a Hip Hop journalist, to launching a Hip Hop advocacy nonprofit.

As Mikal Amin Lee highlighted, a lot of us Hip Hop heads can be pretty nerdy. So was my friend. His family were early adopters of the home computer, and we spent countless hours exploring the burgeoning world of programming, and—to a mostly innocent extent—hacking. We both kept that love of technology through the years. In fact, while my friend went on to become a highly successful emergency room trauma surgeon, he would also work on several innovative medical technology projects.

One day, knowing all of this, I was excited to tell him about an event I was going to be involved with. Hip-Hop Hacks was an initiative launched by Regan Sommer McCoy[1] "that explores and promotes ways in which hip-hop interacts with and inspires technological innovation." She was organizing a major event, a "Hip Hop Hackathon," which would feature workshops, panel discussions, and performances. The event aimed to demonstrate how Hip Hop music and culture could be used to increase interest in technology, improve access to these fields, and spark innovation within various technology disciplines.

My friend was... confused. He knew about Hip Hop—or at least rap music. And he knew that hackathons were gatherings focused on technology and programming projects.

Putting the two together, however, didn't quite compute.

This confusion is understandable and aligns with the common misconceptions we've covered earlier. Those less familiar with Hip Hop often know it only for rap music. However, as we've explored regarding fields like education, mental health therapy, and cultural studies, what should be starting to become apparent is that Hip Hop can be integrated into *all sorts* of disciplines in exciting and innovative ways, integrations that create new avenues of access and engagement, particularly for individuals who might have been traditionally excluded from these fields.

Technology is no different, and in fact is particularly well suited to help bridge these gaps. The hackathon was a rousing success, and exposed dozens of eager young people to several folks working along these lines, including Richard Achee.

Richard was demonstrating an initiative that he helped develop that teaches computer coding to teenagers through Hip Hop music production, commonly referred to as beatmaking. By connecting the rhythmic patterns and potential arrangements of Hip Hop beats to the logical structures of coding, Richard's project perfectly encapsulated the promise of making programming more accessible and enjoyable for young people.

At the time, the project was called PythonMC—it has since been rebranded as BreakBeatCode—and it remains the very first example I give when talking to folks like my friend who might not be immediately able to envision how Hip Hop can help young people—particularly those from underserved, underrepresented, and underestimated communities—find creative, effective, and inspiring ways to get their foot in the technological door.

The Interview

Manny Faces: Richard, let the people know who you are and how you define yourself from a professional standpoint.

Richard Achee: I'm Richard Achee. I work at Google in Strategic Partnerships. In my "20 percent" time,[2] I created something called PythonMC. It's a collaboration with Code Next at Google which helps bring computer science to underserved communities, and Rapport Studios, who helps bring culturally responsive pedagogy into tech.

Manny Faces: How long have you been at Google?

Richard Achee: 9 years yesterday, actually.

Manny Faces: Happy Cake Day! Happy GoogleVersery! Do you share the same anniversary as Gmail?

Richard Achee: Gmail and I came roughly the same day. And fun fact, I was born August 11, 1973, which is arguably the day Hip Hop was invented.[3]

Manny Faces: There you go. You have some lineage. So, what is your day-to-day at Google?

Richard Achee: I work with technology partnerships. Basically, Google has lots of technology that a third-party company could integrate with. So, if you're developing a product, you can hook into different parts of Google. I help them understand what they can do on Google technology and pull in the right resources to help them do it.

Manny Faces: What kind of projects, what are some examples?

Richard Achee: I work in Chrome—the Chrome browser and the Chrome device—and we help bring this to enterprises. Companies have lots of different technologies that run on a device or in the browser, so we'll work with everyone from Citrix to Salesforce to SAP and all these big enterprise companies to help them run properly and effectively on our technology.

Manny Faces: Got it. Now, for those who don't know, Google does allow its employees to work on side projects. . .

. . .I guess you can't, you know, be a stripper. . .

Richard Achee: [LAUGHS] Right.

Manny Faces: [LAUGHS] . . .but they give leeway to work on different projects. You work in education-based projects. What is your connection to the education world?

Richard Achee: My first job ever after college—besides waiting tables—was an English teacher, for a year. I was convinced I was going to be an English teacher. I had my little English teacher suit, my jacket and everything, and I was trying to be an adult. I was really getting into that role. I absolutely loved teaching. I still do.

But about six weeks in, in the middle of class, a student raises his hand. I'll never forget this. He says, "You don't look like an English teacher." I was like, "Wait, is that a question?" He said, "No. It's just that you just don't look the part. This is not you. I think you should wear a suit. I think you should work for a company. We're having fun. You seem to be doing a decent enough job. I just don't think this is, like, your thing."

If he was a student today he'd be saying, "This is not your jam." Basically, he was saying English teaching is not my jam. And I kinda laughed, and then I went away and said to myself, "He's right. I don't know why he's right. He's just right. I know education is for me in some way. I just think this is probably not the right space."

[At Google though,] I finally got this opportunity to teach computer science to students through Code Next and that's where I really got properly reconnected with education. One thing that we did with Chrome is become the number one device in education, and I was part of the team that was helping schools understand how to use Chrome in the classroom.

Manny Faces: Got it. First of all, before we get into how you came to create PythonMC, give your best elevator pitch for what PythonMC is all about.

Richard Achee: The idea behind PythonMC is to use the music and the movement of Hip Hop to teach computer programming.

Python is one of the most popular computer programming languages. It's used by Google and Instagram and NASA—many of the large organizations out there. Teaching it in the traditional way of teaching computer science goes something like this: They teach you the language and the syntax and how complex it is. You go through all this effort just to learn how to type a little program to write, "Hello world," on the screen, and you get a little bit further than that. And the first thing you do—your *payoff*, as I like to call it—is to write a program to do something like check whether a word is an anagram or a palindrome.

For certain types of learners, that is an awesome payoff. I happen to be one of those types of learners. I really get into that. I also think it falls short. For many learners, it's just not enough. They wanna feel like they're doing something that's that is a bit more impressive, a bit of a bigger impact than checking for anagrams.

So I was teaching myself Python, and I was listening to a Hip Hop track. The particular track I was listening to was "The Choice Is Yours," by Black Sheep. Do you remember the intro of that song? It goes "This or that. This or that. . ."

That sounds like an "if, then" statement. I started to think, what if you could rap in code. And what if you could teach coding through rap?

So I started working with Rapport Studios—these guys have been doing culturally responsive pedagogy for years. This is their jam. They do a great job. They've been doing it with history and English and all these other topics but hadn't yet done it in computer science. I said, "Well, what if we could do this?" That's when our collaboration started, and then it went off from there. We just started to riff on different ideas and eventually started to realize you can really integrate Hip Hop into computer programming in so many different ways, and that's how PythonMC started to take off.

Manny Faces: I sat through one of these workshops, and that payoff is there because you're immediately seeing the results of their work, and it's not just something displayed on a screen. It's not just "Hello world." It's something you can actually dig, and jam to, and have a good time with. It's gotta be one of the most engaging ways to teach computer programming that's ever existed.

Richard Achee: I really appreciate that. The feedback from students is pretty awesome. They get that within the first hour, because they've written enough code to start to create their own beats and remix their own beats and their eyes light up and they're in. They're in for good.

Manny Faces: And they don't have to have any computer coding experience the way you're presenting it.

Richard Achee: Right. And no music-making experience either.

I had stumbled upon this platform called EarSketch. It's made by Georgia Tech's School of Music. Jason Freeman and his team there are absolutely brilliant people deeply steeped in computer science, music production, and music theory, and they created this platform called EarSketch.

It's basically a digital audio workstation, similar to Ableton or Garage Band—it's actually based on one called Reaper. For those computer scientists out there or people that have a strong technical acumen in the space, it's basically making API calls to Reaper. In normal everyday language, what that means is you are writing code, but instead of dragging and dropping, that code is taking those actions for you—to put in a sound file on a track, stretch it out or shorten it, put in effects. . .

And you write that in Python. You can do that with just a little bit of Python code. Just by knowing how to create a variable—which takes me maybe five to 10 minutes to teach someone—they can then use the template, and all of a sudden, they're throwing in beats all over the place. Then, with a little bit more, they're doing a four [bar] loop. And after that, now they have a sequence of beats that they're doing interesting things to.

In that workshop, we basically get through five and a half to six weeks of content in the space of two hours. It's sort of a crash course in coding. And, yeah, you don't really need any background.

It's primarily suited for school students—our sweet spot is around 7th to 9th grade, but younger students can definitely do it. DJ Will Rock was in our session, and he's eleven years old. We've had eleven, twelve-year-olds before, and you can have older students that are in college or older. Anyone can start from scratch in this space.

Manny Faces: Learning the variables, learning the *if, thens*... are the foundations of programming anyway. So, if you've never been exposed to that, you're immediately exposed to the foundational concepts [in this workshop], but in a way that you can relate to and understand because of the way it's presented.

Richard Achee: That's exactly our intent. The idea is to learn what we call The Big Four. The Big Four, like you said, are the fundamentals of coding—variables, loops, conditions, and functions. If you know variables, loops, conditions, and functions, you now can learn any programming language. It's basically the fundamental building blocks of languages like Python and Javascript. The great thing about coding is once you learn one language, you actually very quickly could learn your second, third, or fourth language, because the fundamentals are there.

That's what we teach in PythonMC, The Big Four, and then we expand from there.

Manny Faces: What have you heard from other program administrators or teachers in these computer science classes or in schools that don't have any comp sci, from the educator standpoint, seeing how the music specifically engages kids? A lot of times it might be the first time they've seen that hybrid or that intersection of music being used as a tool to educate. What is some of the feedback you've gotten from teachers and administrators?

Richard Achee: Many teachers have said, "This is just a great way to engage students." Some have said, "This is *the* way we need to engage students," and that this is the sort of thing we should be doing.

I'm not the trailblazer in culturally responsive pedagogy—that is an area people like Rapport Studios have been doing for a very long time—nor did I create EarSketch, but mixing the two together has been a new thing and the reaction is extremely positive. [It's now] a question of how many people can we connect with and how fast we can do it.

What I've been doing is going to places like conferences, like the Carnegie Mellon University Hip Hop Hackathon,[4] and places like that. My goal in each of those is to find one person there who wants to volunteer. If I can get one more volunteer each time I speak, then this thing will start to grow more and more.

But the administrators and the people that teach, they absolutely love it. They want to get into it. Some just don't know how. They might not have the coding background, so we offer free coding workshops. We do that through Google Hangouts,[5] through webinars, as well as face to face training. I can get someone up to speed within a few hours, and then it's up to them to go and study the content on their own.

If they already have a coding background, sure, that's a bit easier, but the sweet spot actually are people that don't have a deep coding background. People that maybe have, for example, a little bit of PHP, or a little bit of JavaScript. They've dabbled to some extent and aren't professional programmers, but they are eager to learn. That eagerness to learn really inspires them to get into the content. The fact that they get to teach it very quickly after they learn it is a great opportunity to reinforce their learning and test their knowledge. We find people that are either just starting their career in computer science or maybe just starting their career in computer teaching, that seems to be the sweet spot for us.

Manny Faces: When a lot of people think about teaching with Hip Hop, they tend to think it's very linear or direct. In other words, if you want to teach a subject, you make a rap that contains a bunch of facts, you have kids learn it, and now they know those facts. And that's great. That works.

But Hip Hop-based learning can go a little deeper than that. I think people think programming is very strict and rigid, but learning programming—and I think learning it through Hip Hop especially, let me know if you agree—also teaches more than just a way to program. These things reinforce other values like critical thinking and problem-solving and other aspects of learning. Do you find that is the case with teaching computer programming with this intersection with music?

Richard Achee: Yeah. It's a great question. And, by the way, I absolutely love your [keynote] presentation.[6] I think it articulated so many of the different ideas I had in a very clear way. You talked about how Hip Hop can *hack everything*. And when we think about Hip Hop and education, sure, you can use things like call and response. You can use rap as mnemonic devices, and we definitely do that in PythonMC. We call it the ABC's of Coding, where we do a little bit of rap about The Big Four, about variables, loops, conditions and functions, but that's definitely not where it stops. That's just a starting point.

It's more like you talked about in your speech, how Hip Hop was fundamentally all about hacking from day one. I love the way you talked about the invention of, effectively, the turntable and the breaks and how that all evolved, that you couldn't just take a turntable and expect to be able to scratch on it. You had to hack it before it got to where you want it to be.

This is very similar because in PythonMC, these students are writing code to ultimately create art and create something that they want to put their name on. We make sure that everyone on day one has a DJ name, so from day one they're thinking, "I'm an artist now." They're *creating* something.

It's less about needing to learn syntax just to learn syntax, or coding for coding's sake. It's more like, "I need to get to this outcome. I need to hack through all the different ways. I can use the code to get to that. I want this beat to drop in every eight measures and then fade while this other beat is layering on top of each other in different sort of phrases..." They describe what they want. Well, what does that sound like? What about this other one that I don't know how to do? I don't know how to drop it in every eight measures. So maybe you should think about different types of four bar loops and record that a little bit. And then they just start to try different things with code.

That's exactly how a natural programmer would work. It's not that someone gives them a problem statement and says, "You gotta figure out some sort of function to do that and you need to fill in the blanks." You gotta think. You wanna create. And there are definitely different paths to get there.

Computer programming at its best is when it's really a work of art and it's telling a story. That's exactly what you see these students doing. They have some musical idea that they wanna express, and now they just have to figure out what code is gonna get them to that outcome. The way they're learning— through Hip Hop—is actually much closer to what they would do in reality, in terms of how they would solve problems.

We're learning how much Hip Hop actually can directly tie into computational thinking, the fundamentals of problem-solving like a computer scientist.

Manny Faces: I love to hear these things. "Hip Hop can help with computational thinking..."

Richard Achee: Yeah. Initially, in my mind, my starting point was exactly what someone would expect—"Oh, I'm just gonna rap about code." But then the further we went along, the more conversations I had, speaking with people like yourself who are looking at this from a much broader perspective, and I started to see how Hip Hop has much deeper implications for not only the way we teach, but about the way we think and the way we problem solve and the way we approach different aspects of life. So when you talk about Hip Hop hacking everything—when you really start to think about what that means—it's true. You can see how it's been happening for a very long time in various ways.

It's just interesting to see how much it actually relates to not just computer science, but tech in general, and how it's shaped technology in many ways—many of the things you talked about in your presentation.

Manny Faces: Indeed. And it's super important to take this concept to the areas, the schools, the communities that don't necessarily have those resources as an everyday thing, that don't have computer science classes. Communities of color, poorer communities. . .

But one thing I love to point out about Hip Hop in educational circles is that a lot of times it gets pigeonholed into, "Oh, this is great for the 'Black and brown kids. . .' I can't use this anywhere else." And of course, that's silly. You would agree?

Richard Achee: Yeah. I 100% agree. The fact is, my focus is teaching Black and Latinx students, because my ultimate purpose is to improve diversity in the technology industry. That is a complex problem. One part of that problem is increasing the number of students that are interested. That's not the *whole* problem—there's definitely a bigger conversation to have about diversity in tech, about unconscious bias, and the way people hire and things like that. Google is definitely working hard on this problem, and has a lot to learn still. But yes, it's just as interesting and attractive and awesome for students of any color—the same way Hip Hop obviously is.

Hip Hop has definitely transcended every possible barrier at this point and actually, when people start to create different things in EarSketch to the PythonMC curriculum, it's not always a Hip Hop track. It's gospel. It's rock. Students' music interests are diverse. Hip Hop's the launching point, and how they drop in beats and remix them is very much a Hip Hop process. But the actual finished work, that might be a lot more like a funk track or some-thing else.

Manny Faces: Right. There's a wide range of genres to pull from. Hip Hop, or any 4/4 kind of music is obviously best suited for this, but because you have this wide range of multi-genre sounds, you can create hybrids of music while you're working on this as well. . .

Richard Achee: Yeah. And this is an after school program so we don't have quizzes. It's not about passing state exams. The way we check a student's work or quiz is very organic. I would look over students' shoulders, and first I would ask them to hand me their headphones, like "Can I listen to that?" And very naturally, students would get excited like, "Oh, yeah. I think it's ready," and they'll give me their headphones. We hear what they did musically and then might say, "Oh, that's really cool. What if you could create a drop here? How would you do that if you could reverse the list of beats that you had in there? And how would you do that in code?"

And then they would say, "Ahhh!" and then go away and think about it. So, the fact that they have this identity as a DJ, their pride is not just about the code. It's more around what they created with the code.

Manny Faces: I think that's what drives that engagement and interest. I saw everyone completely into it all the way through with great presentations at the end, showing off their work.

You know, we used to have to read our stupid essays in front of the classroom. I'm like, "Oh God. I gotta stand in front of everyone and read my poem." You know? But this is something you actually want to get up there and be like, "Yeah! Check out what I've done. This is dope!"

Richard Achee: Yeah. And during the Hip Hop Hackathon at Carnegie Mellon, they had a PSA on staying in school with a whole rap and a video on Google Slides along with the beats they created. They were getting really, really super creative, and that was exciting to see.

Manny Faces: That's good stuff. Just a couple more questions and I'll let you get back to "not being evil" or whatever it is Google says. . .

So, what's next? Are you trying to expand the program? Just get more instructors? Get into more spaces, as you alluded to earlier?

Richard Achee: Yeah. First, it's free. Anyone can go to our website and see the free curriculum. Anyone with any background at all in computer science could probably just pick it up in a few hours.

If it's someone without experience, they can contact us directly, and we would absolutely love to teach people more about this. I can take someone with no coding background and ramp them up [quickly].

So, to scale, we just want to get this out to as many schools and after school programs as possible. It's just about getting out there to more schools.

Another thing we're going to start working on is teaching teachers how to use the curriculum. Right now, it's all about one-to-one coaching. We're trying to figure out the best format for that, whether it's videos or books or some other twist on that concept, to enable teachers to do this in a self-serve way, to just pick up the content and run with it with minimal prior experience.

Manny Faces: Got it. You're looking for the next line of people who'd be interested in teaching it, not just the participants. You might have young people at the workshops, but you're also looking for older folks who might be interested in paying this one forward.

Richard Achee: Exactly. For example, seniors in high school who are interested in computer science and just up for it. It could be a more experienced high school student or college student. . .

It could be a music teacher, in theory. That's one of our hypotheses at this point is that we might be able to get a music teacher really excited about this as a way to create. That's another thing we're thinking about in the future is how we can bring out more musical pedagogy within the program. Because right now, music is the payoff. How do we make that more part of what they learn in the process? That's another thing we're gonna start to experiment with.

Manny Faces: I'll wrap it with this. This is, sort of, the *payoff* of this podcast, the thing I like to ask everyone who blesses me with their time. The title of the podcast is *Hip Hop Can Save America!* It's a lofty idea, and I think we need a lot more than *just* Hip Hop to save America. But I think, honestly, that Hip Hop can actually be a big part of that.

In your experience, from a grander perspective, a holistic view, what are the reasons that people should be considering Hip Hop music and culture when they're looking for ways to truly improve lives, livelihoods, communities, and industries across the country.

Richard Achee: My simplest and easiest response is that we have tried a lot of wrong answers to change different things about our culture, our society, and the way things work. Clearly, those wrong answers are not ones we want to reuse. If anything, we want to *hack* through them, take bits of them, remix them, rethink them, and come up with, hopefully, some unexpected solutions that might work.

Manny Faces: Well, Hip Hop's full of unexpected solutions.

Afterthoughts

In my lecture that Richard alluded to, I talk about how Hip Hop and technology have worked hand in hand since the genre's inception. From early turntable re-engineering to mass-produced mixtapes, from sampling to peer-to-peer filesharing, from SoundCloud rap[7] to AI—Hip Hop has consistently pushed technological boundaries, creating new use cases and, many times, entirely new products and industries.

The Hip Hop Hacks hackathon demonstrated this historically symbiotic relationship's modern potential.[8] Presenters wove Hip Hop music and culture into their demonstrations, exposing young attendees to worlds that previously might have been inaccessible, if not entirely unknown.

Having witnessed BreakBeatCode's transformative power on several occasions, I've noticed that most young participants enter these sessions never having considered computer programming as a possibility. Despite being bright, savvy digital natives, this field often remains foreign to them, especially when their schools lack early computer science education. Yet by the end of even short sessions—half-day workshops and hackathons—teenagers with no prior experience find themselves programming, creating, sharing, and enjoying access to an exciting field they may never have imagined possible. This represents just one way Hip Hop can help fuel interest, access, and excitement in technology, a field that remains highly segregated.[9]

It's worth noting that this was when I first started expanding my closing question about Hip Hop's role in improving society to include "industries."

While my focus remains on uplifting people and communities—and though capitalism often creates or exacerbates the very problems requiring correction—we can certainly, as a society, seek to amplify thoughtful approaches to making the business world more equitable. As with other fields we've explored, Hip Hop might very well be uniquely equipped to help guide such a transformation, and to me, BreakBeatCode is one inspiring piece of that puzzle.

In the years since we first spoke, BreakBeatCode has continued expanding, reaching more and more young people globally through virtual and in-person hackathon events while recruiting more partners and instructors to help sustain its growth.

Key Takeaways

1. BreakBeatCode uses Hip Hop music and culture to teach computer programming, specifically Python.
2. The program engages students by allowing them to create and remix beats while learning coding fundamentals.
3. The program teaches "The Big Four" programming concepts: variables, loops, conditions, and functions.
4. The approach allows students to see immediate, exciting results of their coding efforts, making it more engaging than traditional methods.
5. Hip Hop's inherent "hacking" nature aligns well with computational thinking and problem-solving skills.
6. The program encourages creative thinking and artistic expression alongside technical skills.
7. The program is designed to be accessible to students without prior coding or music making experience.
8. The curriculum can be adapted for various age groups, from middle school to college level.
9. The program aims to increase diversity in the tech industry by making coding more accessible and engaging for underrepresented groups.
10. The program demonstrates how culturally responsive pedagogy can be applied to STEM fields.

Discussion Questions

1. How might other STEM fields adapt the BreakBeatCode model to create more engaging and culturally responsive educational programs?
2. In what ways can tech companies collaborate with educators and artists to develop innovative learning programs that appeal to underrepresented groups?
3. How can the principles of Hip Hop culture be applied to problem-solving and innovation in various industries beyond tech and education?
4. What strategies can nonprofit organizations use to scale programs like BreakBeatCode to reach a wider audience of young people?
5. How might the integration of arts and culture into STEM education impact long-term career choices and diversity in tech-related fields?
6. In what ways can the concept of "hacking" in Hip Hop culture be applied to other areas of business or social innovation?
7. How can companies in non-tech industries use culturally responsive approaches to attract and retain diverse talent?
8. What potential benefits and challenges might arise from incorporating artistic expression into traditional STEM curricula?
9. How can educators and program developers ensure that culturally responsive teaching methods remain authentic and avoid becoming gimmicky?
10. In what ways can the success of programs like PythonMC/BreakBeatCode inform broader educational policy and curriculum development?

This podcast episode was originally released on October 5, 2019.

Notes

1 Regan Sommer McCoy is a community archivist, curator, and arts administrator. She is the founder of Hip-Hop Hacks (HHH) and The Mixtape Museum (MXM) initiatives and is a consulting producer for the *Hip Hop Can Save America!* podcast.
2 A policy that encourages Google employees to spend 20% of their time beyond their regular projects, working on initiatives they believe will benefit the company.

3 While no single moment marks the creation of Hip Hop's diverse culture, August 11, 1973, is widely recognized as its symbolic birthdate—when Bronx, N.Y. resident Cindy Campbell and her brother DJ Kool Herc hosted a party that featured musical and cultural innovations that would come to define Hip Hop.

4 Gabriel Bamforth. (2019, March 31). *Inaugural "trip tech" combines hip-hop and coding*. The Tartan. https://thetartan.org/2019/4/1/news/trip-tech

5 Google Hangouts was a cross-platform messaging service which was discontinued in 2022, replaced by services such as Google Meet and Google Chat.

6 One of several keynote presentations in my repertoire is titled "Hip Hop Can Hack Everything! Tech Inspiration From a Culture of Innovation," which delves into the immense innovative potential when science and technology intersects with Hip Hop. [https://www.mannyfaces.com/hiphophack]

7 A DIY Hip Hop movement prominent in the mid-2010s which used the SoundCloud platform to distribute often home-grown content.

8 Manny Faces. (2017, August 30). *"Hip-Hop Hacks" Event Highlights Youth-Fueled Technological Innovation*. The Center for Hip-Hop Advocacy. https://www.hiphopadvocacy.org/hip-hop-hacks-event-series-highlights-technological-innovation-fueled-youth-culture-lifestyle/

9 https://www.dice.com/recruiting/ebooks/equality-in-tech-report-recruiter/discrimination-in-tech.html

· 5 ·

THE ARCHIVIST | BEN ORTIZ

Like many others profiled in this work, Ben Ortiz has an extremely important job for Hip Hop, even though it's one that wouldn't traditionally be considered a "Hip Hop job."

In recent years, educational institutions have increasingly welcomed Hip Hop into their halls in a few ways. There is the study of Hip Hop as subject matter, typically consisting of classes that examine artists' bodies of work or explore Hip Hop's history. There are music programs which focus on the creation of Hip Hop music. There are interdisciplinary ways of incorporating Hip Hop into more traditional fields—English, anthropology, sociology, etc. There is the overarching field of Hip Hop Studies, analyzing Hip Hop as both an art form and a lens for understanding contemporary urban life, race relations, and cultural production.

Some of these subfields overlap, as we'll explore in a later chapter examining Dr. Andrea Hunt's Sociology of Hip Hop Culture course, where students gain insights into Hip Hop's cultural dimensions and, by extension, the broader society in which it exists by studying rap artists lyrical output. We also see more solidification of Hip Hop Based Education as a field of its own, as we'll learn more about when we hear from Dr. Gloria Ladson-Billings and Dr. Lauren Kelly, both who are educating educators at the graduate school level.

Creating spaces for these studies within legacy educational institutions is as crucial for Hip Hop as it is for other humanities disciplines. For Hip Hop's art and culture to survive the test of time, society must resist two threats: biased limitations on understanding its breadth and depth, and the influence of capitalistic forces that seek to extract only its entertainment value while disregarding its cultural essence. Hip Hop deserves the same scholarly treatment afforded to other major social and cultural movements.

In this spirit, several universities have recognized the importance of doing more than just adopting Hip Hop-based curricula by incorporating the curation and preservation of physical, historical artifacts into the most hallowed spaces within legacy institutions—their archives.

These institutions, alongside their museum counterparts, play a vital, but still burgeoning role in protecting Hip Hop's archeological history. As a culture and set of art forms born in analog times and evolved into the digital age, Hip Hop has left behind a scattered, multimedia legacy for which preservation was not always front of mind. Today, much of the Hip Hop we see and hear is distributed to the world through corporate-controlled media conglomerates, with little incentive or interest in taking part in preserving any historical attributes or artifacts. These factors make the work of collectors, curators, and archivists focusing on Hip Hop particularly urgent.

In addition, in an era of increasing attention to the ethics of preservation, it is incumbent upon these institutions to consider both evolving attitudes to the field as a whole, and the unique nuances specific to archiving Hip Hop. Through the initiatives taken by its founding director, Katherine Reagan, and by bringing on Ben Ortiz as assistant curator, the Cornell Hip Hop Collection has created a framework for Hip Hop archival practice that every similar endeavor should reference.

The Interview

Manny Faces: Ben, if you could just state your name, your affiliation, and how you present yourself to the world.

Ben Ortiz: This is Ben Ortiz. I'm the assistant curator of the Cornell Hip Hop Collection.[1] I'm a Scorpio, and my blood type is O-negative... And serial number, you said?

Manny Faces: We could save that for, you know, the dog tags.

Ben Ortiz: No doubt.

Manny Faces: We gotta keep some things off the Internet. So, like many of us in the game you wear several hats. Besides your title, which is impressive enough as it is, how do you define yourself from a professional standpoint, who you are, and what you do on a day-to-day basis?

Ben Ortiz: My job requires me to wear several different hats. This particular role with the Cornell Hip Hop archives requires me to be a teacher. It requires me to be an educator, formally and informally. It requires me to be a person that is connected in lots of different communities, like the Hip Hop community, our local community here in Ithaca, New York, our campus community here at Cornell University, and so forth.

It's funny. I find myself doing things just like this, talking on interviews for news outlets, podcasts, radio shows, and I find myself speaking in front of formal classrooms, giving lectures at conferences. But I'm also developing the collection and building relationships with people in our community who are looking for a home for their materials, for their archives to be preserved and used for education, for all time. So I seem to be discovering certain hats as time goes on.

I'm also a DJ, and that's an interesting hat for me to wear. I feel like there are certain opportunities for me to do outreach in a different way, to speak to audiences, but not necessarily using my voice. We had a B-Boy jam here in Ithaca. I was the DJ for that. I'm also the staff adviser for the Cornell B-Boy crew, which is called Absolute Zero, and I'm an unofficial adviser for the Ithaca College crew, which is called the Ground Up Crew.

It's just interesting how many hats I actually have, to use your phrase there. I actually sometimes refer to myself as a Swiss Army Knife. Because I got *this*, I got *that*, I got *this*, I got *that*. And it requires a broad skill set and a broad knowledge base. But without question, I have my dream job. I'm loving every second of it.

Manny Faces: That varied skill set, all the things that you bring to the table, emphasizes how important is for someone like you to be in that position. Bridging the gaps or *speaking to the room*, being in front of different audiences, advocating for the things you do, takes someone that can speak to all those different audiences and get them on the same page.

Could you state a little bit of history about how the archive came to be and how you came to be involved with it?

Ben Ortiz: The Cornell Hip Hop Collection started off as one singular archive in 2007 when a guy named Johan Kugelberg deposited the archive that he assembled for the production of his 2006 book, *Born in the Bronx: A Visual Record of the Early Days of Hip Hop.*[2] Johan had assembled an archive of vinyl records of early rap recordings—and I'm saying the word *rap* intentionally because it included some of the songs that definitely fit into the canon of early Hip Hop. From "Rapper's Delight" by The Sugarhill Gang[3], to Grandmaster Flash and The Furious Five, to Funky 4 Plus One, stuff like that, but also all the novelty records that were coming out globally that were trying to cash in on this fad called rapping.

So, Rodney Dangerfield[4] for instance. . . And there was a Muppet thing—this rat—I think it was a British TV show. I think his name was Roland? Roland the Rapping Rat?[5] Something like that. Johan put together this archive of early rap recordings. . . And I think it's interesting, the rat or whatever. They're not good songs. They're poorly produced, un-artful type songs. . .

Manny Faces: Parody type stuff. . .

Ben Ortiz: . . .at best, parody. But, you know, at worst, it's some culture vulture type stuff. Just cashing in on a fad, right? You wanna be able to study those things just as much as the realness, because it helps to gain a scholarly understanding of how Hip Hop has progressed through the ages.

Johan also put together a collection of early party flyers, something like five hundred flyers. He put a selection of those things into the *Born in the Bronx* book, along with working with the one and only Joe Conzo, Jr., [known as] the man who took Hip Hop's baby pictures. And then he also put some artwork, or I should say the *original* artwork made by Buddy Esquire, known as the King of the Flyer, including the actual boards that he was working on where you can see the glue and the Wite-Out[6] and the pencil marks and stuff like that, the thing that they took down to the copy shop. But when the book came out, Johan was looking for an institutional, educational home for this material. So he brought his archive here in 2007, and that became the very first archive relating to the topic of Hip Hop here at the Cornell University library.

Shortly after that, Joe Conzo established his archive. Shortly after that, Buddy Esquire established his archive. Also, *archive* in this sense doesn't necessarily mean a carefully assembled group of materials. It can mean the accumulation of stuff a person produces or acquires in the course of doing whatever it is that they do.

Manny Faces: Okay. A *dump* for a lack of a better term, as opposed to individually acquired pieces that someone might associate with a museum or something like that.

Ben Ortiz: Yeah... Maybe the word *dump* is a bridge too far...

Manny Faces: [LAUGHS] I mean it like a mind dump, you know...

Ben Ortiz: Yeah. There are certain things that we don't necessarily consider too research dense or having a lot of information contained within them. So if somebody was like, "Here's my collection of broken record needles," we'd be like, "Yeah, that's kinda interesting for a museum," but this is a research archive, and we want people to use this material because they can actually gain some sort of information from it. Not to say that we don't have some sentimental items, but we would love to have a box full of documents much more so than a box full of used microphones or something like that.

So this was founded in 2007 with that very first archive, but now it's grown into a collection of roughly forty individual archives over the eleven years that we've been in existence. We estimate that the very first collection that Johan brought us contained about 5,000 individual artifacts. But we estimate that today we have roughly a half million artifacts. So it's been a steady, steady growth over the last 11 years.

Now you also asked how I got involved. When the collection was brought here back in 2007, the person who worked with Johan to make that happen is my supervisor, and she is the curator of rare books and manuscripts...

Manny Faces: The collection falls under that umbrella. Right?

Ben Ortiz: Yeah. The Cornell Library System is huge and contains, like, twenty different libraries. But the Library of Rare and Manuscript Collections is where we're housed. So my supervisor, Katherine Reagan, is the curator of rare books and manuscripts. Her job is basically developing these collections across all the topics you can think of. Anything that is deemed important to human culture. That can be anything, which is actually how we look at stuff. Our overall mission is to collect and preserve artifacts documenting the whole human experience.

But when she brought that stuff here back in 2007, she only really knew one thing about Hip Hop, that it's an important cultural, musical, historical movement, which is arguably the most important thing to know about Hip Hop. But beyond that, it wasn't like she knew a ton. So she assembled an advisory board of people to help guide the direction of this material and the growth of the collection going forward. So, questions like, "How should this material be represented in exhibitions?" "How should this material be represented in the news media?" "Who's the one to talk about this stuff when reporters are asking about this material?" "Who's the person that can teach classes using this stuff from an informed perspective about Hip Hop."

So she put this group of people together, most of whom were local people here in Ithaca, staff members, faculty, graduate students, people that really did have a deep amount of Hip Hop knowledge, myself included. I was actually the third person asked to join the advisory board back in 2007. At that time, I was the coordinator of K-12 outreach for Cornell University, so I was working in a whole other field. I remained on the advisory board for four years up until 2011, and I was then offered the position of assistant curator to work formally with the archives here, which was the moment we kicked everything in the super high gear because we finally had a person who's deeply knowledgeable about Hip Hop, somebody able to field all the questions from researchers and teach all the classes and put exhibitions together. Whereas before that, there was no one person who was able to devote their full time to that stuff.

Manny Faces: I interviewed Joe Conzo so I learned about his involvement, and he was telling me that some of his photos are on the same shelf as the Gettysburg Address. It's amazing to hear him tell that story and it's amazing that you can help make that happen and put Hip Hop in its rightful place in history.

Some of the big names we hear, like Afrika Bambaataa,[7] Joe Conzo, Buddy Esquire… Give me a couple of names that maybe wouldn't have made the news necessarily, that aren't the biggest names, but are super interesting to have in your collection.

Ben Ortiz: I don't even wanna talk about anybody as if they're not *big names* or whatever, but I'll phrase it as some of the people who you might not know. We have their archives. Everybody knows we got Bambaataa. We got Kugelberg. Everybody knows we got Charlie Ahearn's *Wildstyle* archive.[8] Everybody knows we got Buddy Esquire. Everybody knows we got Ernie Paniccioli's photographic archive.[9] Everybody knows we got Bill Adler's archive.[10] Crazy Legs archive.[11] Grandmaster Caz archive.[12] Pop Master Fabel archive.[13] But some of the things people might not really know too much about? I got a whole bunch that I could mention.

Let me start by mentioning my man Eric Orr. Eric Orr created a comic book in 1986 called *Rappin' Max Robot*. It's the first comic book that ever used Hip Hop culture as the plot point or the backdrop of the premise. It was a complete do-it-yourself, independently produced comic book he put together and distributed by hand in comic shops and record stores. It's a pretty brilliant, fascinating project. That's the premise of his archive and we also have a lot of things that document his other artistic pursuits. One of the famous things about him is that he used to run with Keith Haring.[14] They were producing some art projects together, graffiti style meets gallery style type of stuff. Eric is a brilliant cat, and I hope people will wanna learn more about his archives as time goes on.

Manny Faces: That's one of the things about the archives in general, big names and lesser known but no less important names, is that everything is open to the public. Yes, it's for research purposes, and it's great on an academic level, but it also serves a purpose for the public.

What I love about the Cornell Hip Hop Collection is that people are often amazed to find out that it exists. I tell people about it, "Cornell has this great collection," and they're amazed. At the same time, what I *hate* is that people don't know it exists. [LAUGHS]

Ben Ortiz: [LAUGHS]

Manny Faces: So how much of your work goes past the curation and administration, but into the outreach and, for the lack of a better term, the marketing, to let people know that you guys do exist and that you're a resource for education to the public, not necessarily just for faculty, students, staff, and graduate students.

Ben Ortiz: Yeah, there's a big chunk of my time that is what you might call outreach. It's funny how impactful social media can be in that regard, that's a very important aspect of this type of outreach. Beyond that, like I said earlier, I'm speaking at conferences. I just talked at Emerson College in Boston. They had a Hip Hop month taking place, and they invited me to be one of the featured speakers. So, I'm very privileged and humbled to be to be able to do that sort of thing.

We have reporters all the time. Somebody's doing a blog here and there. International people too. Just recently, a German magazine hit me up to interview me to find out what this archive is all about.

It's funny. A ton of people *do* know about this. And then a lot of people are still learning. We're not *Avengers: Infinity War*. We're not that kind of famous. But we are still growing and still expanding, and my feeling is that we are just at the tip of the iceberg with this type of work. We're not slowing down anytime soon.

Manny Faces: The general public tends to not always be as knowledgeable as we would like them to be when they think of Hip Hop. They sometimes stop at music, or rap music, or rap music on the radio. They have a very limited understanding of Hip Hop as a culture. So when you have an organization like yours, if you have institutional integrity behind it, it does perk up the ears in the right manner when they do hear about it. How important do you think it is for Cornell, or for any archive that deals with Hip Hop, to make sure that they're dealing with the broad cultural, social movement aspects—all the things—not just the music?

Ben Ortiz: You know, as much as I want them to be doing that, I think that it's important that each of these archives understands their own purpose and goal. So if somebody says we are going to do a Hip Hop archive, OK, fair enough. But we wanna, obviously, make sure that whoever's doing that is doing so with good intentions and trying to do right by the culture that they wish to archive. Ostensibly, they see some value in it beyond it [being just] cool, fun, or cute, or something like that.

I'm not saying I've actually heard of anybody setting up a Hip Hop archive who feels that way about Hip Hop. Nevertheless, as time goes on, it's possible that somebody's not gonna have altruistic reasons when they set up their Hip Hop archive. So I think it's important that they have knowledgeable people in the mix from day one. I think that's what happened here at Cornell, starting with Johan, who got all his knowledge in a rapid amount of time because he was putting this book together. But in the process of doing so, he made mad connections with people like Joe Conzo, Buddy Esquire, and so forth.

Manny Faces: Straight from the source. . .

Ben Ortiz: Straight from the source. And he was, by the way, a former executive at Warner Brothers Music. He had connections all over the place. Then when the archive actually came here, as I said, my supervisor did the right thing in bringing this advisory board together, saying, "Look, as a person who doesn't come from this culture and doesn't know about this culture, I can't just be archiving this culture, and talking about this material to audiences and reporters and whatever. We need to do the right thing and have people who are seriously knowledgeable and coming out of this culture doing that sort of work."

I think that's the most important thing for people to know.

Now if somebody says, "We wanna start a rap music archive or a turntablism or DJ culture archive," or whatever—that's a specific aspect of Hip Hop that they can focus on. Tulane University has a New Orleans Hip Hop archive, which is focusing geographically on their city and also on their homegrown branch of Hip Hop, which is bounce music—among others, but, you know, that's the most famous.

So it's important, again, that everybody understands their purpose. But what you might have been trying to get at, correct me if I'm wrong, is about the holistic attention to all of Hip Hop's elements, as opposed to just focusing on the music. . .

Manny Faces: Right. As you say, if you're not in a specific niche. . .

Ben Ortiz: That's one of the things about us is that we make a great deal of effort to focus on things beyond music that has been produced [by] the music industry. [For instance,] grassroots music that was coming out of Hip Hop's pioneer days, we have cassettes documenting live shows, block parties, stuff like that. Graffiti, for example. We've got the *IGT* archive. *IGT* at one point stood for the *International Graffiti Times*—it changed its name a bunch of times—but it's this 'zine that was produced in the 1980s and 1990s documenting *street art culture* as it's sometimes called. You know, we call it graffiti and style writing culture. We have the archive of SEEN, one of the golden age graffiti gods. It's very important that we do that sort of thing in order to produce a holistic record of this culture for all times.

Part of my job is thinking about what people 500 years from now are gonna think of this stuff. I need to make sure that these people 500 years from now are able to assemble a clear understanding of everything about Hip Hop because [of how] we put it all together at this point in time.

Let me give you one more little anecdote. Just this past Friday, I was giving a presentation for a student group here on campus who call themselves the Cornell Hip-Hop Heads. What they're basically doing is analyzing lyrics— like a book club for Hip Hop lyrics. So that's pretty fresh.

In the course of talking to this particular group, one of the students asked me, "So who's your favorite Hip Hop artist?" The fact that the person said *artist* and not *emcee* made me say, "I bet I can flip this whole thing on them." So I started naming B-Boys and B-Girls, DJs and graffiti writers, and they were all like, "Wow, we haven't heard any of these people." And I said, "That's because you guys might be thinking that they're emcees, but you need to expand your horizons on what your understanding of Hip Hop is."

That's part of the educational piece. I love talking to young people who are open-minded enough to hear about Hip Hop culture in this bigger, holistic sense. I mean, the freshmen coming in this fall, they were born in the year 2000! You cannot expect them to have as clear an understanding as you and I, and that's why I'm an educator first. Being able to talk to people about the way things evolved and the history behind a movement is an important role that I don't take lightly.

Manny Faces: That's important. You hear a lot of [older Hip Hop heads] complain about what the younger folks may or may not have a perspective on. But at the same time, that work has to be done to deliver that perspective. It's not gonna happen magically on their own.

Ben Ortiz: That's exactly right. Because everybody's gotta learn from somewhere. And I very much embody *each one, teach one* as a guiding philosophy. Because, trust me, these kids are putting me on to stuff I never even heard of. And I love that. I like that I'm becoming more knowledgeable because of *their* knowledge and perspective. The exchange of knowledge—I know what I know, and you know what you know, let's talk about it—that's the essence of the cypher.[15] That is Hip Hop. So, the old heads lamenting that the young kids aren't *with it*, I think is a misplaced frustration.

Like you see interviews with young trap rappers talking down about [older artists like] Biggie Smalls or DJ Premier and stuff like that. That's very clearly a manufactured beef which is a tried-and-true method of the music industry to stimulate attention to their product. You generate some controversy, everybody's gonna start talking about you. Everybody gonna start paying attention to you.

As much as I've known Kanye West is certifiably insane for a long time, all of this stuff happening with him [like] when he said, "Slavery was a choice..." He's insane to begin with, but I also think he's crazy like a fox to be saying that. He's totally getting all this attention, which is gonna make everybody pay really, really, really close attention to his project, to his next move. They're gonna keep his name on their tongue. And it is kind of crazy how he is a lot like Donald Trump in that regard. It's depressing, but you gotta have some media literacy about this stuff to understand what's really happening.

Manny Faces: Well, that's why it's important to help bridge the generation gap as well, instead of just sitting back and lament. I don't like to throw out the babies with the mumble rap bath water. You know what I mean?

Ben Ortiz: [LAUGHS] That's right! That's a great way to put it.

Manny Faces: Well, I appreciate your work reaching out to people, especially in the academic field, who might not have the real authentic foundation needed for the archiving work, or don't quite get to that level of understanding [as to] how important that is. They stay in their academic towers and don't realize that it's about reaching back into the community and helping this culture evolve and move forward, all together. That's the way it's supposed to work.

Ben Ortiz: Yeah. That's well stated. Hip Hop has been documented in formal academia since the very late 1980s [and] Hip Hop in academia is huge right now, much more so than it ever has been. And if people like you—well, I wanna say people like me, but I got my feet on both sides of the tracks—but people like you, you gotta be watchdogs. You gotta be cultural watchdogs and make sure that the people who are in positions to control the knowledge for entire swaths of the population [know] what Hip Hop is, what its history is, where it comes from, what it is supposed to be. Or [else] it's gonna get lost. It's gonna get twisted.

Just think about this. There are no more cultural watchdogs in existence for things that happened over a hundred years ago. The American Civil War era, for example. Nobody's alive who was there. There are no more cultural watch-dogs and the information is gonna continue to get shaped almost exclusively by the academics. Who knows if that's for the better or for the worse? I'd like to think for the better, as academics get a little more woke about including the narrative of slaves and what their experiences were like going forward...

Manny Faces: ...stuff that might have been left out. But, again, you don't have those sources anymore...

Ben Ortiz: Yeah. So it's important that people really get interested in the academics of Hip Hop because anybody can participate. It should be a grassroots enterprise that anybody can be down with. I love that Hip Hop has produced more organic intellectuals than formal academia has produced formal intellectuals who have been handed a piece of paper with their name on it at some point. Again, I'm just using the Civil War as an example because it deals so heavily with the topic of slavery. And you got [Kanye] talking about, "Slavery was a choice." Well, you know what? Kanye West is an incredibly important figure in history. And a hundred years from now, 200 years from now, people might get it twisted. And go, well, "Kanye West said..." And that's why it's very important that people are really speaking truth to that sort of power wherever possible.

Manny Faces: I take that responsibility of cultural watchdog myself pretty seriously. That's kind of the role we all need to play. Because even with the academic field, it's not like the entertainment business where it's clearly based on, obviously, what's gonna sell. But in some cases that academic world—even though it's supposed to be rigorous and integrity filled—is going to say, "Hey. This would be cool to have..."

It's not about being cool. It's about being authentic to the roots and the people that made it happen.

Ben Ortiz: Most definitely. Well said.

Manny Faces: So, I've got one more question. The name of this podcast is *Hip Hop Can Save America!* Now it's probably a lofty idea—it's not the *only* thing that we need to save America. But I want to ask you, based on all your experience and perspectives, why is it important for people to consider Hip Hop music and culture when looking for ways to truly improve lives, livelihoods, and communities. What does Hip Hop bring to that table?

Ben Ortiz: I'm gonna echo my previous point. People who are coming out of Hip Hop culture—and I mean people who are deeper into Hip Hop beyond, "I like to sing along to every Cardi B song," or whatever—people who are exposed to Hip Hop's philosophies and history and the deeper sociological reasons behind it all, I think it's important that we recognize that there are all these organic intellectuals being created by Hip Hop culture.

To the point of how it can save America, I'm thinking pragmatically about that, actually. If you've got people coming out of the particular grassroots branch of Hip Hop, not the commercial music shit, but, you know, getting involved in politics, getting involved in leading swaths of society, I think that's an interesting way of thinking about how Hip Hop can actually save America. One interesting thing about Hip Hop is that it often, as Public Enemy said, likes to fight the power. I think it's intriguing to think about what would happen if instead of trying to *fight* the power, we *become* the power. And how do you become the power? Well, power is defined in many different ways. But at this particular moment in time, we're talking about elected officials, law enforcement, the people in positions like mine, in academia. If we can infiltrate—as the Hip Hop community—infiltrate those particular spheres and really get these people with that particular underpinning of Hip Hop as their core philosophy, core identity, core lens through which they look at the world... That just actually might change America. . . . I should say, *save* America. That's the name of the podcast. . .

Manny Faces: [LAUGHS]

Ben Ortiz: That just might save America. And it's a pretty simple concept in terms of just getting more people who are interested in social justice and changing society for the better in elected positions or law enforcement positions. Hip Hop, again, is producing more organic intellectuals, more people who are woke about this stuff than any other movement that's not founded in something formal like academia.

I think that's really a fascinating question. Because you're right. The first time I heard the title of this podcast, I was like, "OK. But can it, though!? Can it?" Because in the same way that you say Hip Hop can save America, we also got—once again, I gotta reference this because it's just been on my mind lately—Kanye West showing his Make America Great Again hat on social media. He's saying Trump is his homeboy. That's actually an example of Hip Hop not, in any way, helping America. That's an example of some aspect of Hip Hop contributing to the decline of many things that are supposedly important about America. So it's important that we don't just talk about Hip Hop as if it's one monolithic thing.

Manny Faces: Right. I think that's the problem. That Hip Hop's rep gets shaped by the Kanye Wests of the world, and not enough by the Ben Ortizs of the world.

Ben Ortiz: Oh, snap! That right there, I'm putting that one on my resume right now.

Manny Faces: Quotable! [LAUGHS]

Ben Ortiz: I might get that as a tattoo, B. [LAUGHS]

Manny Faces: [LAUGHS] That's what up... We'll talk about [royalty] percentages.

Ben Ortiz: Right! [LAUGHS]

Afterthoughts

The push to properly study and archive Hip Hop in academia came to prominence in 2002 with the launch of the Hiphop Archive & Research Institute at Harvard University, and has continued to expand over the years. Aside from Cornell, other examples include the William & Mary Hip Hop Collection, the Atlanta Hip Hop Archives at Georgia State University, the Seattle Hip Hop Archive at the University of Washington, and the Massachusetts Hip-Hop Archive at the University of Massachusetts Boston. There are also archives unaffiliated with universities, such as the National Hip Hop Museum based in Washington, D.C., some focused on particular regions like the Bay Area Hip Hop Archives, prominent displays of Hip Hop memorabilia and artifacts in museums like the National Museum of African American History and Culture, initiatives launched by individuals like The Gates Preserve, digital endeavors such as The Mixtape Museum and the Internet Archive's housing of the DatPiff archive of digital Hip Hop mixtapes, and more. Of course, there are many Hip Hop archives throughout the world, and the eventual expected completion of The Hip Hop Museum in New York City should attract more mainstream awareness to the concept.

The real importance of this work, however, isn't only in the collecting of things—it's in the proper telling of tales. With Hip Hop entering its sixth decade, documentarians have the advantage of being able to source material from pioneering figures, in many cases while they are still alive, to help protect against what has become a troubling trend throughout history—that to the victors (or oppressors) often go the stories.

With the advent of digitization and other technological tools, curators now can ensure many of the culture's original artifacts and oral histories will be preserved in ways that other massive social movements in the past did not have at their disposal.

Ben Ortiz and others involved with the Cornell Hip Hop Collection have set a standard of care for the preservation and protection of Hip Hop culture that should inspire not only those interested in archiving Hip Hop, but anyone involved in the archival field as a whole. As for the saving America angle, Ortiz himself demonstrates what he suggests—that having culturally conscious individuals and forward-thinking leaders inspired by the innovative and inclusive spirit of Hip Hop serving in legacy institutions that have traditionally been less than equitable when dealing with marginalized communities, could indeed be an effective way to help ensure power is more fairly shared among all the people.

As of this writing, the Cornell Hip Hop Collection has continued to nurture and grow its archive and has added artifacts from several more prominent figures from Hip Hop history, including DJ and pioneering figure in U.S. West Coast Hip Hop, Lonzo Williams; creator of iconic rap TV show *Yo! MTV Raps*, Peter Dougherty; and renowned DJ, radio host, filmmaker, and author Bobbito Garcia.

Key Takeaways

1. The Cornell Hip Hop Collection started in 2007 with a single archive and has grown to more than 40 individual archives containing approximately half a million artifacts.

2. Ben Ortiz describes his role as multifaceted, requiring him to be an educator, community connector, DJ, and adviser in addition to his curatorial duties.
3. The collection aims to preserve artifacts documenting the entire human experience of Hip Hop culture, not just music.
4. Ortiz emphasizes the importance of having knowledgeable people from within Hip Hop culture involved in archiving and educating about the culture.
5. The archive includes materials beyond mainstream music, such as grassroots recordings, graffiti art documentation, and early party flyers.
6. Ortiz sees his role as an educator crucial in teaching younger generations about the broader aspects of Hip Hop culture beyond just rap music.
7. The collection serves as a resource for both academic research and public education about Hip Hop culture and history.
8. Ortiz stresses the importance of "cultural watchdogs" to ensure accurate representation and preservation of Hip Hop's history and origins in academic settings.
9. He highlights the potential of Hip Hop culture to create "organic intellectuals" who could positively influence society by entering positions of power and leadership.
10. Ortiz suggests that Hip Hop's potential to "save America" lies in its ability to produce socially conscious individuals who can effect change in various sectors of society.

Discussion Questions

1. How does the concept of "cultural watchdogs," as mentioned by Ben Ortiz, relate to the preservation and representation of marginalized cultures in academic and legacy institutional settings?
2. Discuss the potential benefits and challenges of having "organic intellectuals" from Hip Hop culture in positions of power, as suggested by Ortiz.
3. How does the Cornell Hip Hop Collection's approach to archiving, which includes grassroots materials and various cultural elements, differ from traditional archival practices?

4. Analyze the importance of including diverse artifacts (e.g., party flyers, graffiti documentation) in Hip Hop archives. How does this contribute to a more comprehensive understanding of the culture?

5. Examine the role of academic and other traditional institutions in preserving and studying popular culture movements like Hip Hop. What are the potential benefits and drawbacks?

6. How might the archiving of Hip Hop culture influence its evolution and public perception over time?

7. Discuss the challenges of educating younger generations about the broader aspects of Hip Hop culture. How can archives contribute to this educational process?

8. Analyze the potential impact of Hip Hop archiving on issues of cultural appropriation and misrepresentation in mainstream media and academia.

9. How does the multifaceted role of an archivist like Ben Ortiz (educator, DJ, community connector) reflect the interdisciplinary nature of Hip Hop studies?

10. Evaluate the statement "Hip Hop can save America." How might Hip Hop's cultural values and practices contribute to social change and political engagement?

This podcast episode was originally released on August 8, 2018.

Notes

1 Reagan, K. A. (2020). The Cornell Hip Hop collection: An example of an archival repository. *Global Hip Hop Studies, 1*(1), 149—155.

2 Conzo Jr., J., & Kugelberg, J. (2007). *Born in the Bronx: A Visual Record of the Early Days of Hip Hop*. Universe Publishing/Rizzoli International.

3 "Rapper's Delight" (1979) by The Sugarhill Gang and released on Sugar Hill Records, is widely recognized as the first commercially successful Hip Hop song and the recording that introduced rap music to mainstream audiences.

4 "Rappin' Rodney" (1983), written by Dangerfield, R., and Bergman, A., released on RCA Records, was one of the earliest "comedy-rap" crossover singles.

5 Roland Rat Superstar, a British television puppet character created by David Claridge and launched on TV-am (1983).

6 Wite-Out is a brand name correction fluid often used by Hip Hop-inspired visual artists.

7 A pivotal DJ and founder of the Universal Zulu Nation who helped establish Hip Hop culture's foundations, though his legacy was later tarnished by allegations of sexual abuse.

 8 Ahearn, C. (Director). (1983). Wild Style. [Motion Picture]. First Run Features. The first feature film to focus entirely on Hip Hop culture.

 9 Ernie Paniccioli, photographer and documentarian noted for capturing iconic images of Hip Hop culture from the 1970s onward. He appeared as a guest on the September 8, 2020 episode of the *Hip Hop Can Save America!* podcast.

10 Bill Adler, music journalist, publicist, and founding publicity director for Def Jam Records. His Adler Archive, later acquired by the Cornell Hip Hop Collection, documented early Hip Hop media coverage.

11 Richard "Crazy Legs" Colon, B-Boy and president of the Rock Steady Crew collective, helped establish breaking as a global phenomenon through performances, battles, and media appearances.

12 Curtis "Grandmaster Caz" Brown, member of the rap group The Cold Crush Brothers.

13 Jorge "Pop Master Fabel" Pabon, dancer, choreographer, educator, and Hip Hop historian.

14 Keith Haring, American artist whose distinctive style and collaboration with New York City's early Hip Hop scene merged street art with fine art.

15 A cypher is an informal, performative gathering where practitioners—typically emcees or dancers—assemble in a circle and take turns as featured performers.

· 6 ·

THE O.G. |
DR. GLORIA LADSON-BILLINGS

OK, let me get a little academic for a minute.

In 1976, my father published an article in the journal *Theory Into Practice*, titled "The Socialization of Teachers: A Case Study."[1] The article discusses a project where a large Midwestern university attempted to prepare student teachers to work in inner-city schools. The goal was to train teachers who could bring new, innovative ideas to these schools. However, the project ran into problems when two student teachers were placed at a particular junior high school.

The student teachers were trained to be innovative and challenge the status quo, but the school they were placed in was very traditional, highly focused on discipline and authority. This led to conflicts between the student teachers and the school staff.

The main issue came to a head during a P.T.A. meeting where the student teachers allowed students to criticize school policies. The principal and many teachers saw this as disrespectful and undermining their authority. As a result, the two student teachers were dismissed from the school.

The article argues that this conflict happened because the university didn't consider how the schools actually operated when training the student teachers. The innovative approaches the students were taught clashed with the traditional methods used in the school.

At the time that I was learning about the origins and evolutions of Hip Hop Based Education, I couldn't help but connect this incident with issues that led to the development years later of an educational theory called "culturally relevant pedagogy."

The concept of culturally relevant pedagogy was developed by Dr. Gloria Ladson-Billings (1995)[2] and emphasizes the importance of connecting school culture with students' home cultures, particularly for students from marginalized communities. The conflict my father described highlights the challenges that can arise when attempting to implement new teaching approaches in established school systems, which is a key concern in culturally relevant pedagogy (Gay, 2002).[3]

As Dr. Bettina Love and other scholars have pointed out, schools with predominantly African American student populations often have a disconnect between traditional school practices and the cultural experiences of students (Howard, 2003).[4] The innovative approaches the student teachers in this article were trying to implement could be seen as an attempt to bridge this type of gap, making education more relevant and engaging for those students, which aligns with the goals of culturally relevant pedagogy.

However, the resistance they faced from the school administration illustrates a common challenge in implementing culturally relevant pedagogy: overcoming institutional inertia and traditional power structures in schools. This, in part, led to Ladson-Billings' (2014)[5] later work emphasizing the need for *systemic* change, not just individual teacher efforts, to truly implement culturally relevant teaching.

With all of this serving as a backdrop, it is no wonder so many of today's leading Hip Hop based educators lovingly refer to Dr. Ladson-Billings as one of the O.G.s.[6]

The Interview

Manny Faces: Dr. Ladson-Billings, thank you for taking the time out to speak with me, I'm a fan of what you do, and it's a pleasure to spend some time with you today.

Dr. Gloria Ladson-Billings: My pleasure.

Manny Faces: If you could, please, [introduce yourself].

Dr. Gloria Ladson-Billings: I'm Gloria Ladson-Billings. I am Professor Emerita from the University of Wisconsin where I was the Kellmer Family Chair in Urban Education. I'm also a faculty affiliate in education policy studies, education leadership and policy analysis in Afro-AM. I am currently the president of the National Academy of Education.

Manny Faces: How would you currently define who you are right now from a professional standpoint?

Dr. Gloria Ladson-Billings: Well, in many ways, I've become an independent scholar because I've just formally retired from the University of Wisconsin. But I've always said to my students, there's a difference between having a job and having work. So while I don't have a job, I have plenty of work. And much of that work is professional development work with teachers, particularly teachers that are going to be working with kids in urban spaces.

Manny Faces: So your work is largely teaching teachers to be better teachers?

Dr. Gloria Ladson-Billings: Yes.

Manny Faces: Got it. So, a theory that you are widely recognized for is this concept of culturally relevant pedagogy. In recent years, you've remixed that theory a bit. Could you briefly talk about what that theory meant when you developed the concept and how you've now modified it over the years.

Dr. Gloria Ladson-Billings: We're talking work that began some 30 years ago, where I was very puzzled by the fact that there seemed to be nothing in the literature that suggested that we could be successful with "urban" kids, and particularly African American and Latino kids. And I just knew that wasn't so, even with an n of 1: myself. I knew that there were teachers who knew how to work with our kids. So, I began studying these teachers.

What came out of the of that three-year study[7] was what I called culturally relevant pedagogy. If you fast forward to the last maybe eight, 10 years, you'll see a shift to what people like Django Paris, H. Samy Alim, and Dr. Chris Emdin are talking about, notions of culturally *sustaining* pedagogy. And while I still use the term culturally relevant pedagogy, I understand the need to be thinking about pedagogy a little bit different.

One of the limitations of my work is that I was looking in elementary classrooms. I looked in those classrooms because they're more convenient, from a research standpoint. You have one teacher, 27, 30 kids, all day, and it's just easy to manage from a research standpoint. But I have a more secondary background, and I know that's a more complex organization where you may have as many as 150 kids in a day.

By taking the convenient sample of the elementary classroom, a big limitation of my work is that I did not get to what I call *youth culture*. Adolescents are really the carriers of youth culture. It's not to say that elementary kids aren't aware of it, but you're more likely to see the aesthetics, the fashion, the arts, all of the important aspects of youth culture identified with adolescents. You're not gonna see it as much on young kids. I knew I had missed that particular opportunity, and as I began to look at the impact of youth culture, I realized it was important to make a shift.

Manny Faces: Is this where Hip Hop starts to play a role?

Dr. Gloria Ladson-Billings: Yes, indeed. Now in some ways, I backed into to this. The University of Wisconsin-Madison had the nation's first Hip Hop art scholarship program, First Wave. I knew these young people. I went to their performances. I supported them. I sat on the board. But a number of them came to me complaining about our teacher education program, and I needed to figure out a way to try to help them.

Now my immediate way to help them was by helping them design what we call on our campus *independent majors*, where they come up with a coherent rationale for why they needed to have a particular plan of study. When they do that, we come up with the courses that make sense for that plan. I thought that was going to be satisfactory for them. But over time, I kept getting young people saying, "No. We want more." In some ways, it was just their way to say, "We need you to *teach* us something."

So, we came up with a course idea. We had a series on campus already called Getting Real, which was a lecture series. We brought in a combination of scholars and artists to talk to students about making that transition into art and the kind of pedagogy or the kind of teaching and learning that their art encapsulated.

We had wonderful people. We had Mark Lamont Hill. We had Dr. Elaine Richardson out of Ohio State. We had Dawn-Elissa Fischer and Davey D. We had Ebro Darden to talk about the business end. We had Mark Anthony Neal from Duke. Colman Domingo, who was a fabulous artist of stage and screen. They gave public lectures, but they also interacted with our students one on one.

We did two courses. The first course was called Pedagogy, Performance and Culture. The second course was called Pedagogical Flows: Hip Hop in the K-12 Classroom. I had H. Samy Alim present virtually. I had Dr. Chris Emdin come and interact with the students. Martha Diaz out of NYU. David Kirkland. So that's kinda how the ball got rolling for me with Hip Hop and education. We just had great people come to work with our folks.

Manny Faces: You speak in one of your talks about students needing to be "multicultural aware." How does Hip Hop enable that.

Dr. Gloria Ladson-Billings: One of the things that we did by design with the courses is that while I reserved about half of the slots in the course for First Wave students, I didn't want it to be a First Wave-segregated classroom. The other half was open to the general campus community. What we saw when *mainstream* Wisconsin students were in those courses is that they were often struggling to keep up culturally. That had never happened to them before. There was just stuff they didn't know.

That was an important revelation for them because they had always been advantaged. They're at the state's top institution. They were the cream of the crop in their high schools. They were kids who always *knew*.

I'm reminded of one of my assignments. Students have to do an artist study. So they pick an artist, tell me why they chose the artist, give me some biographical background, give me the discography, and then put together a mixtape[8] of that artist's work, [explaining] why that work is significant for education. After all, this was an education course. In one of the papers, a young white Midwestern woman said, "I chose Lauryn Hill because one day in class everybody was talking about Lauryn Hill, and I said, 'Who's Lauryn Hill?' And they all looked at me like I was the stupidest person ever."

Now I know what kids feel like in my practicum classroom when I ask something that I just assumed they should know. It was a [bit of a] revelation that there was knowledge out there that many of our students had no way to access yet. They would be going out in the schools and classrooms, talking to kids who are very much steeped in this knowledge, so it was an important aspect of developing what we're calling this cultural competence.

Manny Faces: As you started to bring these concepts together from a teaching standpoint, was there any pushback, any hindrances on an institutional basis? You said there were already things happening at the university that were open to this way of thinking, so how difficult was it to incorporate some of these things into curriculum and do the work you were trying to do?

Dr. Gloria Ladson-Billings: Well, it wasn't hard for me because I was doing this near the end of my career and I had already been somewhat celebrated. So, in other words, it's like, "Let's just leave her alone." It might have been harder for some of the younger folks who want to do this work, but I think what made the university embrace it were the networks we were able to build. We were bringing people from some of the top institutions, Stanford, Teachers College, Harvard. There's already a kind of cachet that was there.

The other thing is that the university had really taken advantage of the way in which the First Wave program put it on the map. Our First Wave folks are so fierce. I mean, these are young people who have performed at the London Cultural Olympics. They've been on Broadway. They've performed for NCAA conferences, for the National Council of Teachers of English, the American Sociological Association. . . We're not talking about a group of ragtag individuals here. These kids are artists.

In fact, my one complaint is that I think we use them too much, you know? In some ways, we do them like we do the athletes. And I always have to explain to people, we don't actually have a Hip Hop major, just like we don't have a football major. They have to take the coursework that the university offers. Their art is what funds their scholarship. I guess my deepest concern is that as someone who is transitioning out of the formal structure of the university, I don't know who is going to be willing to take this up.

Manny Faces: Do you find that now that the #HipHopEd movement[9] is gaining popularity, it's becoming easier for educators to bring these concepts to the schools?

Dr. Gloria Ladson-Billings: I think it's easier when they get the right grounding. To me, the thing I hate most is to see somebody *using* Hip Hop as a gimmick. I really dissuade teachers from doing that.

I was just in Baton Rouge last weekend working with teachers who are engaged in, what they call STEM. I call it *STEAM* because it's not just science, technology, engineering and math. We add the arts. So the very first question that I asked these teachers was, "How many of you have seen *Black Panther?*" 75% of them had seen *Black Panther*. Next question was, "How many of you have used *Black Panther* in your classroom?" Not one hand. And these are science teachers!

So, I made them go through a process of looking at all of the science, technology, engineering, art, and math elements in the film. There are tons of them. I said to them, "This is what I mean by *being* Hip Hop. You think it's all about the music. First, Hip Hop is made up of four elements and the fifth element, of course, is knowledge."[10]

I don't want teachers to *use* Hip Hop. I want them to *be* Hip Hop.

What do we mean by that? I'll give an example of a teacher I know, a fabulous teacher. I always tell him that he's Hip Hop, and he's like, "Doc, I have never played a Hip Hop record in my life in my classroom." And I said, "That's not what I mean. What I mean is, you use the *elements* of Hip Hop in your teaching." Number one, he knows how to flip something out of nothing. He's teaching a course that didn't exist, a course on global poverty and global health. An amazing course, getting his kids connected with people from around the world.

So, to me, if you use *Black Panther*, that would have been flipping something out of nothing. You had no *Black Panther* curriculum before you went to the movies. But when we saw it, you're like, "Oh, I can use this!"

I asked those STEM teachers, "How many chemistry teachers in the room?" They had a bunch of chemistry teachers. I said, "Here's an exercise. Where would you place Vibranium on the periodic table?" There's a logic to the table, so if you really want to understand that the kids *understood* the table as opposed to trying to get them to *memorize* the table—which to me makes no sense—but there is a logic to the table. The gases are all together in a particular place, the hard metals in another. It's a thought exercise. We know Vibranium is a made-up thing, the whole thing is made up, come on! It's a comic! It's Marvel! But if you could get kids thinking that way... This is the notion of flipping something out of nothing.

The other thing that's so emblematic of Hip Hop is the notion that a fresh beat yesterday is a fresh beat yesterday. Stop doing that same old stuff because it was cool and hip in your day. Not unless you can connect it up with what kids are dealing with today.

And then the third thing I try to get teachers to look at is being creatively resourceful, figuring out how you might do a new thing despite some constraints or limited resources. To me, if you do those three things, I don't care if you never play the music because Hip Hop is more than the music. It is the culture. To me, that's *being* Hip Hop.

I asked the teachers, "How many of you have a playlist in your classroom." Nobody had a playlist. I said, "You gotta have a playlist!"

One of the things you get to do as the teacher is moderate. You get to curate. You can tell the students, "If you bring me a song that's obscene, if you bring me a song that uses bad language, it's not gonna make the playlist." The kids will look for the right songs. But the idea is, you're not trying to *be* them, you're trying to say that what they bring to the classroom is of value.

One of the ways in which I started using music was as a young teacher in the Philadelphia school district. Every morning when I got in—and I got in early—I always turned the radio on and I'd be working. When the first bell rang, I turned the radio off and then the kids would come in.

One day, I was rushing to get something done, the bell rang, and I didn't turn the radio off. The kids came in, and I got up to turn the radio off and one of the kids said, "Oh, Miss Billings, don't turn that off." And I was like, "Wow!" So then, I began bringing in albums, and I had different things I would play for the kids at different times. I also exposed the class to music they would never have listened to. I introduced them to classical music. If what we wanna do is have a really calm and relaxing time, you know, it's not time to "Knuck If You Buck"...[11]

Manny Faces: [LAUGHS]

Dr. Gloria Ladson-Billings: And sometimes I'd ask the kids, well, "What do you guys wanna hear?" I'll never forget, I had a kid in class who could only be described by every other teacher in the school as disaffected. He said to me, "Can you play that song, you know the one that goes 'Dunn dunn dunn dunnnn... Dunn dunn dunn dunnnnn.'" I said you, "You wanna hear Beethoven's Fifth?" He said, "Aw man, thats my jawn!"[12]

See? How does that get to be his jawn if he never gets exposed to it?

So [after that], I always had music. If you come by my office, I'm the one with the JBL speakers. I'm the one with the wall rattling sometimes, because that's just who I am. And I realized I need to do this with the students. It's a good management tool. I played Al Jarreau right after he had died. We had an open discussion about who Al Jarreau was. Why is he significant? Why would I play Al Jarreau here in Wisconsin? Well, Al Jarreau was from Milwaukee.

And [in fact], Al Jarreau was very dedicated to public education and left a part of his estate to education. They didn't know that. It's those little tidbits.

Manny Faces: There's always a way to tie things in. What I like about the #HipHopEd movement is that some of the younger instructors also help by bringing in artists or making connections to artists in the Hip Hop landscape that aren't in the mainstream. You know, the perception is that rap or Hip Hop is just what you hear on the radio, and that's it. That there aren't any [artists] today making music or giving perspectives that have substance or positivity. Of course, that's not the case. I think what the educators are doing in some ways by looking at the newer crop of artists like Kendrick [Lamar] and Chance [The Rapper], and sometimes local artists who are often artist-activists and bringing them into the mix as well, helps fight back against the perception that Hip Hop doesn't have *that* anymore.

Dr. Gloria Ladson-Billings: Right. I mean, I use Jasiri X all the time. His work is just so politically motivated. Most of the teachers, they don't know that. I say to them, "For you to say, 'Well, I don't wanna use Hip Hop because it's racist or it's violent. . .' That's like saying, 'I'm not gonna go to the movies because in *The Godfather*, they killed all these men.'" It's a genre. It's like saying, "I'm not gonna read a book because I've read *Lady Chatterley's Lover*, and it was pornographic." It's a genre. You need to say, "This is the kind I like, and this is the kind I don't like."

I work with a cohort of high schoolers helping them get prepared to write their essays for college, and I always use the same piece—Kool Moe Dee's song, "I Go To Work." I love that piece. I'm showing my age on that one. . . But I used it because, first of all, the lyricism is incredible in that piece. But he's bragging. And I say to the students, "This is not the time to be the shrinking violet. You're supposed to explain to these people why you are a better choice than every other 3.6 varsity letter winner or orchestra member that they're looking at." We have a lot of fun with that, where they look for metaphors to describe who and what they are. And they loved the video because it's got the whole James Bond theme to it, the white dinner jacket, you know?

Manny Faces: That actually leads me to something you touched on a little bit before. What I'm trying get across to people by talking to individuals like yourself, is that Hip Hop used in educational settings, as well as in all kinds of settings, from health and wellness to science and technology, the public perception might be, "Well, that's a great way to reach African-American youth," or 'inner city' youth or whatever they're gonna call it. But I suggest that there are some universal applications to this kind of work. Certainly, the work being done to help young African American youth connect to the subject matter or industries that they've been traditionally shut out of is super important, but what are some of the universal ways that Hip Hop works for people that are not necessarily from a Hip Hop oriented community?

Dr. Gloria Ladson-Billings: Let me respond to that in two ways. The first question I often get is, "Well, what if the kids aren't into Hip Hop?" You know, these people are thinking they're teaching in the suburbs, or wherever they think they are. I explain to them that the commercial Hip Hop industry couldn't exist without suburban kids. So, number one, your kids are support-ing the industry. But [going back to] the idea of, what if they're not into it... Let me flip that...

What if they're not into Shakespeare?

We teach what we value. Most kids are not into Shakespeare, trust me. But we have decided that it's of value. So, I think it's really important for people to understand that it's not merely about *Black culture*. Hip hop is the most commodified, monetized culture. I've been everywhere in the world. I've been to six of the seven continents. I was in Edinburgh, Scotland, coming out of having dinner one night, and I heard this beat in the club next door. I'm like, "Wait. Let me go ahead and see what this is." And no one in there looked like me.

It's not limited to Black or "urban." Did it originate in the Black community? Yes. There's a whole aspect of Hip Hop that is linked to Latino culture that we often don't talk about. All of the early B-Boys. All of them. All the best were coming out of the poor working communities of New York. So we need accurate histories of Hip Hop to be able to respond to this question of, "What if our kids aren't interested in it," or "Oh, that's OK for *those* kids."

The second thing that I want to say, again, harkens back to my experience this weekend, because I started talking about the knowledge economy that our kids were entering. Most of the kids who are deeply into Hip Hop also have mad tech skills. . . You have to if you're gonna do your own mixtapes, or if you're going to do any of the technical aspects of the work. And our kids are entering an economy that we just couldn't predict. Who knew that there could be a point in your life that you could use your phone and just call some guy with a Toyota Camry to come pick you up. That's just not imaginable. Who knew that you could turn your house into a little hotel on a part-time basis, you know? Hip hop is perfect for this gig economy. The skills that you can learn and understand from Hip Hop fit so well into this knowledge economy, this gig economy, where people really make their own work.

We want kids to have those skills, regardless of who they are.

Manny Faces: Indeed. And just as an aside, one of the things that I'm trying to do as a journalist, what I talk about and think about is the danger of Hip Hop's true and vast culture and its associated art forms being erased or pushed back because of the focus on entertainment and pop culture. And, again, that's where it ends for a lot of people. There are media and corporations who largely control a lot of the imagery that's put out there, and they have little incentive to promote anything that doesn't feed into their corporate profit machine. Bringing it into the education space when you're dealing with young people, either K-12 or the collegiate level, helps that cause as well. It helps protect Hip Hop, the *culture*, from being co-opted so much.

Dr. Gloria Ladson-Billings: Right. That's always gonna be a danger. One of the reasons why I have such a simpatico relationship with this generation of young people is that I'm a child of the sixties, so [for me it was] The Last Poets. Nikki Giovanni. You know? When I play that for my students, they're like, "Oh my god. That's so dope!" Or, "That was sampled on a song!" They see the connections, and they are a group who want their art to be used for social justice and activist purposes.

Manny Faces: Right. That helps inspire those movements to grow and continue. We need that.

Dr. Ladson-Billings, you've answered all of my questions with brilliant perspective. One more, if that's cool with you. The audacious name of this podcast is *Hip Hop Can Save America!* Maybe a lofty theory, but in your experience, what are the best reasons to consider Hip Hop music and culture when we're looking for ways to truly improve lives, livelihoods, communities, and relationships, and fix this crazy country of ours?

Dr. Gloria Ladson-Billings: Well, I used to be a history teacher, so I'm always going to default to historical perspective for most things.

Think back to the early days of Hip Hop in New York, and one of the things it did was decrease the violence. New York was being overrun with street gangs, but once Kool Herc, Africa Bambaataa, those folks started having these dance parties... We've seen the evolution from the DJ to emcee. We all talk about dope emcees, but really, the early Hip Hop was all about the DJ. You get that loop going over, that calmed the community in a powerful way that has never really been acknowledged. I believe Jeff Chang, in his book *Can't Stop, Won't Stop*[13] looks at the police records that the decrease in violent crime was simultaneous with the rise of Hip Hop. So we know that it's a good outlet.

If our young people don't have something creative to do, if they don't have a chance to express themselves, they'll destroy themselves, and us with them. I think the arts and the humanities are indeed what make us human. We can't just be technical. We have to be artists.

It was fun when I was doing the exercise with the teachers about *Black Panther*. I said, "Let's not forget the art. Where's the art in this?" And, you know, they certainly recognize that in almost every representation in Shuri's lab[14] or the community, you saw these cultural paintings, because it's the art that keeps us... That holds us together... Not just the science. So Hip Hop as an important art form is always gonna make it significant.

I remind the teachers I talk to, "Raise your hand if you ever heard someone say, 'Oh, that Hip Hop stuff ain't gonna last.'" We're 40 years into *not lasting!*

And my question to the students that I teach is, "Who introduced you to Hip Hop?"

The answer is almost always, "My parents."

So, I'm teaching the children of Hip Hop heads. It's going to last. Will it change? Will it shift? Of course, because that's just how art is. It has a long history. Let's go all the way back to "The Message" by Melle Mel and The Furious Five.[15] Let's look at that. What were they trying to do? How has that changed over time? Who's still doing that? Who's doing something different. Look at the way in which people have used Hip Hop as a springboard to other things.

We know that in the same way that sports and athletics provide more than entertainment, they do show some level of hope and encouragement.

Hip hop has that same potential.

Afterthoughts

In The Notorious B.I.G.'s song "Ten Crack Commandments," while listing said commandments, he states, "Number nine shoulda been number one to me..."

First, this always struck me as ironic. This was *his* song after all—he could have simply *made* it number one. But I digress.

In the context of this book, Chapter Six could have been number one to me, and I think it's safe to say no one who followed would have felt the least bit slighted.

After speaking with nine brilliant Hip Hop innovators before her, Dr. Ladson-Billings put a perfect punctuation mark on the first season of the *Hip Hop Can Save America!* podcast. Her decades of teaching experience were on full display as she elaborated on every aspect that my show—and now this book—had delved into, delivering insight with a brilliantly down-to-earth style that just makes things make sense.

Dr. Ladson-Billings touched on so many key aspects I was trying to show-case, from the basic concepts at the core of culturally relevant, responsive, sustaining, and affirming pedagogical approaches that undergird all of the work I had been discovering, to her brilliant-in-its-simplicity method of using modern, real-world references to better connect with and build trust among young people.

She reinforced the importance of protecting against commercialization of Hip Hop's educational and social justice-oriented characteristics. Most profoundly, she delivered a statement that should be foremost in the mind of anyone exploring Hip Hop's intersectionality as a collaborative tool for improving societal institutions like the education system: one must not simply *do* Hip Hop; instead, one must *be* Hip Hop.

This emphasis reinforces one of the key throughlines in these explorations—the need for legacy institutions to better facilitate the partic-ipation of practitioners and cultural members in teaching their own culture.

We'll continue to explore some of these themes again in upcoming chap-ters. In the meantime, it is worth reflecting deeply on Dr. Ladson-Billings's les-sons, as few have come to understand and represent this intersectional world better than the O.G. herself.

Before we move on, a personal fun fact. In the mid-1980s, one of the students in my father's sociology class at the State University of New York at Old Westbury was scheduled to perform at the college. Though I remember asking to go, my father didn't oblige. Maybe he thought I was too young. Maybe he just didn't understand why I would want to see some guy he knew as Mohandas Dewese perform. Of course, I knew him as Kool Moe Dee, whose music Dr. Ladson-Billings now uses to inspire her students.

Full-circle moments indeed.

Key Takeaways

1. Culturally relevant pedagogy has evolved to include youth culture and Hip Hop as essential components in education.
2. Hip Hop in education is not just about playing music (though that can be a part of it), but about embodying the culture's creativity, resourcefulness, and adaptability.
3. Incorporating Hip Hop into education can help students develop multicultural awareness and expose them to knowledge they might not otherwise access.
4. Teachers should aim to "be Hip Hop" rather than just "use Hip Hop" in their classrooms.
5. Hip Hop can be a powerful tool for teaching across various subjects, including STEM fields.
6. Music in the classroom, including Hip Hop, can be an effective management tool and a way to engage students in learning.
7. Hip Hop culture is not limited to any one demographic; it has global appeal and relevance.
8. The skills learned through Hip Hop align well with the demands of the modern gig economy and knowledge-based industries.
9. Hip Hop has historically played a role in reducing violence and providing creative outlets for youth.
10. Hip Hop's longevity and intergenerational appeal make it a lasting and influential cultural force in education and society.

Discussion Questions

1. How can educators in non-arts subjects, such as mathematics or science, incorporate Hip Hop culture's principles of creativity and resourcefulness into their teaching methods?

2. In what ways can businesses and organizations outside of education adapt the concept of "being Hip Hop" to foster innovation and adaptability in their work environments?

3. How might community leaders and policymakers use Hip Hop's historical role in reducing violence to inform current strategies for youth engagement and crime prevention?

4. How can educators in predominantly non-urban or non-diverse areas use Hip Hop to promote multicultural awareness and global perspectives among their students?

5. What strategies can be employed to bridge the gap between older educators who may be unfamiliar with Hip Hop culture and younger students who are immersed in it?

6. How might the principles of culturally relevant pedagogy and Hip Hop education be applied to adult learning and professional development programs?

7. In what ways can the tech industry collaborate with Hip Hop artists and educators to create innovative educational tools and platforms?

8. How can the concept of "flipping something out of nothing" from Hip Hop culture be applied to solve challenges in fields such as environmental sustainability or social entrepreneurship?

9. What role can Hip Hop play in promoting intergenerational dialogue and understanding in various social and professional contexts?

10. How might healthcare professionals incorporate elements of Hip Hop culture to improve patient education and community health initiatives, particularly in underserved areas?

This podcast episode was originally released on August 29, 2018.

Notes

1 Conforti, J. M. (1976). The socialization of teachers: A case study. *Theory Into Practice*, *15*(5), 352–359.

2 Ladson-Billings, G. (1995). Toward a theory of culturally relevant pedagogy. *American Educational Research Journal*, *32*(3), 465–491.

3 Gay, G. (2002). Preparing for culturally responsive teaching. *Journal of Teacher Education*, *53*(2), 106–116.

4 Howard, T. C. (2003). Culturally relevant pedagogy: Ingredients for critical teacher reflection. *Theory Into Practice*, *42*(3), 195–202.

5 Ladson-Billings, G. (2014). Culturally relevant pedagogy 2.0: a.k.a. the remix. *Harvard Educational Review*, 84(1), 74–84.

6 The term O.G.—originating in 1970s Los Angeles gang culture and later popularized through film and Hip Hop—refers to an originator or pioneer, derived from "original gangster."

7 Ladson-Billings, G. (1992). Culturally relevant teaching: The key to making multicultural education work. In C.A. Grant (Ed.), *Research and multicultural education* (pp. 106–121). London: Falmer Press

8 Mixtapes, popularized by Hip Hop DJs in the 1980s and 1990s, began as custom compilation albums on cassette before evolving through CD and digital formats. The term now can refer to any curated music collection resembling a traditional album, regardless of artist count or medium.

9 The Hip Hop Ed movement, often identified by its hashtag #HipHopEd, is a loose collective of educators, professionals, advocates, activists, Hip Hop fans, practitioners, and others who support Hip Hop as a valuable educational tool.

10 Hip Hop comprises four primary artistic "elements" or pillars, with a fifth element acknowledging its broader cultural significance: DJing, emceeing (rapping), graffiti art, breaking (dance), and knowledge (of self). While some organizations recognize additional elements, these five remain the most widely accepted foundations of Hip Hop culture.

11 "Knuck If You Buck" (2004), a rap song by Crime Mob, frequently inspires rambunctious physical responses from listeners.

12 "Jawn" is slang originated in Philadelphia that can refer to a person, place, thing, or idea. While it can describe just about anything, it's often used when talking about a favorite song.

13 Chang, J., & Herc, D. J. K. (2005). *Can't stop won't stop: A history of the hip-hop generation.* St. Martin's Publishing Group.

14 This refers to the laboratory in the *Black Panther* comics and movies run by Shuri, sister to King T'Challa, otherwise known as the Black Panther.

15 Grandmaster Flash and the Furious Five's *The Message* (1982), led by Melle Mel's vivid portrayal of urban poverty and struggle, marked Hip Hop's first mainstream social protest song and remains a defining example of rap as social commentary.

· 7 ·

THE MUSIC MAN | JARRITT SHEEL

At one point earlier in his life, my father wanted to be a radio disk jockey. During his coming of age in the 1950s and 1960s, radio was in its heyday, with musical genres blurring and crossing demographic boundaries while television's increasing popularity helped music propagate geographically. Being the next Alan Freed[1] would certainly have been an aspirational goal for music lovers like my dad, and although he would eventually gravitate to academia for his career, his love of music never waned.

Growing up, I would be showered by his musical preferences. He was primarily a jazz, blues, and early rock and roll and R&B enthusiast, so on any given day or night our house would be filled with the sounds of Count Basie and his orchestra, Duke Ellington, Ella Fitzgerald, Bo Diddley, B.B. King, Lightnin' Hopkins, Little Anthony and the Imperials, Frankie Lymon, and other titans of Black American musical brilliance.

In fact, when my elementary school music teacher asked which instrument I would like to learn, I'm certain it was Muddy Waters' influence that led me to request the harmonica.

(It should probably be no surprise that blues harmonica was not an option.)

So, I ended up rather unenthusiastically choosing the trombone which, by soulful swinging brass standards, isn't necessarily the worst choice; I just found that whatever we were being taught simply didn't excite me enough to stay engaged. In retrospect, it might have simply been that it wasn't anything like what I was used to hearing—and certainly not what I would have *liked* to learn.

I ended up switching to the cello. That was even worse. Before long, I gave up on school music classes altogether. Despite my dad's love for music, I don't recall him having a problem with that. Perhaps he understood what has become evident across multiple fields we've explored: that clinging to outdated methodologies, even when built on solid foundational principles, can create barriers for students whose lived musical experiences differ from a traditional curriculum. It wasn't that I didn't want to learn music; I just didn't want to learn *that* music.

To that point, as my generation would become more and more influenced by the electronic productions of 1980s Hip Hop and R&B, and the music-making technology those genres were employing were becoming more accessible, my inert musically creative spirit would awaken. I scraped up enough savings to buy basic equipment, including a turntable from Radio Shack, a BOSS Dr. Rhythm DR-220E drum machine,[2] and, eventually, my holy grail at the time, an Ensoniq EPS sampling keyboard workstation.[3]

Since I was also beginning to fancy myself an emcee, I began producing beats for my own raps, and would later branch out to provide backing tracks for other fledgling neighborhood wordsmiths, forming a small, home-based collective of aspiring artists—a Long Island, New York operation in the mold of Atlanta's Dungeon Family,[4] albeit with none of the commercial success.

I did go on to attain a small bit of recognition as a DJ/remix producer, creating and releasing my own versions of commercially popular Hip Hop and R&B songs, and, humbly speaking, I suppose at one point I could have been a professional beatmaking contender, though even after a couple of brushes with actual industry interest, nothing like that ever happened. Nonetheless, my glorified hobby ended up teaching me a plethora of skills that have helped fuel many of my professional pursuits since, not the least of which being my award-winning work producing, editing, and providing sound design services for audio journalism and podcasts.

In fact, I would argue that Hip Hop taught me *all* the life lessons—and perhaps more—that traditional K-12 music education might typically instill on all those students who take band class but never go on to play in an actual band.

So, for me, it all worked out. I still would have liked to play the harmonica though.

All of these personal anecdotes came flooding back to me during the Hip Hop education discovery journey I've been describing, once I came across a Twitter hashtag and Facebook group dedicated to the advocacy of Hip Hop music education.

The Hip Hop music education movement differed from the #HipHopEd[5] initiative mentioned earlier in this book. While the latter tended to focus on supporting the work of educators using Hip Hop to teach other subjects or those who might cover Hip Hop through a historical or sociological lens, #HipHopMusicEd was advocating for teaching Hip Hop *as* music.

One might think that, with decades of creativity under its lucrative belt, *Billboard* and GRAMMY categories, millions of fans worldwide, and an ever-increasing influence on society at large, Hip Hop *music* classes would be more prevalent.

Acclaimed musician and educator Jarritt Sheel thought so too, and along with like-minded colleagues, helped create a digital community to share resources and discuss ways to make it so.

I welcomed Jarritt to the podcast in October of 2019 to share his insight and outlook on the complexities of Hip Hop as music, and the work he personally was doing to address and correct these institutional shortcomings, including the #HipHopMusicEd movement.

It also must be noted that, to the great sadness of that community and the many students, faculty, fellow musicians, music lovers, and Hip Hop heads whom he touched during the course of his many endeavors, Jarritt passed away on November 12, 2022. It remains a great honor and privilege to have had the opportunity to speak with him and record his viewpoints. Our interaction continues to be one of the guiding principles of my work.

The Interview

Manny Faces: Mr. Sheel, I appreciate you taking out the time to kick it with me on this lovely afternoon. It's been a long time coming.

Jarritt Sheel: Yeah, man. This is dope.

Manny Faces: I appreciate it. Let's get into it. As many of us do, I think you wear many hats...

Jarritt Sheel: Yes.

Manny Faces: ...if you could just introduce yourself, describe how you present yourself from a professional stance.

Jarritt Sheel: Well, first, I would say I'm Jarritt. Secondly, I guess if I had to identify myself, I'd say I'm an educator who's a performer who likes to do research about popular music education and contemporary practices for schoolteachers, so kids can go into the world trying to learn about art music in a freer space.

I also identify as an amateur DJ. I identify as a graphic artist. I did a little graffiti when I was younger. . . Nobody knew that until now...

Manny Faces: Exclusive!

Jarritt Sheel: [LAUGHS] Yeah. . . I'm not gonna tell anybody what my tag name was. . . But I draw a lot. I do a lot of comicing at home, and I draw stuff for my kid to color in. So, I'm an artist and I'm a photographer.

Manny Faces: Creative mix right there.

Jarritt Sheel: Yeah, man. I'm also a doctoral student, a candidate in a really cool school called Teachers College.[6] So I'm also a frustrated creative.

[LAUGHTER]

Manny Faces: I can relate. I suspect a lot of people listening might as well. Now, let me ask you. . . There's Hip Hop, and there's *Hip Hop ed*... And then there's Hip Hop *music* ed.

Jarritt Sheel: Yeah.

Manny Faces: Explain this offshoot mixing Hip Hop with education that you've been involved in.

Jarritt Sheel: I'll tell you the history first. In 2004, I took a class when I was going to Northern Illinois University for my master's in music and jazz studies, and I took a course—a pedagogy course, a research course. When I took the course, I could've written about jazz stuff, which I was gonna do at school. But

I was like, "Nah. I wanna do something different." I was an older student, and so I wanted to do a paper about Hip Hop and music education. I did a little scant Google at the time—it was the early stages of Google in 2006. I look it up on Google Library, Google Scholar, and there was very little knowledge out there in music ed. There was a lot in other forms of education—science, literature, even theater, but for music education there were maybe two articles, maybe four at the most, whereas for other fields there were a hundred.

That was interesting, so I wrote a research paper about it. Fast forward, I hadn't really been in a lot of Hip Hop bands, but I was a huge fan. As I graduated and moved to Orlando, I started getting tied up in what people consider Hip Hop music band situations, [bands like The Roots]. So I found it, head on. This experience was very interesting, and so I went back and got my other master's in this Ed.D. program at Teachers College. I did some more research and I ran into people like Chris Emdin[7] who was one of the figureheads for #HipHopEd, and I'd read Bettina Love and a variety of other people who had written in that vein—Mark Lamont Hill and Greg Dimitriadis[8] and all these other people [like] Adam Kruse,[9] who had written about things, but there wasn't a lot in the space of music ed. So I started having these conversations on Twitter with people, and I hooked up with Adam Kruse, and he wanted to do this website, HipHopMusicEd, where there's a repository and resources for music educators because that seems to be the least free space to talk about Hip Hop... Which is so weird because it's music, and we study music so you would think...

Manny Faces: ...explain that. Why is it so empty in the music education space?

Jarritt Sheel: Well, music education—and I'm sure somebody's gonna get upset when I say this, but, oh well, it's the truth.

I'm a big fan of Duke [Ellington]. Because art is placed in this rarefied space, this commodified space in America, somebody has to be in charge of what art influences us. We're so still stuck on the Germanic European model of aesthetics here in America, we can't get into our own love of ourselves, let alone minority groups.

And Hip Hop is so *Black*. Let's be just very truthful. You cannot separate the body from the culture. They've tried it many times with other forms. I was just having a conversation about jazz—that's the one that's spoken about so much. Blues, R&B, so many varieties of things have been co-opted, but because Hip Hop has been so entrenched in the Black visual, and it's associated with it...

So, "you can't do it unless you're Black, right?" I mean, that's the thing people talk about. . .

Manny Faces: Right.

Jarritt Sheel: So that makes it weird because music ed can be a very prickly space with people of color.

Duke Ellington, for Christ's sake, just became a standard norm because of the Essentially Ellington program.[10] Before that, it was only if your teacher *knew*. Now everybody's like, "Oh, Duke Ellington is one of the patriarchs of jazz." People weren't talking about that all the time. That was a nascent name, even though he's always been the titan he is.

So now you have people that see a neoliberal artifact that they can kinda control and monetize. But they can't do it without the Blackness. That's the truth. Because look at the economics. . . Look at the people on the top of the charts. . . It pushes the narrative of this monolith. . . So people in music ed don't wanna deal with it because we can't really deal with race that well in music ed. And that's very apparent.

Some might be mad that I'm saying this, but as a student of color, anecdotally, I can tell you the amount of experiences—even going to a historically black college where I really dug into the study of Black music. In every book, there's that one chapter about it, and it's *really skinny*.

Manny Faces: [LAUGHS] Right.

Jarritt Sheel: You know what I mean? Come on, man. And it's always, like, *The Music of the Diaspora*. But then it's always a skinny little chapter. I'm like, do you know how much music Black people have done? You could write volumes of books about it. So, if we treat it like that in the research and the reporting. . . And then on top of that, most of the teachers aren't coming from those Black spaces. Then there are people who are gonna be less likely to deal with the subject in a really humane and holistic way.

I don't blame everybody. That's why HipHopMusicEd is supposed to be there, to enlighten people who really wanna know.

Manny Faces: Right. So how do you do that with HipHopMusicEd? There's a website, there's some social media interaction and some programs and stuff. . .

Jarritt Sheel: We do symposiums and conferences and professional development workshops. Adam Kruse does a lot of work up in Illinois. Carla Becker, who's one of the founders—she does stuff at Delaware State. Johan Söderman is one of the founders, he's at Gutenberg University and does a lot of that stuff all throughout Europe.

And there are many other people who do it, I don't wanna just limit it to those names. There are tons of people who are doing stuff in the space of Hip Hop music education. I'm just speaking about the people I'm most closely tied to. There are people at NYU and at Columbia and at Temple and University of Georgia, people all over the country doing it.

And then there's all of the people who are really doing the work in the K-12 schools. I see that all the time. That's my jam, working with those people, because I wanna make it so that every kid—if they want to or not—gets the opportunity.

Manny Faces: Why is that opportunity so important? I know that we might be preaching to the choir—but I'm always trying to bring in people, the outsiders who don't really get the nuances of Hip Hop music and culture—who don't even recognize the *culture* part. They only recognize the music to a tiny degree based on what's on the radio or what they might have come across in a cursory manner. But those folks are in these education spaces or they're gatekeepers or greenlighters—and they *need* to know.

So, what is that message? The most basic fundamental reasoning behind the importance for Hip Hop music education... Hip Hop being taught *as* music. Why is that so important?

Jarritt Sheel: I think the answer to that is, "Why do we do any of the other stuff?" You know? That's the question I ask back. "What's the rationale between any of the other things that we've chosen to showcase to the kids or the people that we're working with?" And then when we get to the nitty gritty of that, most of it is based on epistemological reasoning. Somebody said, "This is the truth and knowledge. . ." You don't really know why it is or if it is. There's tons of facts that have changed over history. We were, like, "Oh, the Earth is at the center of the universe."

Manny Faces: [LAUGHS] Right.

Jarritt Sheel: And then it was, "The sun rotates around the Earth." And then somebody said "The Earth is flat"—which that's a new thing right now. . .

Manny Faces: Retro. . . [LAUGHS]

Jarritt Sheel: [LAUGHS] Right. . . Going way back. . . Throwback Monday!

But all these facts, somebody later checked. My thing is, why do we have to wait to check this? Because we know Hip Hop is a music in a culture. We know Black people are part of the culture here in America. So why don't we just do it justice and do it right the first time? Why do we have to come back 40 years later and go, "Oh, that should have been included." Have we not learned anything?

That's my first thing, because understanding difference is super important. Because we're not the same. That's a lie. We're all different, and it's a good thing. There's nothing wrong with different. If I bring in a narrative that you're uncomfortable with, guess what? That's how I felt studying classical music for twelve years of my life. It didn't represent who I was. It wasn't played at home or on the radio. It's not like it was we were *anti*-that, but I was listening to Stevie Wonder, and Smokey Robinson, and the Temptations. . . Run DMC and that kind of stuff.

So for me, I think it's another voice in the room, and if you don't like it, you should question why you don't like it. The critical part of it is asking if we're just doing social replication? Or are we really doing fact finding missions?

Like, what is the biggest conversation we had in the 20th century? Race. And what's the biggest conversation we're having in the beginning of the 21st century? Race. We do these students no service by ducking and dodging from the thing that we are most uncomfortable by. We're not doing them any favors.

That's how I come at it with teachers because I've done things like a DJ meetup—a study group, which I did for a year and a half—in which we just sat down and talked and read stuff. We listened to music and we deciphered it. We DJ'd a little bit. We made meaning around what Hip Hop is and how we can use it in our classes.

What I'm trying to do now is engender people to study it and do it in a very humane, holistic way so that when you do it in your class, you're not just doing the thing, you're doing a long, longitudinal study with kids about what it means to put odd things together and how we all fit. It's very democratic.

Manny Faces: And it encourages other things like creative thinking and problem-solving and all the other things that you want a student to learn. You get it through these channels.

Jarritt Sheel: Right. You have to be a problem solver if you're a minority. If you wanna win. You have to be a critical thinker. That's why whenever they do that educational talk stuff about grit and persistence, I'm like, "Look. They got receipts. Their grandparents were slaves. So what do you mean persist?" [LAUGHS] "What do you mean problem-solving?" Some of these kids gotta catch three trains and a bus to get to school. That's not problem-solving?

It's just acknowledging all the critical, great, good, gooey stuff that's in Hip Hop so we don't have to use it just like, "I'm DJing," or "I'm rapping." Like, that's really cool, but there's something deeper about Hip Hop that we have to acknowledge.

Manny Faces: Past the "entertainment."

Jarritt Sheel: Right. It has to be deeper. I work here at Berklee College of Music. And one of the things I do with students that I'm so grateful to work with, is "Why are you choosing that piece?" "What does it say?" "What do these words say?" "Are you playing this because the melody's pretty?" OK. "Are you playing it because of the lyrics?" Alright. "Do you really like the chord structure?" "What is it?" Why are you doing this?" Like, don't just do it because it's on the list.

There's something deeper about it. They get that with a lot of the teachers, I'm sure, because there's really a lot of great teachers. But for me, personally, I think there's something deeper about studying music. Let's study something that's challenging, that challenges the status quo because nobody's really doing it. That's why we're having discussions here at Berklee and a lot of other places about how to bring that into colleges.

Manny Faces: I wanna amplify that as much as possible. I think that we have, again, perceptions that have to be pushed back against so often. My dad was a jazz and blues head, and he played a lot of vinyl—I got a big vinyl collection from him. I listened to all this stuff back in the day... And then we used to have these arguments about Hip Hop's musicality, right?...

Jarritt Sheel: [LAUGHS]

Manny Faces: ...about whether it has melody or not, that kind of thing. Because, of course, his exposure was, you know, maybe Run DMC... OK. I get that you might not think that there's a big musical factor. There's a lot of hard-hitting drums and grittiness and such. But, obviously, we're talking in the

1990s when A Tribe Called Quest was out, and Guru was doing *Jazzmatazz*.[11] And there's a whole bunch of things where I could point and say, "No. No. No. You can't say that Hip Hop is non-melodic if we're sampling things that have melodies." Even now, we've expanded past that because—and I don't mean some of the simplistic stuff on the radio—but there's a great range of musicality in Hip Hop in the genre past what's on the radio, past the mainstream stuff. That's still hard to convince people of. Yes?

Jarritt Sheel: I totally get what you're saying, so I'm not disagreeing with you. I'm just like, "Why?" "Why do you feel that?" Because I'm like, "What have you heard? Are you talking about 'Old Town Road'?"[12] And even that, there's a melody in there. Like, what do you mean?

I think these are people who were born in the 1920s. I don't know. . .

Manny Faces: [LAUGHS]

Jarritt Sheel: Maybe they're affected by [the lack of] a bridge. . . and I get that. I love Stevie Wonder, every Stevie Wonder song has a bridge or two or three other parts. But if you're looking for that in Hip Hop, that goes somewhat against the premise of Hip Hop. It's a repetitive, iterative space so that you are able to get out what you wanna say or do. Constant change is already the experience of a majority of the people who were rapping, and they wanna be in a homeostasis space, a comfort space, where they can do and say anything. . . That's what I mean. It's so deep.

Manny Faces: Right. People always complain, especially this *old head* versus *new head* argument. I say, you're trying to put something in a box which inherently can't be put in a box.

Jarritt Sheel: Yeah. If you're trying to compare Hip Hop to jazz, get this. . . *It's not jazz*. Stop. Don't do that. If you try to compare funk to jazz. Guess what? Don't do that either. That's not a good argument. You're gonna lose.

They're all different, but watch this. . . They're all interconnected. And this is when all the old heads get mad at me.

I say, well, "Hip Hop is a child of jazz." And they're like, "What?" And I'm like, "Look, man. Isn't all this music out of the Black experience? Or partly, at least?" And they go, "Yeah. . ." And then when they say that, I'm like, "So is Hip Hop not Black music? A lot of the architects, bruh. . ." And they go, "Yeah. . .?" And then I think we're done with the conversation.

That's it. They're interconnected. We're not Martians. You know, when [Afrika] Bambaataa[13] and all of them, [DJ Kool] Herc...[14] they were all children of the same Black melanin bodies that came over from Africa. They're all interconnected in a way. And it's not a magical way either. This is really straightforward. You can look it up. You could Google it! It's not like we're making this stuff up.

When you talk to these people, especially the teachers, about convincing them, I cannot be overly dramatic with my presentation of this because I'm not trying to *sell* them. . . I don't know if you ever watched or listened to *The Music Man*. It's a theater piece about a guy that goes around and sells band instruments at the turn of the century in America. Kinda like, pulling the rug over peoples' eyes and selling them on the idea. I don't do that when I'm working with the kids and working with the teachers—that's why I picked up the DJ stuff. I just wanted to be authentic. Like, I'm not an emcee. I'm not a rapper. I do think it's really dope. But there was something about doing the turntables that was really exciting to me, and I was like, "I'm gonna pick that up as my lens." So when I'm going there, I'm not gonna go, "Hip Hop is *this*," and take out my trumpet. I'm gonna go, Hip Hop is *this*. Here are some turntables.

Manny Faces: And like you said, you're not even pulling out the microphone and rapping, which most people who are outside of the cultural family think that's all there is. I talked to people outside to try to get their perspectives, and I remember someone telling me, "I used to love breakdancing. That was fun." And I'm like, "It's not dead. It's not gone!" They just believe that doesn't exist anymore, and all we have is rap. So I like that this is an angle that you push. And shouts to DJ Raydar Ellis[15] up there too. . .

Jarritt Sheel: Right. And Raydar is super dope at what he does. He inspired me a lot, because he's one of the foundational people in schools in a university setting really doing turntablism. Are there other people? Yes. But Raydar's been doing it for a minute. And he's killing.

So there are lots of other really dope people that are doing the work. That's why I try to have the dialogue online because the #HipHopMusicEd hashtag wasn't about me or anybody else. It was like, if you're doing it, tag it so we can know, so we can check it out.

Manny Faces: For sure. Each one teach one.

Jarritt Sheel: Yeah.

Manny Faces: Let me ask you. When it comes to the students that you work with and you're getting these concepts across to them—we could talk about convincing the establishment, blah blah blah. But you say the receipts come from working with students, and the work usually speaks for itself. That's how most Hip Hop educators or Hip Hop-based educators talk about it. They say, "Look, we could try to convince you, but when you *see* it, everyone's won over." You see it work.

From your experiences, do you have some milestone moments where you had a student or somebody you're trying to get across to that maybe doesn't quite get the whole thing, or you really find someone who excelled at picking up what you were putting down. Does anything come to mind? Like a case study...

Jarritt Sheel: Oh, yeah, man. One of my former students... I taught at a charter high school up in Marble Hill, [New York City] and I was starting the DJ stuff when I was there. And because the school waited—and this is the truth, I'm not making this up—I tried to tell them, because they didn't have a music program before me, that they needed to order the instruments before school started. They didn't. And so for the first eight weeks of school, I had no instruments in classes that were filled with, like, 30 kids.

It was so awesome... *not!*

After the third or fourth day, I was like, "Eff this, I'm gonna bring my turntables in. I'm gonna connect it to the projector, and we're gonna do a couple weeks on DJing and Hip Hop." Easy. Do some activities, creation, collage, whatever. It worked for a little while, and then [school officials] were like, "You should do worksheets." And I'm like, "What? In music class? *Just get the instruments!*"

So in that class, there was a senior by the name of Rameen. And Rameen graduates. Great guy, got kids, I love him and his daughter and his girlfriend. They were both my students. He's a professional DJ now, but then...

Well, I was leaving at the end of the day, and he was like, "So mister, you made money DJing the other day?" And I was like, "Yeah." And he was like, "Well, how much did you make?" And I thought that was an interesting question. But you know, these are kids from the Bronx... He knew where I lived. We talked many times in a very truthful, straightforward way. So I was like, "Well, I made 400 dollars." "How long did you work?" "Maybe two hours." And he was like, "You made 400 dollars for working two hours?" And I was like, "Yep." And he was like, "Can you show me how to do that?" And I was like, "I was waiting for you to ask."

So I showed him a couple of rudimentary things, and we talked through a lot of stuff. I showed him a lot of videos. We would practice during his lunchtime, and I saw he really wanted it. He bought a laptop, and I gave him my turntables—my little digital mixer—and I bought a new one. And he got good at it. And then he bought some really nice turntables and became a professional DJ before he graduated high school. This is a kid who is on his own. He was living on his own, literally.

For me to see somebody so interested in something, always negates all of the conversation about minorities in inner cities or achievement gaps, because the kid is super smart. He was just like most kids that are just not interested in school [saying], "You're not doing stuff I want to do. I wanna make money..." But he has to know about signal flow. He had to understand the mixer board. I had to show him that. He knows all the terminology. He's one of those kids that, if you give him a problem, he'll go watch all the videos all night long and come back the next day and have everything figured out. He'll tell you the name of the board... That you don't wanna turn it to *this* frequency because of the feedback... So for me it was just a really great opportunity to place [these things] in concrete terms.

A lot of the stuff we do in education falls flat because we try to make abstract stuff more abstract. We say "Well the philosophy is..." and then we give them some weird abstract thing. And I'm like, "No. No. No. Place it into real world terms. It's a concrete thing." So that's what [philosopher and educator, John] Dewey would say, "It's all in the doing."

Manny Faces: And it's the meeting them where they're at. Right? Culturally relevant connections and all that, because this is not foreign to them...

Jarritt Sheel: No it's not. It's foreign to *us*.

Manny Faces: Yeah. And it's very familiar and it's very comforting. And like you say, it's not just DJing for the sake of DJing. You learn all these other things...

Jarritt Sheel: Yeah!

Manny Faces: It's like, look... Everyone wants to be a rapper. Everyone tries rapping. Right? But when you try to rap, you learn some things about... English...

Jarritt Sheel: Right! And wordplay...

Manny Faces: And if someone points out to you the literary devices that you happen to be using, then you can learn something from it. And there are plenty of programs that integrate rap that way. But it's not just, "I learn how to rap."

Jarritt Sheel: Right. It's transfer of learning. That's what the old people used to tell me. "Well, did you learn something from that experience?" And I would say, "No." And they'd be like, "What do you mean you didn't? I can tell you four things you should've learned." And then I was like, "Oh, you're right." So it's connecting those dots from that one thing to your life, or your life to that one thing.

Manny Faces: Yeah. It's funny... I go back to something I've experienced in my life... Colleges will say, "Oh, you wanna get [college] credits for experiential learning? Sure. Just pay us, and if you could prove that you've learned this thing going through life, we'll give you credits." But then they're the same ones who are hesitant about welcoming these culturally-tinged ways of learning. What difference does it make? If we learn the thing, we learn the thing!

Jarritt Sheel: Right. It's like somebody has to be—sometimes, I don't know if all the time—but somebody has to be the keymaster... The gatekeeper for that, [to be the one to say], "I don't know if we *should* give you credit." Like, what do you mean you don't know? Where's the rubric? Just tell me the rubric and I'll point to where it qualifies.

Manny Faces: I wanted to ask this... I think the priority is that when one talks about minority communities—Black and brown communities—that don't have access to the educational advantages that other communities do, that a lot of times the educational system doesn't favor them in a culturally relevant manner. Right?

Jarritt Sheel: Yeah.

Manny Faces: So everyone looks at that and says, "Great. These are great tools, these are great methods, these are great pedagogical ways to help out or improve schooling for these minority communities." But, of course, I think there's also some universal appeal when it comes to Hip Hop...

Jarritt Sheel: Yeah...

Manny Faces: ...and you talk about it as a way of using it to understand other people's perspectives and other people's points of view, and I've talked to people who teach in majority white colleges, and they teach sociology of Hip Hop courses, and they say that there's value in that. You would agree to that?

Jarritt Sheel: For me, as a practitioner, I support any authentic use of Hip Hop. If they're authentic or not, I can't judge from here—I'd have to go see it...

Manny Faces: And I understand that. Because—let's not get it twisted—there's some of that in academic circles where it's more of the... I don't wanna say gimmicky, but it could be, you know, inauthentic...

Jarritt Sheel: No, that is the right word, that is totally the right word...

Manny Faces: I'm trying to be diplomatic. But, you know...

Jarritt Sheel: But that is diplomatic because you were just naming it what it is, which, is... It's a gimmick. Where people go, "I'll just use it to do this thing," but they don't understand it. That's a gimmick.

You know how to use tools. I know how a hammer works. I've studied the hammer...

Manny Faces: ...you could also bust someone's thumb if you're not using it right.

Jarritt Sheel: Right. Because you don't know a hammer. If you knew a hammer, then you wouldn't be swinging it around somebody's hand. If you know how to use the tool, then you know the purpose of the tool, and how it should and shouldn't be used. I think that's the thing. When you're doing a gimmick, you don't know how it should be used, and then you do it in these really misinformed ways, and you hurt people.

Manny Faces: Right. But when done authentically, it is something that does have a universal appeal.

Jarritt Sheel: Of course! Look, I like all types of music. I don't care what community it comes out of. As long as it's good.

Manny Faces: And like you say, there's a lot of ways to connect the dots between communities, between cultural perspectives through music. That's always been done, not just through Hip Hop. But Hip Hop is really well suited for it because it is so expressive.

Jarritt Sheel: Super expressive. One, because it's the most listened to music in the world right now. Two, it's everywhere on TV, movies. . . It's changed how America's dressed. It is a global force. . . Again, to go back to the abstract, there are some really pragmatic reasons why we would use it. So when you bring it up, it's like, "Well, you know, it's popular." I'm like "Yeah. So why wouldn't you use what's popular. . .?"

Manny Faces: [LAUGHS] Right.

Jarritt Sheel: What is it with this morbid obsession with classical stuff? I don't get it.

Manny Faces: It's that proverbial *resistance to change*, I suppose. It's like, well let's not use the Internet then.

Jarritt Sheel: Right! Are we all luddites? We're afraid of technology? Like. . . No.

Manny Faces: We'll segue that into this as we wrap it up. . . I'm hoping to incite more of these kind of conversations and more of those perspectives. . .

Jarritt Sheel: I would love to have more of them with you, that'd be great. . .

Manny Faces: Absolutely! And I hope people listen to it. My interest is bringing in people from the outside as much as possible so that y'all could do the work and not have to market yourselves so much. You know what I mean?

Jarritt Sheel: Word! I appreciate it, man.

Manny Faces: I appreciate the appreciation. Now, the name of this podcast is *Hip Hop Can Save America!* . . .

Jarritt Sheel: Yeah.

Manny Faces: . . .and it might be a lofty theory. But I do ask folks like yourself who's been involved in these movements, what are the best reasons to consider Hip Hop music and culture when looking for ways to truly improve lives, livelihoods, and communities in this country?

Jarritt Sheel: Ooh. . . That's a big one. . . I think if we had to look at reasons, just for the sake of understanding difference and giving voice to the voiceless and the concept of power to the powerless and how it talks about agency and how it *is* agency. . . How it talks about rallying for your community, and repping your hood, without saying everybody else must go. . .

It really argues for inclusion. I think a lot of it right now is that America just has to be real with itself—that's, I think, another rationale—and say that understanding ourselves involves listening to one another, and that if we're really trying to move toward a more inclusive space, one of the easiest ways of doing this is including Hip Hop and a lot of other musics into our space. I think Hip Hop's rationale is not to only bring itself, it's like, "You have to bring all my boys with me too."

Manny Faces: Right.

Jarritt Sheel: And I think that's the wonderful thing about Lil Nas X was that country [music] could gain so much with Hip Hop. We can all make money. We can all be creators. We can all be relevant. We're just trying to cross into new spaces. To not take over and destroy it, but to enhance.

I think that's great, and it can happen in really organic ways. I think that's a lesson for us, as people. That same thing which is—it could all be great.

We don't have to exclude anybody. We can include each other. I think that's just one of the really beautiful lessons from Hip Hop. Look at all the elements that you don't think should belong together, but they work. Look at all the people that shouldn't be mega hit stars, but they are, because the power of their message. . . or at least their messaging. Or their art, or their music, or any of those things. I just think we can learn a lot by looking at Hip Hop and difference. Because Hip Hop is so big. There's so many different types. Like there's no Black monolith, there's no Hip Hop monolith. There so many different types of Hip Hop right now.

Manny Faces: That's right. I tell people, "Anything you want, you could find it. It's being done. Someone's doing it and doing it well." It may not always be on the tip of an iceberg. You might have to dig a little, but you'll find a lot of inspiration from all across that spectrum. I don't think there's anything that's been that vast in terms of creativity, except the written word. You know?

Jarritt Sheel: Yeah. There's definitely been what they would call, a turn, an aesthetic turn. I think that's really awesome. I mean, like, right now, I'm learning in Boston there's this dope Hip Hop scene. And so this guy, Cliff Notez, I started playing with him and his band. And I see the scene at the Strand Theatre the other night down here in Dorchester, and there's a healthy music scene. And I've never heard of these artists. I'm like, "Who are they? They're dope!"

But they all look different. There's women and Japanese dudes and all kinds of people involved in this scene. It's not all Black people.

Manny Faces: I've been covering New York Hip Hop for over ten years. I say the same thing. Whatever you want, I'll find it. It's here. It happens.

Jarritt Sheel: Dude!

Manny Faces: And then there'd be stuff you don't even think exists, and you walk in on a random place and you find it.

Jarritt Sheel: Right. But people get twisted by the commercial view of what that stuff is, so they just think, "Oh, it's just *this*." But in actuality, it's so much more. We only just look at one little part of it. That's my thing with the teachers when they say, "You know, I don't know where to start." I'm like, "Well, pick a tune. If you don't like it, go to the next one." There's plenty of listening lists. They're called the *Billboard* charts.

Manny Faces: [LAUGHS] Right.

Jarritt Sheel: Just go to any year and select Hip Hop / R&B and look for the top hits. And then if you don't like that, go to the next year, the next month... Like, it's super easy, man. I'm like, do I have to put it in a book?

Manny Faces: [LAUGHS]

Jarrit Sheel: I mean, but that's what I do in my work. Because people want you to just give them a thing to read, but then, it puts it out of context. You gotta do some of the work.

Manny Faces: I think you're doing the work. That's why I wanted to talk to you and get this on the record. I draw inspiration from folks like yourself. I know that we all, like you said, teach each other a little bit, and we all draw inspiration from one another. I respect you for your work and how you not only do the work, but spread the word about the work. You and your cohorts at the HipHopMusicEd collective you have. I enjoy learning from the things you guys share and put out.

If there's anything else you wanna say to just send out to the universe, the floor is yours.

Jarritt Sheel: Sure. I wanna shout out to all the kids that might listen to this that are in high school somewhere, or young adults in college. I just wanna let you know that you can study any and every thing that you want in music, and Hip Hop is one of them. It's one of the ways that you can know the world. If you wanna be a Hip Hop musician, you can make tons of money and you can survive in the world. If you want to be a producer or a beatmaker, that's dope. You can be a Hip Hop philosopher. Any of those things can exist. I just want you to be your authentic self. You don't have to be any color. You just have to be yourself and tell your story. I think that's really what matters the most. And for the people who are out there doing the work, be safe. Find some cohorts of friends. Do the work. There's tons of people I like to work with. Toni Blackman, and I've worked with Chris Emdin before, Bettina Love... I think you have to find people that support you and will tell you truths so that you can be not just only successful academically or professionally, but in life. So, hang in there.

Manny Faces: That's well said, my friend...

Jarritt Sheel: ...and thank you for doing this show.

Manny Faces: I appreciate it, man. And thank you. I'm glad we finally got a chance to link up.

Afterthoughts

After talking to enough teachers, you understand why they excel at teaching. Jarritt Sheel personified the down-to-earth, plain-spoken, unpretentious voice of reason that makes Hip Hop-based intersections so inviting and promising as vehicles for social uplift. Echoing Dr. Ladson-Billings' assertion that "we teach what we value," Jarritt made the compelling case for Hip Hop's place in music education, proclaiming it no less valuable than "the other stuff" we do.

Jarritt's bird's eye analysis of how the music education space has long been devaluing or even wholly ignoring the artistic genius of Black America, only adds to the urgency of his pleas to not have to "wait 40 years" to make it right when it comes to Hip Hop. On a more granular level, Jarritt pointed out, again, why nuanced cultural understanding is so vital, noting how traditional music educators might overlook rap's oft-repetitive musical stylings as a creative comfort zone for artists and listeners, seeing it only as representative of a musical void. This recalls Dr. Love's insight about teachers only seeing "banging on a desk" instead of recognizing rhythmic drumming perhaps being used as a tool for emotional self-regulation.

We also heard further validation that Hip Hop music-making can be more than the sum of its parts—how working turntables can develop transferable life skills, and that guiding students to be able to truly connect with Hip Hop musical pieces can foster introspection and critical thinking just as much as, if not more than, any other genre.

Of all the intersections we've explored, it seems most ironic that Hip Hop music education has struggled so much to gain a foothold in academic ecosystems. Yet the work of Jarritt Sheel, his #HipHopMusicEd collaborators, and countless others inspired by his efforts have make remarkable strides to highlight the inequities and create impactful opportunities for more diversity and inclusion in the field.

In fact, since his passing, several colleagues have continued the annual Hip Hop Pedagogy for Music Educators workshop that Jarritt helped create with arts advocate and music teacher Randal Swiggum. I had the great honor of keynoting the 2024 iteration, which highlighted and honored Jarritt's work and legacy.

I'd also like to point out that when asked if there was anything else he wanted to add, Jarritt didn't take the opportunity—as many of us would, myself included—to promote his own work, direct people to his website, or shoutout his social media. Instead, without missing a beat, he directly addressed the young people he dedicated his life to helping, offering words of motivation and encouragement. Having just discussed Hip Hop's extraordinary ability to bring people together, this moment served as yet another example of the many indelible lessons Jarritt Sheel left for the world to learn from.

After our interview, Jarritt and I exchanged several emails about my potentially visiting Berklee to build on our podcast discussion in person and in public. Unfortunately, the COVID-19 pandemic derailed those plans, and we never got the chance to reconnect before his untimely passing—a fact that makes our conversation even more precious, and one that I will continue to reference to help guide and inform my work.

For these reasons and more, it was of utmost importance to include his words in this book, and I want to express my deep and heartfelt gratitude to Jarritt's wife, Dr. Antonia Sheel, for her blessing.

Key Takeaways

1. Hip Hop music education has historically been underrepresented in formal music education spaces, despite Hip Hop's global cultural impact.
2. Traditional music education often remains tied to European classical models, creating barriers for incorporating other musical traditions.
3. Hip Hop music education should be authentic and not treated as a gimmick, requiring real understanding of the culture and its elements.
4. Hip Hop music education can serve as a bridge for teaching technical skills, problem-solving, and critical thinking.
5. Hip Hop's inclusivity and ability to combine different elements makes it an effective tool for teaching across cultural boundaries.
6. The commercial success of students (like example with DJing student, Raheem) demonstrates how Hip Hop music education can lead to many viable career paths.
7. Hip Hop music education can help address racial and cultural gaps by acknowledging and celebrating diverse musical traditions.
8. Hip Hop music education extends beyond just rap to include various elements like DJing, production, and music technology.
9. Hip Hop's adaptability allows it to be integrated with other musical genres and traditions, creating new possibilities for music education.
10. Success in Hip Hop music education, as with other Hip Hop and education intersections, often come from meeting students where they are culturally and building on their existing interests.

Discussion Questions

1. How can traditional music education programs be redesigned to incorporate Hip Hop elements while maintaining academic rigor?
2. What technical and cultural training might music educators need to authentically teach Hip Hop in their classrooms?
3. How can music programs use Hip Hop to create bridges between different musical traditions and cultures?
4. How might performing arts organizations incorporate Hip Hop education to attract and engage more diverse audiences?
5. What role can technology companies play in developing tools and resources for Hip Hop music education?
6. How can community music programs use Hip Hop to create more inclusive and accessible music education opportunities?
7. In what ways can Hip Hop music education inform the development of culturally responsive teaching in other artistic disciplines?
8. How might music industry professionals collaborate with educators to create more authentic and practical learning experiences?
9. What innovative approaches could be developed to assess and evaluate student progress in Hip Hop music education?
10. How can the success of Hip Hop music education programs inform broader discussions about cultural representation in arts education?

This podcast episode was originally released on October 24, 2019.

Notes

1 Alan Freed was an influential radio disc jockey widely credited with popularizing the term "rock and roll" while promoting rhythm and blues music to mixed-race audiences in the 1950s.
2 A programmable digital drum machine featuring 12 drum sounds that could be triggered by tapping on rubber pads.
3 A groundbreaking digital sampling keyboard/workstation that combined sequencing, effects processing, and sampling capabilities.
4 An influential Atlanta-based Hip Hop collective formed in the early 1990s, which included OutKast, Goodie Mob, and Organized Noize Productions.
5 The Hip Hop Ed movement, often identified by its hashtag #HipHopEd, is a loose collective of educators, professionals, advocates, activists, Hip Hop fans, practitioners, and others who support Hip Hop as a valuable educational tool.

6 The graduate school of education, health, and psychology of Columbia University

7 Dr. Christopher Emdin, a leading figure in the Hip Hop education movement, focuses on science education. He co-founded the online community #HipHopEd and its related conference series, and has authored several books exploring the connections between Hip Hop and education.

8 The late Greg Dimitriadis was an influential scholar in education and cultural whose work examining Hip Hop culture, youth literacy, and qualitative research methods helped shape contemporary approaches to critical pedagogy and urban education.

9 Adam Kruse, a music education scholar whose research focuses on Hip Hop pedagogies, informal music learning, and culturally responsive teaching in music education.

10 Essentially Ellington, established in 1995, is Jazz at Lincoln Center's flagship education program providing high school bands with Duke Ellington scores and culminating in an annual competition in New York City.

11 A genre-bending series of albums by rapper Guru that merged live jazz instrumentation with Hip Hop production, featuring collaborations with noted jazz musicians like Donald Byrd and Roy Ayers.

12 A 2018 record-breaking country-rap single by Lil Nas X featuring Billy Ray Cyrus.

13 A pivotal DJ and founder of the Universal Zulu Nation who helped establish Hip Hop culture's foundations, though his legacy was later tarnished by allegations of abuse.

14 DJ Kool Herc is widely credited as one of Hip Hop's founding DJs, developing a technique of isolating and repeating the "breakdown" part of soul and funk records that would become foundational to Hip Hop and DJ culture.

15 A Hip Hop producer, DJ, and educator who helped develop formal Hip Hop production curricula for higher education.

· 8 ·

THE CONNECTOR | DR. ANDREA HUNT

It should be pretty clear by now that my father, a distinguished professor of sociology who taught at the university level for decades, is a large influence on me and my work. Having such a towering educator and researcher as a dad, I inherited natural curiosities about people, places, systems, and cultures, and despite initially deferring my own pursuit of a higher education, I was lucky enough to have picked up a few collegiate-level ideas and advanced thought processes through a lifetime of direct conversations and intellectual osmosis.

My dad specialized in areas referred to at the time as "urban studies" and "sociology of minorities," publishing dozens of papers breaking down all sorts of research he conducted: Italian American bias in popular culture;[1] low birth rates in Japan;[2] even some issues that I would later examine conducting my own independent Hip Hop journalism and scholarship, such as the legitimation of inequality in American education.[3]

I often joke that I knew what "gentrification" was when I was eight. It's funny, I suppose, because it's true.

Our conversations weren't only of a scholarly nature, of course. As we learned in the last chapter, my dad was an avid blues and jazz connoisseur, and we would often debate about the worthiness and musicality of rap music—or lack thereof, in his mind. I would, of course, wholeheartedly attempt to defend my favorite genre, in the same way many of my generation had to spar with their parents—just as *they* undoubtedly had to defend their own choices to *their* elders. As I got older, however, and started down the path I'm describing in this book, I began to share with my dad thoughts and findings about the fuller breadth and depth of Hip Hop culture, beyond just the music, and it pleased me to no end when, ever the social scientist, he would show interest in the stories and data I was collecting.

Unfortunately, my father passed away in 2010, before I became fully engaged with the purposeful journey of exploration that led to my podcast and, by extension, this book. These days, I like to view my father as something of a guiding muse. I often imagine the questions he might ask and how I might answer them. It's a good practice since, if you knew him, you knew he was the personification of "You better come correct."

Still, not being able to engage with him directly is one of my life's most disappointing ironies.

Luckily, I can find some solace in the fact that several sociology and anthropology educators and researchers respectfully and enthusiastically weave Hip Hop music and culture into their work, so I was genuinely excited when I came across the work of Dr. Andrea Hunt.

At the time of our conversation, Dr. Hunt developed and was teaching a course at the University of North Alabama called Sociology of Hip Hop Culture. While Dr. Hunt is also very much involved with the regional Hip Hop community, what really struck me was that she was teaching this course in a college with a predominantly white student body—in a politically "red" state to boot.

While many of the innovators in this book attest to the positive impact of incorporating Hip Hop subject matter and pedagogical approaches into schools in urban and minority communities, and that Hip Hop's universal appeal also allows for many of these techniques to be successful in other communities as well, we have also been exploring the idea that certain strains of Hip Hop studies are uniquely suited to help foster deep, cross-cultural dialogue and understanding—much more than being a fan of the genre could. Dr. Hunt's experience in her neck of the educational woods shed direct light on this intriguing possibility.

The Interview

Manny Faces: Dr. Hunt, how would you currently define who you are right now from a professional standpoint?

Dr. Andrea Hunt: I'm an assistant professor of sociology at a regional institution in the South, so a lot of my time is spent in the classroom with undergraduate students. I teach introductory sociology courses, but I also teach our Sociology of Hip Hop Culture class. I also teach courses that are related to family diversity, because inequality is one of my areas of specialization. In addition to teaching, I also do a lot of research on diverse families, and I'm doing research right now on how Hip Hop shapes the identity development of undergraduate students and how it shapes their racialized and gendered identities.

On top of all of that, I am very involved in the community working with at-risk youth. I go out to juvenile diversion programs and to our middle and high schools and work with kids on a variety of topics from making good life choices, using poetry as an entry point into writing about feelings, and how poetry connects to Hip Hop.

Manny Faces: Fascinating and noble work. I'll have you know that I am the son of a distinguished professor of sociology. . .

Dr. Andrea Hunt: Oh wow!

Manny Faces: Yeah! So we have, you know, kindred souls. . .

Dr. Andrea Hunt: Yes, exactly!

Manny Faces: I want to touch on the Sociology of Hip Hop Culture course. What would be your elevator pitch to describe what that class is about?

Dr. Andrea Hunt: A lot of times students think that it's just about music, that we're gonna go in and listen to music. And that's one part of it. We listen to music every class period, but it's much more than that because Hip Hop is much more than that. We are using Hip Hop as a way to critically discuss issues in the world around us. We're looking at race, gender, sexuality, identity, faith, capitalism, cultural appropriation, and urban policy, all through the lens of Hip Hop.

Manny Faces: What were you teaching previously or otherwise, and what led you to develop that course?

Dr. Andrea Hunt: I teach about inequality, so I teach our race, class, gender course, which is a course really on intersectionality, and I teach a diverse families course. So I was already immersed in the literature on inequality, race, gender, and capitalism. I'm an avid Hip Hop fan since 1988 who needed music in my classes anyway, so when I had an opportunity to develop a special topics course, I thought, "Wow. This is the time to do this!"

This is an area to get students engaged in and an avenue for us to critically discuss the things that are going on in the world around us. It's a way to hook students in these conversations. I had an opportunity to develop the course, and I jumped right in.

Manny Faces: In an article I read about your work,[4] it describes how your class looks at song lyrics as a form of journalism, a method by which artists speak their perspectives or the perspectives of their communities. One example was the use of "America," by Nas.

What I like about that is it pushes back against what is often the public narrative that rap music does nothing more than glorify negative behaviors or celebrate materialism. You said many students come in thinking this is going to be all about music—how many come in thinking of Hip Hop as only pop culture, a music genre—radio rap—as opposed to the more complex, artistic, and lifestyle-driven culture that it is.

Dr. Andrea Hunt: Most of them come in with familiarity with what is mainstream right now. They are very familiar with trap music because that is what is getting a lot of radio air play, so that's often times the range of experience. I do have some entertainment industry students, as we have a major here for students that are interested in going into the production side of the entertainment industry. Several of them are artists themselves. They have a different perspective because they're writers, but for the most part, students don't have as much familiarity with what we may think of as the classics and the foundation of Hip Hop.

I also have been interviewing students over the last year for my own personal research, looking at how Hip Hop shapes their sense of self, how they think about themselves as young people today with racialized and gendered identities. And many of them are really only familiar with some of the mainstream artists and don't know the depth of Hip Hop.

Manny Faces: What's the racial makeup of your school or your class, generally?

Dr. Andrea Hunt: The university is a predominantly white institution, about 70% of our students are white. But I am embedded within our Hip Hop community in this area. I help with spoken word events on campus and I'm plugged into some other communities on campus. Because of that, students see my classes as a safe space to be able to talk about these things, so I often get a much more diverse racial makeup in my courses than many of our other professors do. In this Hip Hop class though, the students are still [mostly] white.

Manny Faces: That's one thing I want to ask you about because I think that a lot of times when we talk about Hip Hop education or Hip Hop being used in education settings, the general public, and even people within Hip Hop, might think that this is an *inner city* thing. That Hip Hop can be integrated into educational settings within African American communities. We see great successes at this, for sure, but I'm curious about that from a perspective of where you're teaching and who you're teaching.

Dr. Andrea Hunt: One of the things that I see from those white students is their ability to interrogate white privilege through music, to be able to address racial oppression, exploitation, systematic inequality, in a way that maybe they wouldn't in other classes.

Through music, they feel that they're learning much more about social issues that different communities are dealing with in our society. We're using music as a way to facilitate cross-racial interactions, and discuss these issues in a way that is also educating students about what is going on in the world.

Manny Faces: That's interesting. There's a quote in that article where one of the students referred to one of Nas's songs, saying, "I immediately envision the American dream and how it's different because he's Black." Can you talk about how analyzing the lyrics and the performances are opening up perspectives to people who maybe, again, are not from those communities, and not directly familiar with the plight.

Dr. Andrea Hunt: We start with the history of Hip Hop, and then we kind of arrive in this space of talking about race, social activism, and how Hip Hop can be used in educational settings. That's kind of where we have been at the first part of the semester. This week, we talked about intellectualism and Black male intellectualism in particular, for students to be able to see these various roles within Hip Hop.

We've taken a step back from our own personal experiences for them to be able to say, "You know what? Other people have stories too that are legitimate sources of knowledge." These artists are creative thinkers, they're critical thinkers, and through the lyrics we're able to see that knowledge production [can present] in a variety of different ways. So, I think for students that are not familiar with some of the lyrics and some of the artists, this has opened up this can of worms for them where they're hungry for more. They want to know more. They want to know other artists because it's exposing them to a different way of thinking, critical thinking about the world.

Manny Faces: Are there any specific instances, students, or reactions you've gotten that really stuck out to let you know that this is really making an impact in that regard?

Dr. Andrea Hunt: We're trying to bridge these different forms of knowledge, elevating the knowledge that is coming out of music as a legitimate form of knowledge and the academic work as this accompanying form of legitimate knowledge. And every week, there are these huge epiphanies that students see. I mean, we had talked about white privilege, and we looked at Macklemore's song "White Privilege," and thought about being a white person coming into social movements and being an ally, and what that looks like. For many of them, it's big light bulb moments going off seeing his song and his video and his very critical reflection of himself: To profit off of this industry and be a part of this industry, that means I need to show up when African Americans are being oppressed. I need to use my voice in that platform as well. So, it has really given students the opportunity to take a step back and go, "What am I doing with my life? What am I doing to create greater good?"

And they all develop an individualized project, I call it The Heart and Soul Project, because I firmly believe that we should not be doing work just to be doing work. It should have personal meaning because education sticks with you when there's an emotional connection. So, they conceptualize an individualized project which looks different for different people, but is giving them some leeway to do something that is really meaningful and that has an impact on their future and on other people's future. Several of the students are really thinking about how we can integrate this into workshops and advocacy work and these greater things that come out of Hip Hop.

Manny Faces: That's awesome. I have another podcast, [News Beat], where we use Hip Hop to bring social justice issues to light. We do interviews with thought leaders, and we talk about some of the pressing issues of the day, and then we invite independent Hip Hop artists to contribute lyrics [written specifically about] that topic. We've covered the true origins of the drug war in America. We've talked about being exonerated from prison after spending decades in jail and not receiving any compensation. Things like that. And what we often tell people who are listening to that podcast is that it's great to know about these issues, to hear about them, and say, "Yeah. That's horrible," but it's about the *action* that's necessary after that. It's about taking action.

Dr. Andrea Hunt: Exactly. I've got several artists from the community that come in so the students get to listen to and analyze their music, and then the artists are going to annotate and [show us] what their thought process was.

So these guys get to take over! They'll teach them the course! I get to just be a student in the course. It's really an empowering opportunity for our artists in the community to say, "I want you to come in. I'm gonna learn from you. You're gonna be the professor because you are producing this knowledge. You're gonna be seen as this legitimate knowledge producer, and you're going to take over the class." Giving other people some room to lead these conversations, I'm just facilitating them. I am not the expert. I don't know everything. I'm a fan as well. I like to be able to facilitate these conversations and bring in other people to help contribute and build expertise as well.

Manny Faces: You referred to Nas, but in the article you also mentioned Chance the Rapper and some newer artists. When we talk about activism in Hip Hop or social justice, the media often focuses on what the superstars are doing and who's giving money and who's putting their voice behind a cause. Coming from the New York City area, [I knew of so many] Hip Hop oriented artists and activists that are on the ground doing work in communities, bridging those gaps. One, who passed away, was a guy named Majesty, and a brother named Hasan Salaam. When they organized an album release party, they brought in social justice organizations. They brought CopWatch[5], for example, which is an organization that looks at police brutality, to set up a table in the album release party. I think it's often overlooked that new artists, young artists, non-superstar artists, are actually out there putting in that work. Bringing them into the classroom lets a new crop of students understand that this isn't just an old school thing. This isn't just when Public Enemy and KRS-One were doing it. There are artists that are concerned about these issues today.

Dr. Andrea Hunt: Exactly. I show some clips and tell some information about an artist out in Chicago, her name is FM Supreme. Love her so much! An amazing female emcee, but she's also boots on the ground in Chicago and working on ending youth violence. She has developed mentoring programs. She's been all over the world spreading these messages of peace. These are artists that a lot of times our students are not familiar with.

I also share a lot of information about Indigenous artists, because we're not as familiar with artists from other backgrounds. A lot of students think about this as this African American experience, but there are also Indigenous artists and First Nation artists that have been doing this work as well. And the stories that they're telling really parallel oppression, and really parallel these stories of state sanctioned violence. Indigenous artists incorporate traditional Native American rhythms and beats and instruments and ceremonial dress along with [more traditional aspects of Hip Hop music such as] scratching, so it's this really phenomenal cultural experience.

Manny Faces: Thinking about when you started developing this course, we hear often of institutions of higher learning and other more traditional institutions having difficulty opening their arms to this kind of work. Did you have any problems with the institution or were there any problems that you encountered trying to incorporate Hip Hop into your curriculum?

Dr. Andrea Hunt: I have not had any problems at all, and I think a part of that is it all goes back to nurturing relationships and collaborations, not only with the institution that I work with, but with people in the community. This endeavor—this journey as I call it—these students are on this journey with me. [The first group of students] were the foundation. I was just trying to see if this was something that would work or not. Their excitement really showed me that we need to push through with this. So I tied this course to the overall goals of our institution and said, "This is going to help us meet these goals." Not only is it gonna help us meet these goals on campus, but it is a form of outreach in the community. So I've worked really hard and really strategically with key community partners to help facilitate this.

I think you've got to have that buy-in, not only from students, but you have to show the institution that it is viable, that you're gonna have students that come out for this. But I also show the community that I'm not trying to say that I'm the expert here—they are a part of this as well.

Manny Faces: That community involvement is vital. You're at a collegiate level. There have been efforts incorporating Hip Hop and education at the middle and high school levels both as a vehicle to teach other subjects—which we've seen success with—as well as a field of study in and of itself. I know that's not where you're at, but do you think that what you're doing and the success you're seeing could be applied to earlier levels of education?

Dr. Andrea Hunt: Definitely. I have worked with middle and high school youth making the parallels between poetry and Hip Hop, so I think there's definitely some room in those middle and high school years to be able to do this. K-12 teachers are much more constrained with what they have to do than we are at the collegiate level, so it's really about finding ways that you can tie this into the core competencies that you need to achieve at the K-12 level.

The greatest success that I've had with middle and high school youth is being invited in to do writing sessions. I worked with youth that are out at a [juvenile] residential facility and we did parallels between poetry and Hip Hop and we had them write. And they wrote and they wrote, and I told them to write from their heart. Nine young men got up and read their poems, and some of them, you know, kinda have a little flow with it too, which is even better. But these young men that are detained got up in front of a room full of 50 other people and read words from their heart.

This is life changing for people.

I'm also partnering with our local library doing a workshop with teens doing something very similar. I'm going to bring some local artists and we're going to have a writing workshop to think about writing as a tool for expressing emotion, for creative thought, for critical thinking, and then maybe do a rap battle as a part of that.

Manny Faces: Do any of these things go out to the general public—not necessarily the students or these groups, but parents or community members in general?

Dr. Andrea Hunt: Yes. We had a talk by one of our department of art professors on the history of graffiti and street art and its integration within the larger Hip Hop culture, and that was community wide. One of our professors in the Department of Communications did a talk on 2 Live Crew and the court cases around that[6], which was open to the community and widely attended.

We've got some brown bag lunch discussions coming up that are open to the community. We're doing an urban art expo that will be a part of this class, but that's also a part of the larger community.

Manny Faces: You've broken down everything you're doing and why it's so important. I only have one more question. The name of this podcast—and my theory—is that Hip Hop can save America. Now this this may be a lofty theory, but in your experience, can you sum up why it is so important to consider Hip Hop music and culture when looking for ways to truly improve lives, livelihoods, communities, and relationships in this country.

Dr. Andrea Hunt: Well, I'm gonna read you a little excerpt that I have from an article that's gonna be published soon. "Hip Hop is an expression of community needs, serves as a tool for social commentary, and influences the larger popular culture. This has been at the core of Hip Hop since its inception. It also facilitates lifelong teaching and learning through the production of knowledge and creates writers and thinkers. Whether you're an artist or a fan, music inspires critical and creative thought about our own lives and the lives of others. This is the promise of Hip Hop."

Manny Faces: OK. I'm done here. [LAUGHS] My work here is done. . .

Dr. Andrea Hunt: [LAUGHS]

Afterthoughts

This conversation prompts us to consider Hip Hop-based initiatives from an important angle we've touched on from time to time. While Hip Hop's universal appeal is well documented, white appreciation of Hip Hop and other Black cultural contributions often reinforces—rather than challenges—stereotypes, racist tropes, and cultural misappropriation. Given the historical whitewashing and erasure of Black American ingenuity, Hip Hop culture keepers remain understandably wary of the very inclusivity that makes Hip Hop so uniquely powerful as a tool for social uplift.

Yet Dr. Hunt's approach—her intentional methodology, refusal to sugarcoat issues for her predominantly white students, inclusion of the broader community, and willingness to give practitioners equal footing—builds on our earlier guests' cautious optimism about Hip Hop's potential across demographics. Her work raises an intriguing question: Could this model inform and inspire people from all walks of life in ways that truly increase cross-cultural dialogue and understanding to help repair our damaged social fabric?

In our polarized, tribalistic American society, particularly regarding politics, well-meaning activists often suggest a need for people to "meet people where they are." Dr. Hunt's work demonstrates how Hip Hop can serve as that common ground for facilitating such discussions, particularly in helping those from privileged backgrounds comprehend the impact of racist policies and other oppressive forces on marginalized communities.

One of the throughlines of my work that this insight reinforces is that when looking for answers to deep-rooted, seemingly unmanageable societal challenges in our nation, we may be overlooking tools already at our disposal—and that Hip Hop is one of those tools.

This line of thought encourages further examination into ways that Hip Hop might foster greater understanding and perhaps even the de-escalation of conflict between groups with vastly different ideologies—something we'll explore in greater detail in the next chapters as we examine Hip Hop's unique ability to break down barriers and bring people together in powerful ways.

Key Takeaways

1. Dr. Hunt developed a Sociology of Hip Hop Culture course at the University of North Alabama, a predominantly white institution in a politically "Red state."
2. The course uses Hip Hop as a lens to critically discuss various social issues, including race, gender, sexuality, identity, faith, capitalism, cultural appropriation, and urban policy.
3. Many students come into the course with limited knowledge of Hip Hop beyond mainstream and trap music, but leave with a broader understanding of the culture and its social impact.
4. The course helps white students interrogate white privilege and address racial oppression, exploitation, and systematic inequality through music.
5. Dr. Hunt incorporates local Hip Hop artists into her teaching, allowing them to lead class discussions and share their creative processes.
6. The course includes a "Heart and Soul Project" where students develop individualized projects that have personal meaning and potential community impact.

7. Dr. Hunt emphasizes the importance of recognizing lesser-known, independent, and Indigenous Hip Hop artists, particularly those who are actively involved in social justice work.
8. The course has been well-received by the institution, partly due to Dr. Hunt's strategic approach in tying it to institutional goals and community outreach.
9. Dr. Hunt has extended her Hip Hop education work to middle and high school students, as well as youth in juvenile detention facilities.
10. The course and related activities are often open to the wider community, fostering broader engagement with Hip Hop culture and its social implications.

Discussion Questions

1. How can Hip Hop education be effectively implemented in predominantly white institutions or conservative areas to promote cross-cultural understanding and social awareness?
2. What strategies can educators use to help students critically analyze Hip Hop lyrics and connect them to broader societal issues?
3. How can community leaders and local artists be integrated into Hip Hop education programs to enhance learning experiences and create stronger community connections?
4. In what ways can Hip Hop education be adapted for different age groups, from middle school to college level, while maintaining its effectiveness in addressing social issues?
5. How might educators design projects similar to Dr. Hunt's "Heart and Soul Project" that encourage students to apply their learning to real-world situations and personal growth?
6. What role can Hip Hop education play in promoting discussions about white privilege, racial oppression, and systemic inequality in diverse classroom settings?
7. How can educators and community leaders collaborate to create Hip Hop-based programs for historically underserved youth or those in facilities such as juvenile detention facilities?
8. What are some effective ways to incorporate lesser-known, independent, and Indigenous Hip Hop artists into educational curricula to provide a more comprehensive view of the culture?

9. How can Hip Hop education be used to bridge generational gaps and foster intergenerational dialogues about social issues?
10. What potential challenges might educators face when implementing Hip Hop education programs, and how can these challenges be addressed proactively?

This podcast episode was originally released on August 1, 2018.

Notes

1 Conforti, Joseph M. "Good News and Bad News: The Mafia is no Longer la Cosa Nostra, but there are more Mafias than ever". Altreitalie. Edizioni della Fondazione Giovanni 6 Agnelli, luglio-dicembre 2004. Online. Internet.
2 Conforti, J. M. (2007). LOW BIRTH RATES IN JAPAN AND ITALY. *International Review of Modern Sociology*, 33(2), 245–268. http://www.jstor.org/stable/41421274
3 Conforti, J. M. (1992). The legitimation of inequality in American education. *The Urban Review*, 24(4), 227–238.
4 Collier, M. (2018, February 18). *Sociology of Hip Hop culture: Commentary on the world.* TimesDaily. https://www.timesdaily.com/life/music/sociology-of-hip-hop-culture-commentary-on-the-world/article_991a88df-2e38-578e-a280-59f47f6fa2f5.html
5 Copwatch is an initiative shared by a network of activist organizations that advocates for the observation and documentation of police activity and public interaction in order to stem police brutality. One New York City-based affiliate is Justice Committee, an organization that Majesty was affiliated with.
6 The 1990 obscenity trials of Florida-based 2 Live Crew followed a court's ban of their album *As Nasty As They Wanna Be*. The trials established key legal precedents for artistic expression.

· 9 ·

THE PEACEMAKER | DR. MARK KATZ

I am often presented with the proposition that if, as I proclaim, Hip Hop can save *America*, surely those same characteristics can be applied to help save the *world*. I do not disagree. In fact, I have personally been involved with several globally focused Hip Hop endeavors.[1] However, there are unique considerations within the borders of the country in which Hip Hop was formed, initially nurtured, and has become such an integral part of everyday culture, that most of my focus has been on highlighting domestic applications of Hip Hop-fueled innovation.

Still, many teaching artists and artist-activists that I was meeting, like Mikal Amin Lee, were sharing insights gleaned from their extensive, international artistic and educational endeavors. They had acquired salient perspectives on Hip Hop's ability to inspire creativity, build bridges, form collaborations, and foster community—even improve relations between conflicting parties—beyond what I had been exploring domestically. In fact, several artists I met had been participants in a program called Next Level. This program, emerging from a somewhat surprising place with a somewhat surprising mission, purported to merge *all* of those ideals, by championing a concept known as "international Hip Hop diplomacy."

Next Level is a collaborative initiative between Meridian International Center, a nonpartisan, nonprofit diplomacy organization, and the U.S. Department of State, which harnesses the power of Hip Hop music, dance, and visual art to facilitate cross-cultural dialogue and creative exchange across diverse global communities. Key aims of the program include promoting mutual understanding and supporting the professional growth of artists in participating regions. Many past participants speak highly of its focus on bridging cultural divides and encouraging conflict resolution and redirection, through the universal language of Hip Hop culture.

The idea of Hip Hop as a tool for conflict resolution is baked into the mythology of Hip Hop's origin story. In *Can't Stop, Won't Stop: A History of the Hip-Hop Generation*, referring to the era shortly after the fabled 1971 New York City gang truce that would open the door for the birth of what would come to be known as Hip Hop music and culture, scholar and author Jeff Chang quotes DJ Jazzy Jay:

> Block parties was a way to do your thing, plugging into the lamppost. Sometimes we used to play till two in the morning. And we has the support of the whole community. It's like, we'd rather see them doing that, doing something constructive than to be down the block beating each other upside the head like they used to do in the gang days.[2]

In part because of this, Hip Hop's reputation became that of an anti-establishment, self-sustaining, and largely pro-Black counterculture, that also accepted and often relished in its role as one of humanity's most inclusive social movements. For many, Hip Hop represented the next evolution of "power to the people," inspiring the rise of community-based organizations and large-scale gatherings of Hip Hop-fueled political activism.[3]

Many people, however, believe those days are long gone, and that Hip Hop no longer possesses that intent or those characteristics. Critics argue that Hip Hop has devolved completely into a cesspool of commodification, a cultural shell of its former self represented by a genre bathed in imagery of violence, incapable of ever serving as an uplifting force for humankind, much less a conduit to defuse or deescalate conflict.

One of the main purposes of the podcast and, by extension, this book, is to emphasize how short-sighted that view can be. My hope is that as the episode and page counts increase, it becomes more and more clear that social impact through Hip Hop does not need be exclusively reflected in its entertainment silo. A Hip Hop-inspired revolution will not be streamed, and when it comes to seeking real solutions to real problems both here and abroad, we must not be tempted to throw out the Hip Hop activism baby with the rap industrial complex bathwater.

Next Level is one example of the ingenuity which can emerge when we remember this, but most importantly, when we aren't afraid to confront the conflicting realties that have always existed within Hip Hop when looking for innovative ways to confront the conflicts that continue to plague our society.

It was a great pleasure to learn more about this artistic, altruistic, and inspiring program from its founding director, Dr. Mark Katz.

The Interview

Manny Faces: This podcast is purposefully aimed at Hip Hop discussions from a domestic perspective, and it covers largely domestic issues. But a lot of your work around the world has had a distinct domestic foundation, so I think it falls within our jurisdiction. The work I'm talking about is what's known as Hip Hop diplomacy, and in your case, it actually has a direct tie in with American foreign policy.

If you could, before we go into specifics of your history and your work with Next Level, if I was to say to someone who's a bit removed from Hip Hop culture that we were going to talk about *Hip Hop diplomacy*, I'm sure they would undoubtedly say, "What the hell is Hip Hop Diplomacy?" I'm sure you've gotten that a million times.

How do you, as someone who's been immersed in this work, explain that concept to the layperson? And then give us an overview about the Next Level initiative and how it works to achieve the objectives of Hip Hop diplomacy.

Mark Katz: Sure. These terms Hip Hop and diplomacy don't really go together in the minds of most people because you don't think of Hip Hop as embodying what they imagine diplomacy to be. When you think of diplomacy, or when I ask people, "What are the images that come to mind?" Frankly, it's white men in suits shaking hands...

Manny Faces: The United Nations...

Mark Katz: Exactly. Maybe there are flags in the background. That's not the first image that usually comes to mind when people say Hip Hop. So what are these two things doing together? Well, first of all, since 2001, the United States State Department has been hiring American Hip Hop artists to travel abroad to represent the United States. The very first one was Toni Blackman, an emcee, poet, and writer that people who listen to this show might know. She's gone on quite a few of these trips.

Hip Hop diplomacy is a form of cultural diplomacy, which is a way in which countries use their culture as platforms to connect their citizens with citizens of another country. There can be several purposes for cultural diplomacy. One is to improve the image of the country. Another is to improve relations with another country. Another might be to connect with populations around the world that this country doesn't normally connect with. Those are all things that are goals of Hip Hop diplomacy.

There are a lot of different forms that Hip Hop diplomacy could take. It could be sending an artist out to do some shows in various countries, and it's just a concert that's paid for by, say, a U.S. Embassy. It could be a workshop. It could be a collaborative performance, jam sessions, and so on. All of that has happened under the State Department's umbrella.

The particular program that I helped create and served as founding director is called Next Level, and that came out in 2013. So, it wasn't the first form of Hip Hop diplomacy, but it was and still is the only cultural diplomacy program under the support of the State Department solely dedicated to Hip Hop. Next Level sends teams of, usually, four Hip Hop artists representing different elements [of Hip Hop artistry] to different countries around the world for two weeks at a time to run workshops.

So, for example, I'm still jet-lagged from a trip to Mongolia where we had a beatmaker, a DJ, a dancer and an emcee. And each of them ran workshops that were attended by young Mongolians who are interested in Hip Hop. Some of them are Hip Hop artists, some wanted to learn how to become Hip Hop artists, some just wanted to learn how to rap, dance, make beats, or DJ. During those two weeks, there's a lot of skill building, but the ultimate goal really isn't so much about skill building. It's about connection. It's about building, I would say, in the Hip Hop sense. Building with someone. Creating community together. Doing something together that you can't do separately. That's the idea of building, and it's about building global Hip Hop community.

Manny Faces: Why do you think Hip Hop is so well suited for this?

Mark Katz: There are a couple of reasons. One is that it's in every single country in the world. I actually tested this. I tried to find a country where there's no Hip Hop and I went through the list of United Nations member nations, and I couldn't Google a phrase like, say, "Mauritius + Hip Hop," that came up with nothing.

Manny Faces: That's funny! I gotta tell you, I did the exact same thing!

Mark Katz: Oh! [LAUGHS]

Manny Faces: I didn't do all 195 countries, but I went to the most obscure one on the list, a place that I hadn't even heard of, Googled it [and "Hip Hop"]—and you're right!

Mark Katz: Exactly. But isn't that mind blowing that there is not a single country in the world that you could go to where you won't find Hip Hop?

So, everyone's heard of it, young people particularly, in every country. The other thing is that it's accessible. There's lots of [different] kinds of diplomacy. You could have sports diplomacy or traveling string quartets. But, as you know, all it takes to create Hip Hop is your own body. You don't need to spend any money. If you have a voice, if you have a body, you can create Hip Hop.

Manny Faces: It's like the soccer of music. That's why it's so widespread around the world.

Mark Katz: Exactly. It's incredible just how accessible it is—and we could get into this—but I've seen people who have disabilities who can make Hip Hop and do amazing things. It doesn't matter what you have in terms of wealth or privilege, if you have a body and a voice and a mind and creativity, you can create Hip Hop.

Another thing is that the story of Hip Hop is so compelling to people around the world. It's kind of mythic—the story of young people with nothing creating something powerful that can change the world. That appeals to people all around the world. That's powerful.

And then one thing is that it is known to be American birthed. So, for the United States to engage in Hip Hop diplomacy is great because it's a way of connecting with people around the world who might hate us, who might hate everything about the U.S., except for Hip Hop.

All those things together make it a really consensible choice for the State Department to run with.

Now, as you said, there are issues and potential problems, and I do want to talk with you about it. But just from the standpoint of the U.S. using Hip Hop to promote the U.S., it's a no brainer. Many more people love Hip Hop than love the United States.

Manny Faces: It wasn't always a no brainer. You've been saying it's been happening for a long time, but maybe when trying to formulate it as more of the Next Level initiative rather than those one offs, it probably met some pushback.

Mark Katz: Oh, definitely. I've talked with the State Department people who were behind this, and it took a while. In 2001, Hip Hop was already hugely popular—you could make an argument they should have been doing this 10 years before that—but there was resistance. For some people, they didn't like Hip Hop, or maybe they were racist...

Manny Faces: There's that... [LAUGHS]

Mark Katz: ...there's that. But even if we're being charitable and saying that maybe people really like Hip Hop but they were still wary of trying to promote it as a taxpayer-funded program. They might be worried how this would play in Congress. Would people think it's frivolous?

Manny Faces: At a time when, you know, in the 1990s, Congress—the *government*—was taking an active role in trying to squash Hip Hop and explicit lyrics.[4] [The government] has traditionally taken a stance against the genre, [helping give it a] negative perception overall. So that's something that wasn't brand new.

Mark Katz: Exactly. In fact, in the research I did, I was looking at what the media was saying about Hip Hop in 2001. There were polls out that asked people, "Do you think Hip Hop presents a good image for young people?" And the majority of respondents said "No." So there is good reason for the State Department to be wary of putting its money into Hip Hop.

Manny Faces: Of course, the counter to that is that there are amazing qualities within Hip Hop music, culture, and its practitioners. There are tons of artists that have been traveling artists with the Next Level program.

You start your book talking with Frankie Perez, [a.k.a.] B-Boy Frankie. I interviewed B-Boy Frankie for another podcast that I used to host and I tell an anecdote that he told me during that interview. Here's a kid from Queens, New York. He's B-Boying,[5] dancing, getting better. He starts traveling around the world, competing, and he tells me how he goes up to somewhere in the Arctic. A First [Nations], Indigenous community, way north in Canada away from everything.

Like you say, Hip Hop is everywhere.

He's doing a dancing workshop up there and he's telling me that he's not teaching dancing. I said, "What do you mean?" He goes, "I'm teaching *self-confidence*. Because these are young people that don't necessarily feel like they can do these things. And then after a workshop, I've shown them that they can do something." So it's dancing, yes, the technical stuff—but it's so much more.

And one of the things that Next Level touts as one of its main characteristics, or main benefits, is conflict resolution. I think that's fascinating. Conflict resolution [through Hip Hop] is a big one that I don't think people get... Again, because Hip Hop can be... conflict filled...

Mark Katz: Right. Well, first of all, I just want to amplify what you said about instilling and building confidence. I've seen it every single time I've gone on one of these trips. Art is a powerful way of expressing yourself and when you have good teachers you can really pull something out of someone, a hidden strength that they didn't know they had. I've seen this over and over again.

Now about conflict resolution... Actually, we've started to use the term "conflict transformation." The idea is that we don't go in and say, "OK, there are two warring factions. We're gonna battle it out and we're gonna have peace in your country after this." That's not what it's about.

The idea is that conflict exists in every society and within every person, and that art is a powerful way of expressing conflict and transforming it into something constructive and positive. So, when you talk about Hip Hop and conflict, some people might say, "Isn't that exactly the last thing you would wanna use to transform conflict?" But remember, as you know, Hip Hop grew out of conflict, and the birth of Hip Hop is, in a sense, a case study in conflict transformation. It was a way young people used art to transform their circumstances into something beautiful and powerful. So, it really feels organic to Hip Hop when we do this. If you think about what battles do, all these are about transforming conflict through art.

Manny Faces: How does this look in practice? When you say you're doing a workshop and there's either a beatmaker or DJ... And I love that you use all the elements,[6] dancers, graffiti artists, emcees, the whole gamut. But what does a workshop as a way to plant the seed of conflict transformation look like in practice?

Mark Katz: I'll give an example. I was just in Ulaanbaatar, the capital of Mongolia, where we spent a day specifically focused on conflict transformation. For this one, we brought in a professor. His name is Arthur Romano, and he specializes in conflict. He did some workshops where, first of all, you talked about conflict and how it's a part of our lives, and it's not necessarily something that we need to avoid. It's unavoidable. But he has these great exercises that we put into the individual workshops.

A lot of what we do is role play, where we talk about very real scenarios that anyone in Hip Hop might encounter, and then we talk about how to either resolve, transform, or shift the conflict. I went into the workshop led by beatmaker DJ A-L. A group of guys in this workshop came up with a scenario where they go to a club and they bring a DJ. They want this DJ to get on at the club, but the manager hasn't already agreed to it. There's this argument where the guy says, "Oh, but this DJ, every time he's here, he draws a crowd," and then the manager says, "Yeah, but you didn't ask me beforehand. You're putting me on the spot." And things get heated.

There's another scenario where there's an emcee crew, and one of the members of the crew brings in a new person without asking the others, saying, "She's so dope. She's amazing. She's gonna make everything great." Then the other members of the crew say, "Wait. You didn't consult." And this is how— even though no one meant any harm on either side—conflict arises and could really turn into something dangerous or threaten their relationship.

So, we came up with all these real-life scenarios that all these people in Hip Hop have encountered and said, "Ok, now let's break this down. Let's talk about how we could avoid this." [We talk about] what to do when it happens, how to deescalate, how to think from the other person's perspective. All these skills. This is not abstract at all. We have been talking about things that they have actually lived through. We talk about beefs in their communities and how to address them. And we don't try to claim too much. A lot of conflict is deeply entrenched, but we have seen people address these conflicts and start to move them into something that's more cooperative and collaborative.

Manny Faces: Got it. Like you say, it hearkens back to the early days of Hip Hop, the myth of Hip Hop's early days, breaking away from gang violence and the despair in the streets to make something out of nothing.

Now there's a tricky part to this. It's political, but you talk about it in your book, *Build: The Power of Hip Hop Diplomacy in a Divided World*, which details a ton of these amazing examples and experiences that you've gone through in action.

One of the things that you go into fairly early is that this all sounds great if you sugarcoat it and only present one side. But there is a danger to this approach in the way that you talk about resolving conflict. It's kind of ironic to a lot of people that the United States State Department would be sending people across the world to talk about deescalating conflict, because we're pretty good at conflict...

Mark Katz: We are. And you're right. There is conflict at the heart of Hip Hop diplomacy. And some people, when they hear this, they have an allergic reaction to it—I say that politely. They'll say, "What the hell is this? How can you justify letting the imperial arm of the United States government co-opt Hip Hop for its nefarious purposes..."

Manny Faces: ...exploiting the culture...

Mark Katz: Yeah. Exploiting the culture, exploiting Hip Hop, using Hip Hop as their tool of imperialism and unwanted intervention. And I totally get that worry. It's a realistic worry because if you know the history of the United States and its interventions around the world and its bad deeds, frankly, illegal acts... There's no sugar coating there.

Manny Faces: Yeah.

Mark Katz: There are a couple of ways to look at this. One thing I do is ask the artists who have agreed to do this, why they are doing it. Because many of the artists that I work with are not big fans of the federal government. They're activists, anti-imperialists. . .

So, I ask why they're doing it. And I get a lot of really interesting reasons. One is, "Finally, the government is putting money into Hip Hop." And they should be. One artist said, "You know, they're spending all this money on missiles. . . Why don't they give some to me and I'll build songs instead?" So one thought is that it's actually—finally, in some people's minds—a valid use of government funding.

Another thing is that artists want to be able to represent their country to the world. No matter how much the artists that I work with might oppose actions of the U.S. government, none of them claim to be anti-American. They don't hate their country. . .

Manny Faces: The activist artists are patriots. They love their country and want to make it better.

Mark Katz: That's right, and that's a good way of saying it. So, they'll say, "Why not put me on the front lines and have me represent the country instead of that bozo on TV."

Manny Faces: And as you mentioned in the book, the reaction from some people is "Oh, wow. All Americans aren't assholes! Who knew?"

Mark Katz: Exactly. And that's a really powerful use of cultural diplomacy, and it's one that the State Department backs because [not everyone there] loves what comes out of the White House. They don't all love what comes out of the government. They want the people of the world to think of the U.S. as a complex, rich, diverse culture. Instead of, [like I hear when I go to some countries,] "Oh, you're American. Where are your guns? Where is your cowboy hat?" I say, "Well, we're not all like that." So, one reason to do this is to represent what is truly beautiful and amazing and great about the U.S., which is Hip Hop.

Manny Faces: Right. It's a macrocosm, I think, of Hip Hop itself, because people say, "Oh, you do Hip Hop? Where's the rhyming about guns?"

Mark Katz: That's a great point. It's also a way of representing Hip Hop in a way that people don't often get to do because unless you are on TV or a social media influencer, your voice is not necessarily shaping the conversation about Hip Hop. But if you work for two weeks with a group of people who have a certain idea about what Hip Hop is based on what they've seen on TV and social media, you can change the conversation about what Hip Hop is and what it can be.

But that doesn't mean that we can't still screw up or do wrong. . .

I just want to acknowledge that once we get into the country, it's not all cake. We can actually create problems once we get there. We have to be really, really careful about how we interact with people, how we present ourselves. So, we've developed, over the course of the last few years and with a lot of input from these amazing artists and thinkers, a set of principles about how to go about doing this work.

At the top of the list are, show respect, be humble, be self-aware, listen as much as you teach. These are things that are really important.

I'll give you a concrete example of one way we could do things wrong and how we try to avoid that. We have some really amazing artists. We've had three members of the Diggin' In The Crates crew[7], Diamond D, Lord Finesse, Buckwild. . . There's no doubting their talent and their authenticity, so they could go in and say, "OK. We're from the U.S. We're gonna show you how to do Hip Hop *right*." And there's an argument that they'd be right to do that. But now they think about going into a community where people have been practicing and creating Hip Hop of their own and having these superpower representatives from this superpower telling them what to do. Well, that just looks like business as usual from the U.S. Even though that seems justifiable, that's not how we operate. . .

Manny Faces: That can be difficult from a Hip Hop purist, traditionalist standpoint. Some folks are very protective of the "traditional" way of doing Hip Hop in America because we see how far it's [deviated] from its roots, and there's that long argument of whether that's good or bad. But I'm sure you can see that overseas, with totally different cultures, they may approach Hip Hop totally differently. So that approach could be seen as heavy-handed.

Mark Katz: Right. We could go and say, "Look, we're in India, but you gotta keep that Bollywood stuff out of Hip Hop. That's not Hip Hop." And in fact, when we went to India, I was surprised to see how much Bollywood influence took hold in the Hip Hop dance that I saw. But doing that is to say that Hip Hop is not Indian. It's not Mongolian. It's not Serbian. It's only American, it's an American export. But I know from experience that's not how people see it from around the world.

In fact, when I went to Zimbabwe, I asked someone if they were worried at all about having this program come in. He said, "Yeah. I was worried that these Americans would come in and try to 'teach us Hip Hop.'" He said, "We *know* Hip Hop. What we wanna do is *build* with you." And in fact, that's what gave me the inspiration to name this book *Build*, because building is a form of diplomacy.

Even little things like what you do on the very first day. Do you go in, do your bios, and do a showcase? What we usually do is sit down we ask them some questions. "Tell us about Hip Hop in your community. What is it like? What are the beefs like? What are the issues that you're facing."

Manny Faces: Right. Listen more than you teach.

Mark Katz: Exactly. That's right.

Manny Faces: You give so many examples in the book, including what we were just talking about, having to be diplomatic about doing diplomacy. But just as an aside, you talk about these artists that are chosen for the program, a lot of them I know personally, like Farbeon, Rabbi Darkside [now known as Sam Sellers], Toni Blackman. . . They're not only artists, they're not only activists, they're not only teaching artists, but they're ambassadors. They're evangelists. They're just an amazing representation of humanity, to be honest, and of Hip Hop and its cultural greatness. And I think that by taking them on these journeys, not only are you letting them take their skills and their way of seeing the world and seeing Hip Hop to these other places, but it's teaching them vital skills. Again, being diplomatic about doing diplomacy, which then lets them further their work when they come back to the States.

Mark Katz: Yeah. It's really a mutually beneficial arrangement. You know, when Diamond D applied for this—and he applied... It's not like he just got a pass and got to do it. . .

Manny Faces: You still gotta audition!

Mark Katz: Yeah. And I mean, it's a no brainer to take him, but I asked him why he wanted to do it since, as he had pointed out, he would get paid more if he stayed at home. I mean, we pay pretty well, but he could get paid more. He's accomplished pretty much anything a producer would want to accomplish. For him, it was about having a different experience. Not just touring, but really connecting with people on an intimate level, working with people. Going to another country, having that experience, and having that teaching experience.

I hope he doesn't mind me using him as an example, but I've also brought him to the University of North Carolina where I teach, and he's done work there. It's gotten him more into the educational side of things. So as much as I would never have thought that I or this program could do anything for Diamond D, it has, because it's opened up something for him.

And not just a different line on the CV, but it opens up opportunities to do more of this because—I hate to say—people who are not in Hip Hop who don't already know who some of these artists are, don't care how many records they've sold or how many top ten lists they've made. But if they see that he did a program for the U.S. Embassy in Belgrade, Serbia, that gives a different perspective, and maybe they'll hire him to do that lecture.

Manny Faces: Right. It's the validation thing. I don't want artists to be exploited, but I also value the opportunity to go in and present ourselves in a great way. I don't want to put the United States on a pedestal, but at the same time, there's greatness in our country that we should be able to share. I think it gets down to that validation thing for a lot of artists or Hip Hop folks when they say, "We don't *need* your validation. But, you know, we'll take it, if it helps the cause."

Mark Katz: Yeah. [Diamond D told me that] his father was a veteran and fought for the U.S., then said, "Now I'm getting to represent my country doing what *I* do." That's actually something really powerful that I've seen across a lot of these artists. Many of them are very well traveled. But to do it and get paid to represent their country [in this way] has a different meaning.

One interesting thing that I hadn't thought about is that it's often powerful for their families who may not have really approved of them going into Hip Hop. They say, "Wow, I never really got this Hip Hop thing, but wait, you met the ambassador to Cambodia and performed in his residence." [It's that] validation—maybe [they] don't *need* it, but it can be nice.

Manny Faces: And it's not just from the institutions... A very quick aside. My dad was a distinguished professor of sociology, so I grew up under that umbrella. I was a Hip Hop head, and he wanted me to go to school and do all the things. And I'm like, "Yo, I wanna make this music though." You know? And he was a jazz and blues kind of guy, so he was like, "That's not music." That whole thing. He passed away about eight years ago and it sucks because in the past eight years, I've been to Leon, France. I've been to Paris. I've been to Oslo. All for Hip Hop. Either covering it as a journalist, or lecturing, or speaking. I went to about 15 universities. I went to one where he used to teach, The Ohio State University. I spoke there. And that validation would have meant a hell of a lot. So, I know what you mean. My dad would've been like, "OK. Maybe your way was alright. I'll give you that much."

Mark Katz: Exactly. And I see that. I mean, these artists all have families. Another kind of validation that comes up is that this program Next Level is run out of the same office that did the jazz ambassador program that sent Louis Armstrong, Duke Ellington, and Dizzy Gillespie around the world in the 1950s and 1960s. To be in that lineage is very powerful.

Manny Faces: Was that the Louis Armstrong picture with him and his wife in front of the pyramid that I've seen floating around?

Mark Katz: That's right.

Manny Faces: Iconic.

Mark Katz: The interesting thing is—and I'll plug my book—you can read about the connections between jazz diplomacy and Hip Hop diplomacy, they faced the same issues. This was in the era of desegregation, the civil rights movement. To have African American artists representing the country at a time when they weren't really free in their own country... It's the same.

I mean for example, Tef Poe[8] went to Jordan. He was deeply involved in the Ferguson protests. And it's really conflicting to represent your country when you may not even be safe in your own country. You may be safer in the country you visit.

Manny Faces: Right. A lot of Black musicians throughout history—the jazz age of course—felt more comfortable overseas. A lot of talk about authors and musicians who moved to Europe. There are a lot of parallels.

Mark Katz: Exactly. One powerful thing I heard from a number of artists is that when they travel abroad, they're treated differently. One artist, and I think he probably would stand in for a number of artists, Akim Funk Buddha, said that when he walks in stores in New York as a Black man, he feels like people are watching him and waiting for him to steal something. But when he's abroad, that feeling is lifted, and he doesn't feel that way. He thinks that people see him differently. Traveling and being treated well can be a really powerful motivation for doing this type of work.

Manny Faces: Yeah. I think that the rest of the world has a lot to learn from us, and maybe we have a lot to learn from the rest of the world.

Mark Katz: Exactly.

Manny Faces: This is an international program, but a lot of the lessons, the core of the work, can be applied domestically as well. It can be applied anywhere. There's conflict everywhere. There's a need to bridge cultures and communities everywhere. Are there domestic applications for some of the lessons that have been learned and some of the techniques that you guys have used in the Next Level program?

Mark Katz: Definitely. In fact, there is a domestic component to Next Level. For one thing, every country we go to, we select one of the workshop participants and we invite them as a team to the U.S. for a two-week professional development program. We have them visit schools and universities, and connect with U.S. artists. That's an amazing experience for them, but it also brings a lot to the places we bring them to.

Beyond that, what I've been trying to do at UNC Chapel Hill where I teach, is bring a lot of the Next Level alumni to give lectures and do workshops. In fact, along with two Next Level alumni, Junious Brickhouse—who, by the way, is the new director—and Curwin Young, an amazing beatmaker who worked with Public Enemy, we created a Hip Hop summer institute at UNC that replicates what we do in these workshops. In fact, I think one of the most powerful things we could do is do more of this kind of conflict transformation with Hip Hop in the U.S.

And, by the way, there are people doing this kind of work in the U.S. Lots of great work being done. And the artists that I work with have already been doing that in their hometowns. They bring back some of the skills they develop, some of the experiences, some of their broadened perspectives into their home communities. There's this continual feedback loop of promoting the work that we do abroad back at home, developing these principles, and spreading them in communities around the country.

Manny Faces: There are definitely a lot of people doing this kind of work, but it is great to have some institutional support that helps support that, validates it, and gives people a place to present their work, and from that can spring a lot of good stuff, I would imagine.

Mark Katz: Definitely.

Manny Faces: We're winding up. You're no longer at the helm of this. What are the changes at Next Level? What does that mean for the initiative? And then what's next for you besides dropping a book on us?

Mark Katz: Well, I'm glad to be able to mention Junious taking over as director. One thing that we didn't mention, you may be able to suss this out if you're listening to me, but I'll just say it—I'm white. And I'm not a Hip Hop artist. The reality is that because of my institutional connections, my grant-making experience, and my administrative experience, I was able to get the grant to do this. Whereas, I know that extremely well qualified people in the Hip Hop community couldn't, because they didn't have the institutional connections, or a Ph.D. or a college degree. That kind of thing, for what it's worth, is important to the people who give out this money.

Manny Faces: It's how they get in the door...

Mark Katz: Exactly. I always knew when I was running this program that the ideal situation would be for this to be run by the community itself. So, over the course of the years that I was directing it, in collaboration with the artists, I started hiring some of them to run residencies, and then I hired Junious to become associate director and then co-director, and then Kane Smego, another artist who became associate director. I opened a door that, unfortunately, could not have been opened by the artists that I work with, but now by stepping back, they are absolutely eminently qualified to take over. What I did was lay the groundwork.

It's not that I got tired of this—I'm still connected with Next Level. I still travel, I still consult. I give talks and all that. But from my standpoint, it's the ideal scenario that this is now completely run by Hip Hop artists.

Manny Faces: The day to day...

Mark Katz: Yeah, the day to day. And I'm there to be helpful and to write books. It's been such an amazing privilege for me to be connected with this program.

What's next is, I'm just going to continue supporting this program, trying to build some of the capacity domestically. I want to develop my own skills in terms of conflict transformation so I can assist in that. I would like to be able to continue using my privilege and access to raise money for Hip Hop activism, for Hip Hop artists, and Hip Hop communities.

And I hope that this will move a few more units of my book, but all of my royalties I'll be donating to various Hip Hop community organizations in this country and around the world—the ones that I've worked with through Next Level and in other ways—because to my mind, it's the way of paying back, of giving back, because I've gotten so much from them.

I just want to continue using what I've developed, the knowledge, and connections I have to continue supporting the Hip Hop community.

Manny Faces: Well, I'm sure the Hip Hop community is very thankful for that. We need more [folks like] you doing that kind of stuff, so I appreciate you for that.

I'll wrap up with this last question. You've answered a lot of this, but I guess this is the soundbite version. This podcast is called *Hip Hop Can Save America!* I named it that because I think that all of the things that you've talked about and that I've seen through the work of artists and individuals like yourself and organizations like Next Level really show an amazing amount of potential for the ideas, the concepts, the people, the spirit, and the ethos of Hip Hop, to actually solve problems.

And if you take conflict resolution and conflict transformation from this talk—if that's the *one thing* that this program has been able to do—that's an amazing angle to take to address one of our foundational societal issues. Nothing gets solved 100%, but if it could be addressed in an efficient way through Hip Hop—and we have some receipts to show that it can—that's an amazing thing. I think there are a hundred different things that could be helped in a similar fashion through Hip Hop.

From your perspective, why should people be considering Hip Hop music and culture when looking at ways to truly improve lives, livelihoods, and communities in this country, and everywhere?

Mark Katz: Well, I love the title and premise of *Hip Hop Can Save America!* I could have titled my book, *Hip Hop Can Save The World.* I mean, that's kind of the idea. It may sound utopian, but I think in reality, Hip Hop can do great amounts of good, and I've seen it happen. You've seen it happen. The sound bite version is. . .

I asked a B-Boy from Serbia if he was able to work with B-Boys in Bosnia and other Balkan countries, given that they've been at war for so long. And he said, "Of course. I work with them all the time." I said, "Well, why? Your countries can't get along. Why do you get along?"

He said, "You can't fight when you're dancing."

To me, that's it in a nutshell. If we could use Hip Hop to bring people together to collaborate in the creation of art, you can't fight while you're doing that. You have to work together. You have to compromise. You have to think about the other person's perspective and the other person's needs. If we could connect with the young people of this country who see Hip Hop as their culture, and allow them to make art and build relationships and community through this art and culture that they see as their own, then we can do a lot of good and move the needle on this goal of having Hip Hop save America.

Afterthoughts

Unbeknownst and perhaps surprising to much of the general population, one of Hip Hop's most well-known mantras is: "peace, unity, love, and having fun."[9] In fact, in 2001, the culture that had long been derided as one that glorifies violence, misogyny, drug use, homophobia, and everything negative under the sun, collectively came together and presented The Hip Hop Declaration of Peace to the United Nations,[10] a document designed to deliver "advice and protection for the existence and development of the international Hiphop community."

Of the eighteen principles therein, several connect to the aforementioned mantra, particularly regarding the intention that Hip Hop culture be used as a force for good and international unity.

The eleventh principle, for example: "The Hiphop community exists as an international culture of consciousness that provides all races, tribes, religions and styles of people a foundation for the communication of their best ideas and works. Hiphop Kulture is united as one multi-skilled, multi-cultural, multi-faith, multi-racial people committed to the establishment and the development of peace."

The thirteenth principle: "Hiphop Kulture rejects the immature impulse for unwarranted acts of violence and always seeks diplomatic, non-violent strategies in the settlement of all disputes. Hiphoppas are encouraged to consider forgiveness and understanding before any act of retaliation. War is reserved as a final solution when there is evidence that all other means of diplomatic negotiation have failed repeatedly."

The fourteenth: "Hiphoppas are encouraged to eliminate poverty, speak out against injustice and shape a more caring society and a more peaceful world. Hiphop Kulture supports a dialogue and action that heals divisions in society, addresses the legitimate concerns of humankind and advances the cause of peace."

Peace. Unity. Love. Having fun.

While the document originated from the Temple of HipHop,[11] one of several cultural organizations Hip Hop has spawned, nearly every organization or program I've encountered utilizing innovative approaches to problem-solving through Hip Hop music and culture demonstrates its own unique expression of at least some of these tenets.

In 2001, Hip Hop artists, leaders, activists, and allies knew that the principles in the Hip Hop Declaration of Peace weren't theoretical. They knew them to be true, because to them, it was lived experience. They foresaw the importance of this documentation, in a noble attempt to "establish a foundation of Health, Love, Awareness, Wealth, peace and prosperity for ourselves, our children and their children's children, forever," particularly in the face of continued commercialization and co-opting, and a backdrop of historical artistic and cultural whitewashing and erasure.

In a similar vein, the purpose of my work, the *Hip Hop Can Save America!* media ecosystem, is to demonstrate clearly that legitimate solutions to serious problems facing our society, both in the United States and throughout the world, exist in and through Hip Hop. Unique, powerful, largely untapped methods and practices that could be applied to some of these issues today, en masse, regionally, nationally, and locally, if only we were collectively informed and daring enough to try.

Thanks to Mark Katz, we have an excellent example of what that looks like in practice.

We'll examine what other examples of fostering unity through Hip Hop might look and sound like in the next chapters, as we explore Hip Hop's potential as a unifying force—perhaps an unparalleled tool in the ongoing fight for social justice and equality.

As of this writing, Next Level continues to send cohorts of brilliant, talented American Hip Hop artists across the globe as artistic and cultural ambassadors that every American should be proud to have representing them. Mark Katz's successor, Junious Brickhouse, was featured in the November 6, 2021 episode of the *Hip Hop Can Save America!* podcast.

As of this writing, Mark Katz's latest book was *Rap and Redemption on Death Row: Seeking Justice and Finding Purpose behind Bars*,[12] written with Alim Braxton. Braxton, who has been imprisoned for more than 25 years on death row, "uses his rhymes as a form of therapy and to advocate for prison reform, particularly by calling attention to the plight of the wrongfully incarcerated." He and Katz crafted "a hip-hop-rich prison memoir" which "chronicles Braxton's struggles and triumphs as he attempts to record an album while on death row, something no one has done before."

Key Takeaways

1. Hip Hop diplomacy is a form of cultural diplomacy that uses Hip Hop to connect citizens of different countries and improve international relations.
2. The Next Level program sends teams of Hip Hop artists to different countries to run workshops, focusing on skill-building and creating global Hip Hop communities.
3. Hip Hop is well-suited for diplomacy in part because it exists in every country, is accessible, and has a compelling origin story that resonates worldwide.
4. The program emphasizes respect, humility, self-awareness, and listening as much as teaching when engaging with local communities.

5. Hip Hop diplomacy can challenge stereotypes about Americans and provide a more nuanced view of U.S. culture.
6. The program is conscious of, and wrestles with, criticism regarding potential cultural imperialism or co-opting of Hip Hop culture by the U.S. government.
7. Hip Hop diplomacy can be a tool for conflict transformation, using art to express and constructively address conflicts.
8. The program provides mutual benefits, offering new experiences and opportunities for both the visiting artists and the local participants.
9. Hip Hop diplomacy builds on the legacy of earlier jazz diplomacy programs, facing similar challenges related to representation and civil rights.
10. The principles and techniques used in international Hip Hop diplomacy can also be applied domestically to address local conflicts and bridge cultural divides.

Discussion Questions

1. How could we create a domestic version of the Next Level program to address intercultural tensions within the United States? What would this look like on a city, state, or national level?
2. In what ways can Hip Hop's conflict transformation techniques be integrated into formal diplomatic training or international relations curricula?
3. How might we leverage technology and digital platforms to expand the reach and impact of Hip Hop diplomacy initiatives globally?
4. What innovative partnerships between government agencies, educational institutions, and Hip Hop organizations could be formed to create new bridge-building programs?
5. How can the success of Hip Hop diplomacy inform the development of similar programs using other art forms or cultural expressions?
6. In what ways can the principles of Hip Hop diplomacy be applied to corporate diversity and inclusion initiatives or cross-cultural business negotiations?
7. How might we create a youth-led Hip Hop diplomacy program that empowers young people to become cultural ambassadors in their own communities?

8. What strategies could be employed to measure and quantify the long-term impact of Hip Hop diplomacy on international relations and conflict resolution?

9. How can we use the lessons from Hip Hop diplomacy to create new approaches for addressing climate change, global health issues, or other transnational challenges?

10. In what ways can the principles of Hip Hop diplomacy be applied to improve communication and understanding between law enforcement and communities, particularly in areas with histories of tension?

This podcast episode was originally released on December 5, 2019.

Notes

1   As of this writing, I am co-chair of the Global Conference on Hip Hop Education, vice-president of its governing organization, the Hip Hop Association of Advancement and Education, and have presented at international academic conferences including the European Hip Hop Studies Network.

2   Chang, J., & Herc, D. J. K. (2005). *Can't stop won't stop: A history of the hip-hop generation.* St. Martin's Publishing Group.

3   Now-defunct organizations like the Hip Hop Summit Action Network and events like the 2003 National Hip Hop Political Convention have attempted to solidify Hip Hop as a constituency.

4   Several congressional actions and federal lawsuits emerged during this time, most notably the 1990 obscenity trials of rap group 2 Live Crew.

5   B-boying and B-girling are gendered terms for practitioners of breaking, a Hip Hop dance form also known colloquially as breakdancing.

6   Hip Hop comprises four primary artistic "elements" or pillars, with a fifth element acknowledging its broader cultural significance: DJing, emceeing (rapping), graffiti art, breaking (dance), and knowledge (of self). While some organizations recognize additional elements, these five remain the most widely accepted foundations of Hip Hop culture.

7   An influential Bronx-based Hip Hop collective including Lord Finesse, Diamond D, and Big L, known for sample-based production style and clever, punchline-driven lyrics.

8   A St. Louis-based rap artist and activist who gained prominence during the 2014 Ferguson protests following the death by police of unarmed Black man, Michael Brown. Tef Poe would later become a Nasir Jones Hiphop Fellow at Harvard University's Hutchins Center for African and African American Research.

9   The phrase is often attributed to pioneering Hip Hop DJ and founder of Hip Hop cultural organization the Universal Zulu Nation, Afrika Bambaataa. They reached the public zeitgeist in a 1984 song by Bambaataa and James Brown titled, "Unity Part 1 (The Third Coming)" featuring a lyrical refrain that included, "Peace! Unity! Love! And having fun!"

10 *Hip Hop Declaration of Peace.* (2010, December). The Temple of Hip Hop. https://thetem pleofhiphop.wordpress.com/hip-hop-declaration-of-peace/

11 The Temple of Hip Hop (TOHH) was established by artist and educator KRS-One as a cultural organization that approaches Hip Hop as both a cultural and spiritual practice.

12 Braxton, A., & Katz, M. (2024). *Rap and redemption on death row seeking justice and finding purpose behind bars.* University of North Carolina Press.

· 1 0 ·

THE BRIDGEBUILDERS | GANGSTAGRASS

I believe the real genius of Hip Hop happens in the audacious intersections it consistently inspires and produces.

After all, Hip Hop emerged from an almost unimaginable mix of art, music, culture, and multiple diasporic influences, coalescing after centuries in 1970s New York City. As Grandmaster Caz, a revered, pioneering member of the rap group The Cold Crush Brothers, said in the documentary *Something From Nothing: The Art of Rap*, "Hip Hop didn't invent anything. But Hip Hop reinvented everything."[1]

Built on and borrowing from influences from so many other genres, Hip Hop, with its unparalleled lyrical density and musical adaptability, easily rivals most traditional artistic movements in its ability to encapsulate the human condition. When done right, these musical conglomerations can be creative, inventive, and inspiring, helping to build intellectual and musical bridges— think *Hamilton's* merging of Hip Hop and traditional American musical, or Guru's *Jazzmatazz* series.[2]

Yet there are still certain combinations that, to many, seem like oil and water. Country music, for instance, is often considered something of a Hip Hop antithesis. While musically possible to marry the two, perhaps the perceived divides between the demographics of each genre's fans, both in musical taste and ideology, makes the idea less tolerable than merging with the rebellious, grittiness of rock.

Credit is due, however, to the 2019 smash success of Lil Nas X and Billy Ray Cyrus's "Old Town Road" for re-opening a door slammed shut after a previously inglorious rap-country collaboration between rapper LL Cool J and country singer Brad Paisley on 2014s "Accidental Racist." Though to many, "Old Town Road" was still viewed as gimmicky pop schtick, it may have opened up a rift in the rap-country continuum.

Consider that in 2024, a group named Gangstagrass rose to the top of Billboard's bluegrass charts with their album *The Blackest Thing on the Menu*.[3]

As one might imagine, this group consists of an assortment of top-tier bluegrass musicians.

As one might *not* imagine, two frontmen of said group are African American rap artists, often delivering forceful lyrics admonishing prejudicial behaviors and advocating anti-racist ideology.

Talk about reinventing everything.

This dynamic exists under a complex historical backdrop. The United States, as with much of Western culture, has a long history of diminishing or erasing contributions of African Americans across many aspects of society, including music. How this infamous tradition plays out in more modern times is as interesting as it is complicated. In recent years, artists like Shaboozey and Beyoncé have made strides in reestablishing African Americans' often-unheralded place in country and western music history.[4] As might be expected, these developments sparked all sorts of responses—from support to confusion to consternation—from within those respective fan bases, and to some extent, the public at large.

It is within this nuanced landscape that a group like Gangstagrass emerges, somehow as inevitable as it is improbable.

What makes the group stand out for many is their uncompromising approach: they don't sugarcoat ideological differences that most certainly exist between large swaths of fans of the two genres they merge, instead remaining wholly unafraid to forcefully address even the most sensitive social justice issues, in the long tradition of socially conscious Hip Hop. Yet they do so with the kind of musical authenticity that welcomes fans less accustomed to these types of lyrical messages to open their ears and their arms to these messengers.

When I was first introduced to Gangstagrass by their then-publicist Fiona Bloom, I was immediately skeptical—we can largely thank LL and Brad for that. Still, in the heart of decidedly un-bluegrass country—Brooklyn,

New York—what I witnessed was a powerful mix of unapologetic, anti-racist lyricism mixed with top-tier bluegrass musicianship, and I immediately joined the multitude of fans who stand by the conviction that while this sort of thing really shouldn't work, with Gangstagrass, it does.

That experience, our subsequent podcast interview a month ahead of the release of their 2020 album, *No Time For Enemies*, and an ongoing relationship with the band, has led me to believe that Gangstagrass is a perfect ambassador to showcase the very essence of what Hip Hop has always been about, and how that essence can help forge an America that most Americans claim they want to live in.

The Interview

Manny Faces: I'm glad y'all took some time out to kick it with me. We've crossed paths before and I'm excited to know exactly what you're into. For the record, we don't have your whole crew here. Please just quickly introduce yourselves and state your role within the Gangstagrass empire, if you would.

R-SON: I'll go first as the elder statesman. My name is R-SON, The Voice of Reason.

[Clip from "Get Your Cuts Up"][5]

> I amaze a racist // make a Klansman like, "This n-gga writes outstanding gigabytes," and add me to his playlist // take his robes off // throw 'em on the burnt cross // light a spliff with it to blaze with my aces...

I'm one of the emcees, repping Philly in all things at all times and the luckiest dude in the world because I get to rock out with the greatest band ever.

Dolio: I'm Dolio the Sleuth, repping Pensacola, Florida, by way of Philadelphia

[Clip from "Get Your Cuts Up"]

> All up on my suitcase // tell me how the boot taste // chase bread like Pac-Man through the maze after fruit shakes // hit you with the punchline you're giggling for two days // try to bite our style I guarantee you get a toothache

Been with the band since the inception, just like my homie, R-SON here. We've been hella lucky just to be able to still be rocking with it.

B.E. Farrow: I'm B.E. Farrow. I'm playing the fiddle.

[Clip of interpretation of the backing track of Pharoahe Monch's 1999 single, "Simon Says," by B.E. Farrow on "Get Your Cuts Up"]

And I'm the resident youngen' of the band, the newest member, probably about two years in with these dudes.

Manny Faces: Well, two years is a long time. So, you know, you're a toddler now.

R-SON: We got him potty trained and everything.

Manny Faces: There you go. You don't have to put up the gate anymore? Like, he don't go down the stairs?

Dolio: We still gotta use the leash every now and then. . .

R-SON: Yeah. We put a leash on when we're out on the road. . .

B.E. Farrow: I always come back. . .

R-SON: He does. He does.

Manny Faces: All right. Gangstagrass. I don't really like to start with the cliche question, but somebody give me an idea how this band came together, how this concept, this genre mashup of musicians and rap artists came together. How did it start?

Dolio: Honestly, it kinda all started a little bit before Gangstagrass. I was the DJ turntablist in this other band that our producer and mastermind of the crew, Rench, had started called Battlestar America.

R-SON: I met Rench on a Wednesday night in Philly. We did the show. I did some old verses and freestyled some stuff over their music and then hopped in the van with him and drove down to North Carolina, and we did three shows that weekend.

Manny Faces: Just on a whim. . .

R-SON: Yeah. "Let's do it." And I was like, "Cool!"

Me and Dolio met in 1999 up at Penn State just in a cypher outside of a bar one night, you know, when cats used to cypher. I miss cyphers. We were just a bunch of dudes out there rhyming. I'm listening to this boy and I was like, "Yo, my man got bars over here! OK! Who's this cat?" And here we are twenty years later and still there are a few emcees that I use as a level to match and to maintain. This guy is one of them.

Manny Faces: B.E. Farrow, I'll come to you in a minute as the newbie in a group, but let me just focus on the genesis of this thing. When y'all two came across what Rench was doing, this hybrid, mashup of bluegrass and country music, this whole vibe. . .

Listen, I'm a Hip Hop dude. On paper, the concept. . . It can go either way. Let's just be generous.

R-SON: You're right. You're very right. And if you look at the ways it's been done a few times, a lot of it has not been great. I think that's because the people involved weren't really trying to take the two art forms and take what was very similar about them and put them together, as opposed to just slapping these two things together and see what worked.

Dolio: Yeah. With me, it didn't even really seem that out of whack for me. When I met Rench, I had recently moved to Brooklyn, but being from the South myself, we would be watching *Soul Train*[6] on Saturday and *Hee Haw*[7] on Sunday. I had never really heard anything that was putting those two things together so seamlessly until I saw it as a live entity. He approached me doing the honky tonk Hip Hop funk thing, needing a turntablist. So I jumped on as the DJ, mostly because of the fact that, I guess, he hadn't heard anybody scratch like [I did]. I'm a southern DJ. I grew up in Florida. Miami, with booty shake and bass music. Cats in New York weren't used to hearing someone scratching that fast on beats like that, let alone on some country stuff. Which is probably also why I was able to get extra tips when I was DJing at the strip club because I was the one that was playing the Luke[8] records. [LAUGHS]

Manny Faces: [LAUGHS] Right.

R-SON: The other thing you gotta remember about your favorite Hip Hop records is that what really gets you is the loop. When it's happening live, you can be playing that same loop and then change the note, but keep the same loop. And then change the note again, but keep the same loop. So the effect is the same. . .

Manny Faces: The buildup. . .

R-SON: Yeah, the buildup is the same, but you can change so much with it on the fly that it's just as authentically improvisational as most Hip Hop is. Just with instruments. . .

Dolio: . . .plus the bluegrass is hella improvisational. . .

Manny Faces: Yeah. Look at what The Roots can do when they're live as opposed to what just sample producers or loop producers can do. There's always gonna be that extra *thing*.

And again, coming into it as a regular Hip Hop head, like "I don't know about this whole combination, but let me see what happens." And hearing your recorded stuff, it's tight. Everyone's musically talented. The emcees are authentic. Everyone's dope and kicking dope stuff. It's a great vibe. But *live*, you do turn it up a notch. I saw y'all live and there's some nuance that gets hard to capture in a recorded version

R-SON: There definitely is, and that's what really makes it a lot of fun to be able to add stuff to the hook and to be able to bounce off of each other. If you got a chance to check out the live album that we did, *Pocket Full of Fire*[9] some of that stuff you only really hear at that show. You know, because we'll be referencing the city that we're in and that's only happening there. . .

Manny Faces: What I do like is that musically, there's an authenticity there. This isn't, like you said, a slapping together of genres. This is authentic musicians from one genre, emcees that are like, "We're not going to come on and do no half ass Hip Hop ish. . ."

So, B., let me bring you into this. Musically, how did you come across the band? What's your musical background and how did you fall into this obscene mix of music?

B.E. Farrow: You know what. . . My first touring experience... Y'all talk about jumping in the van with four other dudes... I was playing with some bluegrass bands around D.C. and we got invited to this big festival, the Kingman Island Bluegrass Festival. It happens to be the festival I met Gangstagrass a couple of years earlier, the first time I went. I played with this band, the Delafield [String] Band. We played a real early set in the day with, like, five people and somebody's grandma there.

But we have passes for the entire day. I just wandered around the festival, seeing friends, getting drunk, lighting a spliff with a friend or two there. And then this thing just gets packed throughout the day. I don't know nothing about this festival. I don't mean to say it like this, but man, this is some white people stuff. But this is poppin'...

Manny Faces: ...but you were playing bluegrass to begin with, wait a minute... How did you get into playing that style of music?

B.E. Farrow: So, to go back a little bit from that. I was playing rock and a lot of R&B and jazz around D.C. And then one day, I go into a regular punk bar that I really like. There's a bluegrass band playing in the basement and it just blows my mind. I didn't know there was a scene for this music around...

Manny Faces: ...I used to hear it on—you know how on cable TV, you got that one channel—Bluegrass Music...

B.E. Farrow: Yeah. I know exactly what you're talking about.

Manny Faces: I used to put on for my kids as a joke. Like, "It's time to go to bed. Time to listen to bluegrass." So I know the music. I know the genre exists. But like you said, you didn't know there was a scene for it. Especially in D.C. We think, that's down South in the sticks.

B.E. Farrow: Right. And I've since learned there's folks like The Country Gentlemen and The Seldom Scene that are around D.C., and they're great. I really dig the scene around that region.

Anyways, I saw that band in the basement, and I was just like, "I wanna play bass." I know they had a bassist, but eventually, he left the band and they hit me up. So, again, this festival, I'm hanging out. I'm drunk and stoned, just watching shows. I still got backstage passes so I just wander backstage, and there is the most funny looking cat sitting there playing fiddle the most funny looking way. It's just long hair, trucker cap on, Levi's jean jacket on, wearing jeans. It's hot out. But you know, that's his look, I guess...

He is playing some good, groovy, scratchy fiddle, and I'm just sitting there staring at him, and he stops for a second... He's like, "Looks like you need a friend." And I'm holding two beers so I'm like, "I'm about to make one." We just get to hanging out and chatting, and then the rest of his band comes along, and they're like, "Ah, we need to rehearse." And they start practicing.

I noticed they didn't have a bassist. My bass was still sitting over there, and I was just like, "I got a bass, guys. How about I join you?" And at first, they're like, "I don't know. We just lost our bassist. I don't think we're doing bassists anymore." I was like, "Come on. . ." [LAUGHS]

Manny Faces: [LAUGHS] We're biased against bassists right now. . .

B.E. Farrow: It's just guitar, fiddle, banjo, and a guy playing charismo—which is cans. This is The Hackensaw Boys, by the way. And Ferd [Moyse], the fiddle player, was like, "Yeah. Let him come up." They were the headliner. I didn't know that.

[The show] was packed, and I didn't do a bad job, and they invited me on tour. And it's four of the hickest dudes that I could have met in D.C., and they were just like, "Come on tour with us for a couple months." And I'm like, "All right."

Manny Faces: . . .and jumped in a van. . .

R-SON: He jumped in the van!

B.E. Farrow: Starting to play this stuff, I noticed there's not a lot of brown folks around. I did meet up with Don Flemons, and I played with him for a while. It's just great to see other folks touching this music and being a part of it because we got a history in there too.

Manny Faces: For sure. I wrote a piece—I'm still sitting on it—about the word Americana. And how when you look at it as musical history, Americana is like, old country and western, jug band music, American roots, American folk [music]. The definition of it is, [music that was] born and bred in America.

But when you look at early blues, there was genre mixing before we had radio stations that were playing genres. Right? And like you say, Black and brown folk, African Americans, were contributing to all of these genres across the board. And that's what some people don't realize that there's a history even behind bluegrass, country, jug bands, early folk. . .

Dolio: The thing is, those things were all one in the same for a long time. They didn't start to delineate between genres until they've needed a way to market these things to different populations. You would see the same record being listed as two different genres because they were trying to sell one to the

Black folk and the other to the white folks. So one thing would be considered country or folk or whatever, but then it would just be called race records or blues on the other hand. So, when you look at things like rock and roll, country, blues, jazz, all of this stuff, there was no real divisions between the ethnic groups that were predominantly taking part in it until they needed a way to market this stuff. That's when the division started happening.

Before then, the bands themselves would be culturally mixed. Bluegrass is mountain music. You go to the mountains, you go to Appalachia, you go to Lynch, Kentucky, where people are in the coal mines, you're looking at Italian immigrants and Black folks and Irish folks, all crammed into a hole in a mountain. And then after they're done working in the mountains and sweating a mile deep in the ground, they come out and they socialize.

B.E. Farrow: There's a cool fiddler violinist, a jazz violinist, Stuff Smith. There are interviews with him where he talks about there not being a lot of jazz violinists out there. So the other shredding cats, folk violinists that he's hanging out with, are guys like Bob Wills and a bunch of other country fiddlers. And he's a jazz guy talking across the line.

And speaking about Hip Hop and old time, I'm always telling folks about Frank Stokes. Listen to "[It's] A Good Thing," and you'll hear the earliest Hip Hop track that I know of.

Manny Faces: O.K. All that was then. But now, those delineations exist. How is it that this hybrid group decides to go touring in areas that are more traditional bluegrass and country type places, and you come in with this mix up, this mashup. Tell me what that is like.

R-SON: I'ma tell you right now. The thing that I found most interesting—and a guy just sent me a picture of his 81-year-old dad that comes to our show every time we go to Thomas, West Virginia that loves us to death.

I can't tell you how many shows we've [performed as Gangstagrass]. In that time, I've encountered *one* person that was like, "Nah, I'm not fucking with these guys," and bounced. One dude.

Dolio: No. There was the other guy in Chattanooga. . .

B.E. Farrow: There was a guy in Chattanooga? The one I was at?

Dolio: Nah. This was the first time we played at Chattanooga. But he left before we even played a single note. . .

Manny Faces: Sight unseen. . .

Dolio: Yeah, he had his other reasons. He was like, "Nope. There's Negroes on the stage. We're getting out of here."

R-SON: But in general, we've been seen by hundreds of thousands of people. It's something you can really watch—and we do, reading the YouTube comments on stuff. People hear about it, and they're like, "I can't fuck with this."

And then they hear it.

And they're like, "Oh. Well, OK. Alright. Yeah!" Because it is so authentic. And regardless of what you think about one set of music or the other, the cats that are playing the instruments are real talented, amazing musicians. Rench is an amazing producer. Rench got beats. This guy is really able to layer stuff. Everybody in the band, myself excluded, can sing their ass off. I can't sing a lick.

Manny Faces: And those melodies! Those melodies are authentic. . .

R-SON: That's the fellas!

Manny Faces: I'm not a country and western, bluegrass guy, but I'm like, "Well, that sounds authentic to me!"

R-SON: They lay it down, on every level. And because it is so authentic in the genre and because the talent is there in what we're doing, you can't deny that it's dope.

One of my favorite quotes of all time was by Phonte.[10] He said, "Dope beats, dope rhymes. What more do y'all want?" And that's what you get. That's exactly what you get from us. The beats are dope. The music is dope. And as emcees, like I said, Dolio is one of my favorite emcees in the world. I measure myself on his standard, so I have to be at the level of what these guys are doing.

Manny Faces: It's always good to have someone, [in this case] another emcee in the group to make sure y'all both trying to top each other all the time.

R-SON: Yeah. Exactly.

Dolio: Yeah. Steel sharpens steel.

B.E. Farrow: I'm in this band because of these dope emcees. So. . .

Manny Faces: There you go. . .

Dolio: I mean, there's a lot of open-minded folks, especially nowadays in the digital age. Everyone's jumping around with the stuff they're listening to. But it wasn't always that open. When we first came out there, folks came in ready to hate. But like R-SON said, as soon as they heard us. . . There was no denying it.

Manny Faces: Now from the Hip Hop side, I understand. [I started out think-ing,] "I don't know. . . Sounds crazy on paper." Then I got to meet y'all [and now] I'm cosigning 100%. . . And maybe when you go into West Virginia, Kentucky, all these places, they might say, "OK. I'ma rock with them musi-cally. They sound tight. They're doing their thing."

But we had some failure in the past, {coughs} LL Cool J Brad Paisley {coughs}. . .[11]

Dolio: Ooh. Yeah.

Manny Faces: In merging these genres, they went for more of a "Kumbaya"[12] kinda thing. What I appreciate as a social justice minded guy is that you guys don't shy away from being real heavy handed with the message.

R-SON: No. Not at all.

Manny Faces: And this really becomes exemplified by the single "Freedom."

Dolio: Oh, yeah.

[Clip from "Freedom"][13]

> Dolio: Learned from the past // there'll be no more marching // the demons the same as the day that he darkened // the shores of our precious, blessed mother continent // stole our ancestors and put them on the market // they stayed fanning the flames that they sparked with // the evil intentions they've had from the start // if we still have to fight, then we'll tear this apart // peace will be found with a spear through the heart.
> R-SON: Another plan is a brother man in power positions // sisters in greater control of our conditions // even when it happens, a doubt you're gonna listen // But consider yourself somehow a Christian. . .

Manny Faces: Now I've seen you [play] live. I've seen you talk about these things. But I saw you in Brooklyn. I don't know how you are in Kentucky, just to be honest. . .

R-SON: The *exact* same way.

Dolio: Exactly. It's fascinating because I have a friend of mine who came to a show in Lexington, Kentucky. And it was the first time she had ever seen us perform. She knew me as an emcee from when I used to DJ in Boston.

And here we are in this bar, surrounded by rednecks. She's familiar with me. She used to hear me [rap]. And she was not expecting it to be even [more intense] this time. It was like, wait a minute, you straight up told these folks that "my forty acres start here" and you're standing right on the line in front of a bunch of rednecks, and they threw their hands up in the air and cheered for you. And I told her, it's because people appreciate it when you keep it real with them. You gotta keep it a hundred. You gotta keep it a buck.

Manny Faces: That's interesting. So, you're saying that even by coming at the issues harder, you're finding a more accepting audience.

Dolio: Yeah. The thing is that you can't address a sickness unless you diagnose it. You can't treat it unless it's been diagnosed. A lot of times, when it comes to art, and performative art at that, people have a tendency to want to mask the symptoms. You want to dull that pain instead of treating what is actually causing it. We beat past that to get it into their head so they're just like, "OK. I never looked at it that way before." That starts the discussion.

I mean, we still got those party, shake your butt, get down songs, but we're still gonna be talking about mass incarceration. We're still gonna be talking about poverty.

Manny Faces: So, let's talk about "Freedom," one of the lead singles from the new album, which was released on Juneteenth. Again, what I noticed is that you're not [talking about] social justice issues with a, "We're all in this together, Kumbaya" kind of thing. It's like, "No. There's extreme injustice in the country."

And in some ways, you're trying to tell the folks who might be more inclined to listen to your foundational style of music, "Hey. There's something you really need to hear. Thank you for inviting us into your space, but we're gonna tell you something."

R-SON: Yeah. That's exactly right.

Manny Faces: This was extremely prominent on "Freedom." Like, *extremely* prominent. . . I was a little bit like, "Damn. Y'all not playing that middle ground. You're picking a clear side, and you're letting people know this is how we gonna rock. Listen to what I'm trying to say."

This is purposeful. Yes?

Dolio: Yeah. We wrote the song last year. We recorded it in January...

R-SON: Yeah. And then everything [in 2020] popped off. It wasn't even supposed to be a single when it came out. We didn't have plans for a video at all. Then things just started to steamroll, so we were like, "Yo, we need to do something."

Dolio: Yeah. We thought this was the song that needs to come out right now because it is the type of thing that we would like to be the theme for the new revolution. The reason why we came so heavy handed on the song in the first place is because pussyfooting around this situation is how we got here. As long as people think it's just about how you feel and not about whether or not you act, then you're gonna just keep repeating the same thing over and over again, and the situation is never gonna get better. So that's why we hit it with, "We ain't gonna wait no more to get this freedom..."

All due respect to the elders of the movement, but it's important that we learn from what they encountered. The whole thing about learning from your past is seeing where things went wrong, where they turned left, and seeing how to build upon that. And they were like, "OK, we shall overcome someday..."

Someday is now.

Manny Faces: How much of the album is message music or protest music?

B.E. Farrow: The album's called *No Time For Enemies*. I think that declaration of demanding freedom goes into that, because you wouldn't take your freedom away from a friend. You take it away from enemies. We don't got time for that. I think it loops into a bigger message. We can't be fighting over this stuff.

When it comes to race relations, there's a lot of bad blood there and we need to talk about it. We need to be open about it, and we need to be able to hear each other on it. And we don't have time to be enemies because the stuff we're going through now makes us as a nation, as a country, look weak. So we don't have time for that.

Dolio: [There are] many meanings wrapped into the title. Because we're not in the business of making enemies with this. We also realize that there are enemies that already exist. So, it's no time to be making new ones, and the time for the old ones is done. Their time is over.

Which is why things are so tumultuous right now because what we're witnessing is the death rattle of the old guard of the age of injustice. People are tired of waiting. People are fed up.

We've hit a critical mass, which is why we're seeing an uprising, globally. How much of this is protest music? I wouldn't say that the album itself is protest music. It's *movement* music.

Manny Faces: You gave me a quotable! I love it...

R-SON: Hashtag Movement Music. That's the new hashtag right there.

Manny Faces: But you see, I teed it up. I set it up...

R-SON: You did, you get the assist on that one... That was Magic Johnson like...

Dolio: Right. Because to me, a protest is really asking the unjust to become just, whereas a movement is motivating those who injustice is being done against and the allies of those who are witnessing this happen, to come together to make this stop and to move forward with it. Because it's more than just being *against* the injustice. It's about being *pro justice*.

We're artists, so we do our part artistically in addition to what we do in our regular lives outside of our art, but we're motivated by love, primarily. Our love for each other, for our people, for our communities. For those who ally with us on many different fundamental levels. It's about us coming together, having each other's backs and pushing past all of this nonsense to build and rebuild into a new paradigm of justice.

And we know it's not going to be easy, but if we could be the soundtrack to that movement, so be it.

I feel lucky that people even listen to us in the first place. But because of that, I know that each one of us in this group does our best to make sure that when we get in there to create and we put our heads together to make something, we don't want the people who end up picking this up to feel let down or feel like they've been cheated out of the reward of that emotion, that energy exchange that we are trying to push forward.

Manny Faces: That's powerful. It's not just a message, it's a mission. There's something purposeful about the work you're doing. It may have started out as, "Hey, we're gonna be artists. We're gonna do this thing. It's gonna be great. We're mashing up these genres. . ." And maybe I'm speaking for y'all, but in the beginning, you might not have seen the social justice ramifications of what you are doing. But as the years progress—and right now especially—you might really say this is purposeful work.

R-SON: Yeah. Just speaking on it, individually, having listened to Dolio's individual stuff, there's always been something to what we were saying. I've been doing this rap shit for almost 25 years, and I've never made a song that would be "a hit." But there was always something that I wanted you to get from it. And Dolio's stuff has always been the same way. There's always been something. Not only were the lyrics dope, but there was something behind it that you hoped somebody was getting out of it.

When we linked up with Gangstagrass—particularly Rench because not only does Rench got bars, Rench is a G on a lot of this social justice stuff. Rench is that dude. I wouldn't be surprised if he got a warrant or two. He's been arrested several times in a lot of protests down in D.C. Rench is about that life.

Manny Faces: The kind of ally who don't call himself an ally. . .

R-SON: Exactly.

Dolio: Right. He's got skin in the game. He's not sitting on the bench. He's not a cheerleader. He's in the game.

R-SON: Rench is definitely on the front line. Just being able to link up with a guy that was doing that [already], just brought it out for me personally to make the whole thing a little bit more official. A lot of it was me writing raps that sounded interesting, now there's more to it for me. . .

Manny Faces: If you're gonna join a movement, you wanna be aligned with that movement. . .

R-SON: Yeah. This is definitely the one.

Manny Faces: What I feel about this is seeing Black men saying, "I'm gonna team up with this style of music that isn't traditionally associated with me. And I'm going to do this, but I'm not gonna sacrifice. I'm gonna still rock what I feel needs to be rocked."

R-SON: Right. Exactly.

Manny Faces: That's what I feel about y'all. You wouldn't half step this. That's what makes it so powerful. And when you talk about hybrids, and cross cultural connection, to me, this is the way it needs to be done.

R-SON: We went another route with it too. Earlier this year, we came out with a mixtape. . .

Manny Faces: Oh, the remakes!

R-SON: Yeah. *My Brother, Where Ya At?*[14] That was very much for the Hip Hop cats that weren't sure, who were like, "What is this all about?" [And we selected those particular rap beats] because if you're a Hip Hop cat, you know every one of them. You know every one of those samples. And when you hear it, you're like, "Oh, wait. Is that..? OK. Alright! What are you doing with this?"

Again, it was a matter of having the best instrumentalists to be able to do it. Then me and Dolio had to. . . It takes a lot. And I was thinking about this when we were recording it, like, on [our remake of "Boom". . .][15]

[Clip from "Boom Goes The Dynamite"][16]

> R-SON: Set it off, we bussin' off a concussive force // that hit from where I rest way up in the North // to down South where they just found out // exactly what this Gangstagrass sound's about // 'cuz it drowns out all the whack noise // I'm a free born man, you won't catch me in the trap, boys

R-SON: That's a DJ Premier, Royce the 5'9" record. . .

Dolio: We could not come half stepping on that. . .

R-SON: No. Not at all. . .

Dolio: Or on any of them. . .

R-SON: . . .on any of those joints. That's legendary stuff. It's like, look, none of this is fake. This is all authentic.

Manny Faces: I think that it's an interesting time for the work you do. I said this in the beginning, on paper, the concept might be a little bit questionable—no disrespect intended, as you know. . .

R-SON: No. No doubt.

Manny Faces: But also on paper, the concept could be brilliant and what we need.

B.E. Farrow: And you know what? Just to put it out there, you hear bluegrass Hip Hop and you're like, "I don't know." But when you listen to it, you find out that we're using those genres to get in your ears, to get in your eyes real quick, because we all come from a very diverse background of different musics that connect.

R-SON, he's from Philly, so he's got those rap connections. Dolio is from Florida, and he knows about southern Hip Hop a lot more. I'm coming from a background of jazz and old time, and though I played bass in bluegrass bands, I've never played fiddle in a bluegrass band. I got old time chops on that thing.

[Our banjo player] Danjo, he's heavy bluegrass. He's the one person who's heavy bluegrass. But he also does choir stuff. He went to school to be a choir director. And Rench is great with the honky tonk and country. He could sing that stuff all night. So bluegrass Hip Hop gets you in the door and gets you saying, "Oh, what is this?" But once you get in here, obviously, people hear so much more.

Dolio: Yeah. To bring it back to the whole Americana thing. . . These past few years we've been knocking doors down and basically establishing our foothold in these arenas. One, we were establishing that Hip Hop is folk music. And two, over the last year and a half or so, we had been establishing the fact that Hip Hop is Americana.

Manny Faces: That's what I was saying! We are on the same page.

Dolio: First, we did it when we went to Americana Fest in the UK, because, to them in Europe, they didn't really necessarily give us those delineations that you would get stateside as far as this is that and this is the other thing. Over there we're just a bunch of Yanks.

Manny Faces: [LAUGHS] Right. Americans. So, Americana!

Dolio: Right. It was American music. So they were like, "OK. This is dope. Let's rock with it." So last year is when we really set our foothold in Americana, here. We went and we smashed Americana Fest in Nashville. And that's when they were like, "OK. Yeah. Hip hop is Americana."

Manny Faces: Like I said, I'm sitting on a piece where that was my whole editorial. I never published that. But. . .

R-SON: Publish that shit!

Dolio: Yo. For real. R-SON, how many Hip Hop crews were at Folk Alliance the first time we went?

R-SON: Zeeeerooooo. . .

Dolio: Well, there was one right? Us.

R-SON: Yeah.

Dolio: But how many were there the last time?

R-SON: There were a bunch there the last time.

Manny Faces: OK. So y'all lead movements on multiple fronts. You lead musical movements. This is social justice. This is artist activism.

R-SON: Yeah. It's all of that because it's too easy to just come out here and put out a record that will make you shake your butt, but won't make you think about anything. It's too easy. Me and Dolio talk all the time about how if we wanted to be famous, we could make some knucklehead shit and pop real quick.

Dolio: Yo. In between takes in the studio, we've written *thousands* of those records.

R-SON: [LAUGHS] Thousands of just, goofball records...

Dolio: Just freestyling. . .

R-SON: "Kill everybody in the room" records. . . "We sold all the crack" records. . . Like, everything.

Dolio: . . .and then we get in the booth and we're like, "OK, let's make this *real* record"

R-SON: My thing in anything that I'm doing is that I want to leave you with something. I want you to walk away from it and be thinking about it. Not just the words that I was saying, but why I was saying it, and what it was all about. That's the kind of music we've been making on so many levels.

We got a song called "Ran Dry" that's about water and having clean water and having access to clean water.

[Clip from "Ran Dry"]¹⁷

> Dolio: Not a single solitary drop // So thirsty // No relent from the thirst of the drought // So harsh 'til your skin starts to crack on your mouth // Sun beating on your neck // not a shadow of a doubt

R-SON: And even if it's something that you just might be shaking your ass to, once that's your favorite joint and you really listen to it, you're like, "Oh, wow. This is pretty dope…"

Manny Faces: "They're saying something…"

Dolio: Yeah. That's why I don't even say my name in most of my songs because I don't want it to be about me. If I'm talking in the first person, I'm writing it so that whoever's listening to it can sing that as themselves and feel it.

Manny Faces: I'm gonna ask you the question that I ask everybody. The name of this podcast is *Hip Hop Can Save America!* And I think we need more than Hip Hop, don't get me wrong. But I think that a lot of the fundamental things that make Hip Hop what it is, are some of the fundamental things that we need as a society. We talk a lot about Hip Hop advancing education. We talk about Hip Hop in health and wellness. I talk to people who are using Hip Hop in school counseling. There are a lot of ways that Hip Hop has been used in nontraditional ways to benefit humanity that a lot of people are not really up on.

I think your group, your band, your crew, is really interestingly poised to touch upon, from both a social justice and a musical aspect, ways that Hip Hop can help bridge gaps, bridge ideologies, bridge thought processes.

But I don't wanna put words in your mouths. What do y'all think people need to recognize when we say that Hip Hop can be used as a vehicle, as a tool, as an ideology, as a philosophy to help improve lives and livelihoods and communities throughout this country? From your very unique experience merging these genres, traveling the country, going to places where Hip Hop is not front of mind for a lot of people, what inspirational ideas have you come up with that would make a case for that argument?

B.E. Farrow: Man, [there's an album that, until last week,] I wasn't hip to. I don't know why I wasn't hip to this album. It's not like I don't love The

Roots,[18] but I didn't listen to this album. R-SON suggested to me *How I Got Over*, because I've been campaigning for something, and I just needed some real encouragement that day. And it's a lot of Black Thought just talking about how he got to where he is and how he got to his mentality. Hip hop can be such an education and such a therapy sometimes. . . Just listen!

Sometimes in our crowds, we've got old folks just like, "Yeah, I really like it. I just, you know, I don't understand the lyrics." I was like, "You *gotta* understand the lyrics! You gotta! That's the meat and potatoes right there. You were just eating the mayonnaise!"

Dolio: That's one of the reasons why R-SON and I are so adamant about how much we enunciate when we spit because we realized that our demographic is wide open as far as age range and culture.

Manny Faces: You gotta get *Hamilton*[19] on them. . .

Dolio: Right. We don't want people to miss the words. Because the stories are what's important to us. And that's also a big thing in bluegrass, the stories. But Hip Hop, because it's a lyric-heavy genre, the stories become that much more important.

As far as saving America, it acts as a way of giving voice to the voiceless. Telling those stories of the people who were previously ignored or disregarded or overlooked. You see it across Hip Hop throughout its existence. Of course, there's the party records, there's the self-aggrandizing ego rap records. But even in that, there is the struggle and the pain because the very reason people do the big talk is because they were made to believe they were small to begin with. So they paint this picture of this larger-than-life figure of themselves to self-affirm. And that in itself is a positive effect. It's motivation music. It's aspirational. Even when you go to Sugar Hill Gang, they're rapping about taking car services to go to a party because they didn't have rides to begin with. But after they started getting [money], they did. Speaking into existence.

The Word itself says at the beginning, there was the word.

B.E. Farrow: [HITS TABLE] Quotables, dude!

Manny Faces: R-SON. Take us out. Why is Hip Hop the mold for how we can make a better society?

R-SON: I would say it's a couple of things. Most importantly, within Hip Hop, if you're dope, if you're good at what you do, Hip Hoppers will respect you. You could be the fattest, most blind, goofball dude in the world. But if you're dope on the [turntables], you will get represented as a dope DJ. You might have terrible breath and your feet stink or whatever, but if you're doing amazing graffiti pieces, cats will rep for you, for your talent, for your ability.

Within Hip Hop—the culture, not the industry and all that—you have to be good at the thing that you do. If you are good at it, you will get props for it.

There are a lot of people that exist within American society that get props for doing things that they're *not* very good at because they knew the right person or they had the right money or whatever, things that they aren't really about. In Hip Hop, if you are dope at what you do, regardless of what you look like, regardless of anything, if you're good at *that*, you will get respect, you will get represented, you'll get your props.

I think that if we make a better effort for people to get the props that they deserve for the things that they do, that, for me, is part of how Hip Hop can save America.

Manny Faces: Well, listen, to me, y'all are dope at what you do. And again, on paper, we might be a little bit side-eyed, but that's what makes it even more satisfying to see y'all do what you do. To hear what you do on a record. To see what you do live and in person. To know that you're carrying this message to other parts of the country that aren't hearing these messages on a regular basis.

I think [y'all are] part of the reason why Hip Hop can save America.

Afterthoughts

Ironic, I suppose, that when I received word of the assassination attempt on Donald Trump's life at a 2024 campaign rally in Butler, Pennsylvania, I was driving to a Gangstagrass show.

Among all the immediate talk of political division, violence, and pleas for "unity," I reflected back to my initial podcast conversation with members of the group. As I mentioned then, their style of genre mixing—while sacrilegious to some—really does work, and in ways very different from "Old

Town Road," Shaboozey, or Beyoncé's 2024 foray into country with her country album, *Cowboy Carter*. Discussions of Black origins and influence on these genres aside, there is something striking about the fierceness with which Hip Hop and bluegrass soundclash, particularly when each maintains strict adherence to its own aesthetic spectrum.

As the band members suggested, when this multicultural mashup showers crowds that might contain fans of either genre—but almost assuredly not both—something surprising emerges. Something we don't see enough of in our social, cultural, and certainly not our political landscapes these days: a spontaneous, unexpected, and almost unfamiliar feeling of...

Unity?

I'm not naïve enough to think that bringing people who might otherwise have serious problems with one another into a concert hall for 90 minutes will somehow instantly change deep-seated biases and invoke feelings of universal peace and love. Then again, I'm also optimistic enough to name a podcast and book *Hip Hop Can Save America!* Clearly, I believe Hip Hop has certain unique superpowers, among them the ability to address, alleviate, and in some cases help eliminate some of our largest societal ills—racism and inequality among them.

Some of this optimism stems from witnessing a Gangstagrass show in places like Gainesville, Georgia, places where there will undoubtedly be people who harbor very negative preconceptions about Hip Hop—and, if we're being honest, about those folks typically associated with Hip Hop. But if you look for it, you will absolutely witness visible changes in folks' demeanors as the show progresses. Skepticism and denial morph into reluctant respect, sometimes into outright admiration, and occasionally, emphatic acceptance. It's quite a phenomenon.

Hip Hop fans might not be too surprised—we've seen all kinds of genre-bending over the decades—but many will be impressed that it works this well without feeling gimmicky. Bluegrass fans, meanwhile, encounter something far outside their comfort zone, particularly through R-SON and Dolio's direct lyrical messages—yet as the band reports, most stay to listen and engage, which is not an insignificant fact.

To be clear, I'm not suggesting all bluegrass fans are bigots, or that those who are would walk in hateful and walk out magically enlightened. Gangstagrass, while thoroughly enjoyable, isn't by itself a panacea to racism. We must remember that the burden is never on the oppressed or underserved to convince those who hold power or privilege to value their humanity. As essayist and author Robert Jones Jr.'s words, originally stated as a Twitter post in 2015 and widely shared after Trump's 2024 re-election, remind us: "We can disagree and still love each other unless your disagreement is rooted in my oppression and denial of my humanity and right to exist."[20]

In this light, the multi-racial makeup of the group does some of that heavy lifting, perhaps providing a disarming environment where white folks in particular can begin to recognize their own implicit biases and how those biases conflict with reality. As any reformed bigot will probably tell you, something had to spark that kind of revelation. Maybe it was love. Maybe it was a threat. Maybe an act of kindness. Maybe they just one day realized they'd been purposefully led astray by architects of an oppressive societal hierarchy that continuously indoctrinates its own citizenry to be field soldiers in the fight to maintain a white supremacist-fueled power structure.

Or maybe it was just the power of music.

In this case, we're talking about Hip Hop—a powerful, culturally driven musical force that could very easily light a spark that completely alters someone's life in a positive light. After all, it did that for me. It did it for many of those reading, and for millions around the world, and it does it in ways that no other musical genre or artform can.

As we see with other interdisciplinary applications of Hip Hop—in areas like education, mental health therapy, international diplomacy, and conflict transformation—authenticity and respect lie at the heart of creating connections across generational, racial, economic, and yes, even ideological divides.

That's what gives Gangstagrass—and by extension, other bold, experimental applications of Hip Hop music and culture—the potential to do more than just entertain. In fact, for Gangstagrass, bringing people together from disparate walks of life is as much the group's mission as making great music, as guitarist and group mastermind Rench told *The New York Times* "because the rise of authoritarianism and fascism really depends on people being separated."[21]

It's often said that music and sports can serve as universal unifiers, and sure, that happens occasionally. Temporarily. But for most folks cut from a biased cloth, simply enjoying the output of entertainers or athletes of color won't lead to true enlightenment. Never has. As Black folks in particular often lament, other folks sure love the culture, but they don't always seem to love the people.

Still, there is an argument to be made that there is no artform or movement more powerful than Hip Hop at changing hearts and minds, remixing old concepts to create new ones, or breaking down barriers and crossing borders.

And despite the negative perceptions often held against it, the hope is that throughout this book we have seen that, as rapper and lecturer KRS-One stated, "if hip-hop has the ability to corrupt ... minds, it also has the ability to uplift them."[22]

So, while many will undoubtedly remain skeptical that anything can truly sway those who harbor deep racial fear or hatred toward others, I'm going to remain all in on the idea that within Hip Hop's DNA lies something extraordinarily unique when it comes to truly bringing people together.

Often, commentary about Hip Hop's political potential starts and stops with whatever socially conscious song some big-name artist drops, or whatever celebrity endorsement is touted in the weeks before a presidential election. A main argument I'm making in this book is that while those momentary intersectional flashes might make headlines, Hip Hop's *real* political power lies elsewhere—in classrooms, in counseling sessions, in archival spaces, at hackathons, and yes, in local concert halls—but only when those involved truly embrace the tenets of a movement literally forged by those tenets of peace, unity, love, and having fun.

When you do come across that type of Hip Hop-inspired inspiration, don't be surprised if you hear a little bluegrass in the mix.

Key Takeaways

1. Gangstagrass successfully merges Hip Hop and bluegrass by focusing on the authentic elements of both genres.
2. Gangstagrass emphasizes the importance of addressing social issues directly in their music, rather than taking a "Kumbaya" approach.
3. The band's live performances often change perceptions about the compatibility of Hip Hop and bluegrass.
4. Gangstagrass views their music as "movement music" rather than just protest music, aiming to motivate action and change.
5. The band recognizes the historical connections between various American music genres and their shared roots.

6. Gangstagrass has played a role in establishing Hip Hop as part of Americana and folk music.
7. The band members prioritize conveying meaningful messages in their lyrics over commercial success.
8. Gangstagrass sees their music as a way to bridge cultural divides and promote understanding.
9. The band emphasizes the importance of storytelling and clear enunciation in their performances.
10. Gangstagrass believes in Hip Hop's potential to recognize and reward talent and authenticity regardless of background.

Discussion Questions

1. How can artists from different genres collaborate to create new forms of "movement music" that address current social issues?
2. What strategies can be employed to introduce socially conscious music to audiences who might initially be resistant to its message?
3. How can the music industry better support and promote artists who prioritize meaningful content over commercial appeal?
4. In what ways can educators use genre-blending music like Gangstagrass to teach about cultural history and social issues?
5. How might the concept of "movement music" be applied to other art forms or media to inspire social change?
6. What potential impacts could the wider recognition of Hip Hop as Americana have on the music industry and cultural perceptions?
7. How can artists maintain their authenticity and message while navigating the commercial aspects of the music industry?
8. What innovative approaches can be developed to use music as a tool for conflict resolution and bridging cultural divides?
9. How can the principles of Hip Hop's meritocracy (recognizing talent regardless of background) be applied to other areas of society?
10. What new genres or musical fusions might emerge in response to current social and political issues, and how can artists be at the forefront of these innovations?

This podcast episode was originally released on July 11, 2020.

Notes

1 Feltrinelli. (2013). *Something from nothing: The art of rap*. Milano.
2 A genre-bending series of albums by rapper Guru that merged live jazz instrumentation with Hip Hop production, featuring collaborations with noted jazz musicians like Donald Byrd and Roy Ayers.
3 Gangstagrass. (2024). *The Blackest thing on the menu*. Rench Audio.
4 Holley, S. E. (2022, October 21). *The Atlantic*. The Atlantic; *The Atlantic*. https://www.thea tlantic.com/culture/archive/2022/10/black-country-music-legacy/671818/
5 "Get Your Cuts Up" appears on Gangstagrass's 2020 mixtape *My Brother, Where Ya At?*, where R-SON and Dolio rap over the band's instrumental versions of classic Hip Hop songs.
6 *Soul Train* (1971–2006) was a pioneering television show that showcased Black music, dance, and culture.
7 *Hee Haw* (1969–1993) was a popular variety show featuring country music and rural-themed comedy sketches.
8 Luther "Luke" Campbell was the leader of 2 Live Crew, a Miami-based Hip Hop group known for their sexually explicit lyrics and pioneering Southern rap in the late 1980s and early 1990s.
9 Gangstagrass. (2019). *Pocket full of fire: Gangstagrass live*. Rench Audio.
10 Phonte Coleman is an emcee/singer who rose to prominence with Hip Hop group Little Brother, later forming the Grammy-nominated R&B/Hip Hop duo The Foreign Exchange and maintaining a respected solo career.
11 "Accidental Racist" (2013) was a widely criticized collaboration between rapper LL Cool J and country singer Brad Paisley that attempted to address racial tensions through what many considered oversimplified and tone-deaf lyrics about Confederate flags and racial reconciliation.
12 "Kumbaya" is a spiritual song that has become shorthand for superficial or naïve attempts at unity and harmony, particularly when addressing complex social issues.
13 Gangstagrass. (2020). *Freedom* [Song]. *On No Time For Enemies*. Rench Audio.
14 Gangstagrass's 2020 mixtape *My Brother, Where Ya At?*, where R-SON and Dolio rap over the band's instrumental versions of classic Hip Hop songs.
15 "Boom" (2002) is a collaboration between Detroit emcee Royce da 5'9" and legendary producer DJ Premier, known for its hard-hitting beat and intricate lyricism.
16 "Boom Goes The Dynamite" appears on Gangstagrass's 2020 mixtape *My Brother, Where Ya At?*, where R-SON and Dolio rap over the band's instrumental versions of classic Hip Hop songs.
17 "Ran Dry" is a Gangstagrass song from their 2020 album *No Time for Enemies* that addresses environmental justice and access to clean water in American communities.
18 The Roots are a pioneering Hip Hop band known for performing with live instruments rather than samples. Led by drummer Questlove and emcee Black Thought, they've earned multiple Grammys and served as the house band for *The Tonight Show Starring Jimmy Fallon* since 2014.

19 *Hamilton* (2015) is Lin-Manuel Miranda's groundbreaking Broadway musical that reimagines American history through Hip Hop, featuring a diverse cast portraying the founding fathers.

20 The quote, often seen in the form of a meme, is often misattributed to James Baldwin. The original tweet is now preserved on Jones Jr.'s website, www.sonofbaldwin.com. (2024). Sonofbaldwin.com. https://www.sonofbaldwin.com/wp-content/uploads/2023/01/TW-150 808-670x525-1.jpg

21 Stockman, F. (2023, August 5). Opinion | A multiracial, Hip-Hop-and-Bluegrass band wants to fix hate in America. Nytimes.com; *The New York Times.* https://www.nytimes.com/2023/08/05/opinion/gangstagrass-music-america.html

22 KRS-One. (2014). *Hip Hop is one* [Song]. Soundcloud.com.

· 1 1 ·

THE MENTOR | DR. LAUREN LEIGH KELLY

A few years into my journey documenting innovators who utilize Hip Hop music and culture to uplift marginalized communities, I began seeking gatherings where these folks might convene.

The Hip Hop-based education sector hosted several such events, primarily academic conferences at universities, organized by faculty working at the intersection of Hip Hop and academia. Notable examples included the "Hip Hop in the Heartland" conference and teacher training institute at the University of Wisconsin-Madison, the "Show and Prove" conference in New York and California (organized by Dr. Imani Kai Johnson), the "HipHop Literacies Conference" at The Ohio State University (organized by Dr. Elaine Richardson), the "Can't Stop Hip Hop Education" conference at Harvard Graduate School of Education (initiated by Aysha Upchurch), and the Trinity International Hip Hop Festival at Trinity College, among others.

As the field of Hip Hop-based education matured, these gatherings grew and were producing insightful discourse and fostering powerful relationships. I began to establish myself as a thought leader, developing lectures, submitting proposals to these events, and gradually securing speaking engagements. Concurrently, as we'll learn more about in the next chapter, I was producing another journalism podcast which used Hip Hop to highlight social justice issues. So, when I discovered the "Hip Hop Youth Research and Activism Conference" (HHYRA), it sounded like a good place to apply to discuss that work.

However, I soon realized this conference wasn't for people like me to address youth; it was for youth to address people like me.

The HHYRA, conceived by Dr. Lauren Leigh Kelly, then Assistant Professor of Urban Social Justice Teacher Education at Rutgers University, was designed to allow youth leaders, typically late high school and early undergraduate students, to organize and conduct a full-fledged, day-long academic conference. Students determined the conference theme, issued calls for papers and presentations, contacted keynote speakers, secured venues, raised funds, and booked performers—essentially managing all aspects of the event.

While Dr. Kelly arranged for a team of mentors to provide guidance, the conference remained primarily youth-driven, and typically addressed themes of health, well-being, social justice, and education, with "youth design" as its core component. In a post announcing that the conference had received a grant from the National Endowment for the Arts, Dr. Kelly explained, "Engaging in design is a form of activism and of what scholar Robin D.G. Kelley refers to as 'freedom dreaming,' reflecting the combination of agency and imagination in the process of reshaping the world to be free of oppression and injustice".[1]

The concept of "freedom dreaming" and allowing students to design their own educational experiences might seem foreign to many. Admittedly, I was all in on championing the positive impacts of incorporating youth culture, particularly Hip Hop, into legacy institutional spaces. I knew that most concerns about these progressive teaching methodologies were invoked by members of the general public who are less familiar with Hip Hop, but I also wanted to make sure we weren't ignoring potentially problematic aspects of these integrations.

This particular conundrum was expertly addressed in a paper co-authored by Dr. Kelly and Dr. Don C. Sawyer III titled "When Keeping It Real Goes Wrong": Enacting Critical Pedagogies of Hip-Hop in Mainstream Schools."[2]

It was through this work and my discussion with Dr. Kelly that I came to understand one of the most profound, foundational insights regarding *everything* I had been learning about the intersections between Hip Hop and humanity, an extraordinarily important angle that *must* be considered by anyone seeking to fully understand or engage with today's youth culture. In fact, what she detailed was a lesson that can be applied to *all sorts* of intergenerational interactions.

We can find great value in talking with young people about "big booty hoes."

The Interview

Manny Faces: Dr. Kelly, thank you for taking some time and hanging out with me today on this show. Long overdue. We all wear several hats, but I'd like you to tell me how you describe yourself from a professional standpoint?

Dr. Lauren Leigh Kelly: Primarily as a teacher. I am currently a teacher educator. I teach students who are in the master's program at Rutgers Graduate School of Education, so I teach urban education and English education, through the lens of social justice and teaching for equity and inclusivity.

I have a background as an English teacher. I taught for 10 years in New York—9th, 10th, 12th and sometimes 11th grade English. And it's funny... I was at an event this past weekend. I was focusing on Black music and the history of it, and I was asked to participate in this event as someone who was *in the industry*. And I had a moment where I was like, "Is that a thing that happened?" Because I forgot my prior life as a DJ and someone that had a radio show and was a promoter for Def Jam Records, and it just brought back all these memories of my pre-teaching life in the music industry. But yeah, a teacher educator—that's my primary hat for now.

Manny Faces: That's the primary hat. But in your DNA is a whole lot of music and a whole lot of Hip Hop.

Dr. Lauren Leigh Kelly: Yeah.

Manny Faces: How does Hip Hop play a role as a teacher educator—in general, holistically, and specifically?

Dr. Lauren Leigh Kelly: Hip hop is in the DNA of my work as a teacher. When I first started teaching, I was not introduced to Hip Hop as an approach to teaching and learning. I didn't know that this was a field of study or a form of pedagogy. It was just really natural for me to play music in my classroom, because I love music, specifically Hip Hop, and I was teaching in an urban environment where most of my students were also engaged in Hip Hop in some way. Also, as I was beginning my career, I was a lot younger than I am now. I was closer in age to my students so what I was listening to was, in a lot of ways, what *they* were listening to, or what their older siblings, or sometimes, parents were listening to. We just really connected based on the music we were listening to, and I found that was a really great starting place to teach from.

That's really how it started, just being an organic part of the classroom.

Then, over time, especially as I was getting more distant from what young people were listening to, I became increasingly interested in how young people were engaged with Hip Hop—specifically lyrically. What were they understanding from the lyrics? What messages were they getting? How were they interpreting or critically engaging with those messages? If at all.

I started to be more deliberate in how I brought music into the classroom for critical literacy development, having explicit conversations about what they were hearing. What do these words mean to them? How are they understanding it? And I found that became really powerful, not only connecting students to classroom content, but also in developing critical consciousness in the classroom through popular media.

I especially [noticed this when] I started teaching in the suburbs and I brought music into more racially diverse classrooms. We were having really powerful conversations around race, around class, around gender, and privilege. These folks weren't necessarily coming from the same perspective because it was such a diverse classroom, so I found it even more critical to have those types of conversations in those spaces where they weren't really having those conversations outside of them.

Manny Faces: And the pop culture parts of Hip Hop was a bridge you found?

Dr. Lauren Leigh Kelly: It was. For two reasons. One, to walk into a racially diverse classroom space, especially in high school, and say, "Hey, everyone. We're gonna talk about race and class and equity today," that's a very different intro. A lot of folks are like, "Am I in the right place? I think I have to go to cafeteria."

So, it wasn't deceptive, but I think when you're starting with the music they're already engaging with, it's a different type of entrance into that conversation because, ultimately, you cannot talk about Hip Hop and not talk about race.

It's really hard to do. I just sort of extracted one from the other. It became a much more organic link to having those really critical conversations.

I also found that some of the students I taught came from a lot of economic privilege. They had, for instance, front row seats to an A$AP Rocky intimate conversation—spaces that *I* wasn't even in. So I thought it was even more important to engage in critical conversations about the music that they were consuming because they're consuming it without thinking about their privilege and what it meant to be able to score these $500 seats to a concert?

Manny Faces: When you saw some of this in practice, as you were implementing these things, you were discovering this on your own. But there was a burgeoning field of Hip Hop-based education, or Hip Hop pedagogy out there. When did those two lanes cross paths? When did you realize that you're not alone, and that this is a thing?

Dr. Lauren Leigh Kelly: That's such a great question. After my fifth year of teaching, I started my doctoral program at Teachers College at Columbia University. I'm super fortunate that I was mentored and trained by some of the foundational scholars in the field of Hip Hop education. I had classes with Dr. Mark Lamont Hill who wrote the book *Beats, Rhymes and Classroom Life*, which is one of the seminal texts about what it looks like to teach Hip Hop in classroom spaces. He's one of the first people who documented having taught an entire class devoted to looking at Hip Hop as literature. Whereas other folks had units, a week or maybe a month or a summer program, or an after school program, we had an entire course where you're getting a grade in really reading Hip Hop and discussing it. That was really significant to me because that was the first time I realized that one could do this and have it be sentient inside of a school space.

I was also taught by Ernest Morrell who was one of the first people to write about teaching Hip Hop in an English classroom. That was my introduction to the scholarly side of it. During that time, I met Dr. Jamila Lyiscott who was at Teachers College while I was there. She was one of the leaders at Urban Word, a New York City-based youth organization around poetry and Hip Hop and activism. Meeting her and getting connected to her work is when I started to attend Urban Word events, like the Preemptive Education Conference that they were running in conjunction with NYU. That was when I really understood there was an entire community around this work and that it wasn't just professors and grad students. This was an intergenerational community.

Manny Faces: Now you're teaching teachers. So how did those experiences shape what you actually do today?

Dr. Lauren Leigh Kelly: I find this is a *the more you learn, the less you know* kind of thing. I find myself even less of an expert every day as I'm learning more from my students, especially from youth communities. What I really try to do in the field of teaching teachers is to focus on who they should be learning from in the classroom, not only their proffering teacher, or student teachers or their colleagues, but also the students in the room.

And especially, I think about me when I was a new teacher and a lot of the essays that I read when pre-service teachers are applying to the program to get the certification. It's a lot of seeing young people as empty vessels that we're filling up with all of our knowledge. It's a very well-intentioned space, but there's this idea that we are learned. We've gone through the things. We've gotten the degrees, and we are now going to go back into school to offer up our knowledge to students. Because it worked for us. So, I've got this notion that I'm gonna do the same thing to young people that people did for me.

All without really recognizing they're *not* empty vessels. They have so much knowledge and so much cultural production, especially now that they're literally producing things all the time and putting them out on the Internet.

It's really looking to our students to learn from them and make sure their knowledge is honored and valued in the classroom.

Manny Faces: That segues nicely into the paper that you coauthored with Dr. Don Sawyer from Quinnipiac University, *When Keeping It Real Goes Wrong: Enacting Critical Pedagogies of Hip Hop in Mainstream Schools*. What I really enjoyed was that it's a counter to what often happens when proponents of Hip Hop education offer what the paper calls *success narratives*. We're proponents of it, we wanna talk about how great it works and all the successes that we've seen—and there are plenty of receipts. We know that it works in a lot of instances, and we can point to that. We want to amplify that.

But what you and your coauthor noted is that it's also important to look at when the results may not be as effective or as positive as you thought it might be, or what you hoped it might be.

So, what if someone asks, "What's Hip Hop education supposed to look like and what is it supposed to achieve?" Part of it is what you just talked about, learning from students from their cultural perspectives, or the ways they see things. But what's the quick elevator pitch on what Hip Hop education is supposed to achieve—and then we can talk a little bit about some of the things that you saw where it didn't quite work according to plan.

Dr. Lauren Leigh Kelly: I love that you framed it that way because in terms of what it's supposed to do, I think part of the challenge is that we never really know. I mean, look at Hip Hop itself. No one knew in 1985 that it was gonna look the way it looks right now, right? Or even ten years ago. That everyone would be sing-rapping, and that we'd like it! So I think a part of the challenge, and also the beauty of Hip Hop-based education is that we don't really know the outcome, and a part of what we are attempting to do is, in some ways, be OK with that, and reframe Hip Hop education not as, "Do these steps," or, "Do what this person did," or "Do what I did and it's gonna be great." Because it is so context specific depending on who is in the room geographically, linguistically, culturally, racially, economically. . .

Manny Faces: . . .which is Hip Hop!

Dr. Lauren Leigh Kelly: Exactly!

Manny Faces: Hip Hop is the same way. I say to the people [who proclaim something as] not *real* Hip Hop, that they're really attempting to put something in a box that, by its nature, is not supposed to be in a box. It's very difficult to say that these are the rules of the game in Hip Hop, generally and even specifically, in its application in educational spaces.

Dr. Lauren Leigh Kelly: I think that's what young people, especially young people who are creators of Hip Hop right now, are showing us every day. Because we could say, "Well, you need to have *this* many bars. You need to have *this* many verses. You need to have syntax and onomatopoeia. . ." And they're like, "Nope."

Manny Faces: [LAUGHS] Right.

Dr. Lauren Leigh Kelly: I think Drake in some ways is really one of the proponents of defining that. He's like, "I'm gonna sing my hooks and rap my verses. And that's gonna be fine. I don't need to get someone else on this." I remember when he came out with "Coming Home." I think that song only has one verse, but you don't notice that because it's just so captivating.

So you're constantly learning from young folks that there are no rules to this. It's about what feels right in that moment, what hits in that moment, and it's so context specific. I think there's a danger in saying, "Follow these ten steps to Hip Hop education, and your class is gonna be THE class, and everything's gonna be great." In that paper, what we challenge is, what happens when you do that and everyone didn't love the class, or everyone didn't get all As.

I think Mark Lamont Hill's book also gets into that where he says [something like], "...and then someone disappeared for two weeks, because something was triggering in the competition we had..."

So, I think we need to be really honest about what this looks like in classrooms, especially for new and pre-service teachers. When they try these things that we say work and it doesn't work, then they feel like it's on them. Like, somehow they failed or they're not the right person, or [they think they did something] wrong. We need to also be really honest about these moments where it didn't necessarily work out the way we thought it would, because it's a learning experience for everyone, and it also lets us know, it's OK. We're trying this out. No one really knows what this will look like because Hip Hop is shaped every day. It's new every day. Similarly, our pedagogy has to be new every day.

Manny Faces: That's interesting. It's definitely an organic, evolving process. Now here's what I liked. When things didn't work out well you were saying to yourself, "Maybe it's me... Is it *not* me?" It's very introspective, and of course, it's very caring. It's coming from a caring perspective.

There's a lot of people that you could probably find who would attempt to show why Hip Hop-based education is garbage. That it's a stupid idea. It's never gonna work. It doesn't work. They're all wrong, of course. But [there are those who would try and] knock down this practice or these methods.

Yours is saying, "No, no, no. It works. Here's why it should work. Here's where it could be improved. Here's what we were trying to accomplish, and here are some things that are blocking it."

So, what was the class in this piece about? What were you trying to do? And what are a couple of examples from the paper where it didn't quite gel?

Dr. Lauren Leigh Kelly: It was called "Hip Hop Literature and Culture," and it was a high school English elective. It was the first time I proposed the class. I had a director who is a critical scholar and was incredibly open to adding to the curriculum in ways that were culturally responsive to students and not just sitting in the canon. It was offered to 10th, 11th, and 12th grade students. Ultimately, it was almost all seniors, because this was in a school where electives were really pushed towards business and AP, so students are really taking electives that would look good on their college application, or that their parents supported, or that would get some more college credit AP scores. So [it was difficult to find] students who were willing to use their precious elective time to take something that was not necessarily gonna look good on their college resume, their application, or that their parents weren't supporting. I ended up with a lot of students that were either super Hip Hop heads or they just needed a credit. They didn't need it to be AP. They just needed something to make sure they graduated.

So, it was a really interesting group of 11th and mostly 12th grade students. There were two girls in that class, which made for really interesting dynamics. One of them was a spoken word poet who ended up in First Wave at University of Wisconsin.[3] She came in as an activist, in some ways a young critical scholar. It made for really interesting conversations because you had some of the Hip Hop heads in the class that were like, "I just wanna play my favorite songs and talk about why they're my favorite." But they didn't really want to engage with, you know, [asking] what does it mean as a white man to love a song whose chorus says, "N-gga, n-gga, n-gga, n-gga, n-gga..."? And to say it out loud, to be reciting these verses in class. They didn't wanna engage with that.

There were a lot that were like, "I don't wanna *really* talk about the songs. I wanna just talk about the songs."

Manny Faces: [LAUGHS]

Dr. Lauren Leigh Kelly: And then the girls would talk like, "Why are you not OK with me playing Lil' Kim? Why are you not OK with Azealia Banks?" Really critiquing and challenging how some of the young men in the class had a very mono, or singular view of Hip Hop [in terms of] who was great, who they would play, and who they would listen to. They were like, "That's weird. That's uncomfortable. That's not alright." And so it became...

Manny Faces: ...like "barbershop talk." Like, "Top five dead or alive," discussions...

Dr. Lauren Leigh Kelly: Yes! It became such an interesting space... So, ultimately, we had a circuitous route to doing the thing that I wanted to do. I came into it really wanting to unpack structural inequity and talk about race and class and gender and power and sexuality through the lens of Hip Hop text. It started out with everyone sharing their favorite songs, talking about how they connected to Hip Hop, critiquing and challenging each other. And then by the end of class, we came back to that in a very roundabout way. We ultimately were critiquing things like race and class and gender and power. But it wasn't in the way that I intended. It wasn't through the text that I brought in or the curriculum I wrote. I scrapped most of it. It really became the students bringing in the songs that *they* gravitated towards and then us asking each other questions to get to the root of what *we* were gravitating towards. Ultimately, we did the things that I was hoping we'd do, [but] it was really me learning from the students throughout.

I particularly remember... Do you remember 2 Chainz's "Birthday Song?"[4]

Manny Faces: Yeah. I'ma play it on my birthday this week. [LAUGHS]

Dr. Lauren Leigh Kelly: That really became, like, our primary text in this class, surprisingly. I thought it was gonna be just [Jeff Chang's seminal book on Hip Hop history] *Can't Stop, Won't Stop*. They were like, "This is mad reading!" [LAUGHS] And I remember one of the students said, "You *have* to watch this video." And I didn't know if I'd heard the song before but I was like, "'Birthday Song,' sure, let's play it." And then once it started, I was like, "Oh, *this* song!"

So we listened to the song multiple times. We watched the video on mute. There were times we could only get through certain chunks of it because we would have these conversations... Something happened that was really, really important for me, as an educator. There was a moment where we watched the video and I told them, "Alright. I know I'm a little bit uncomfortable about the song and the chorus," ["All I want for my birthday is a big bootie hoe..."] And especially when you watch the video. It's a lot of women's bodies, and a lot of times you don't see their heads, you don't see their face. There's a cake that's in the shape of a woman's body...

So, of course, I was very judgmental, and I was like, "Why do you like this?" And they're like, "Well, you know, we relate to it." And I said, "What exactly are you relating to? Does it reflect your life? Is this what your life looks like?" And they're like, "No. No. No. But it's what I wanna have. . ."

I just kept posing questions. "Do you want your birthday to look like this? Is this what inspires you?" And they're like "No. We don't really want *this* this, but we want the power to have this if this is what we wanted."

So, through these questions, I'm understanding that what I think they're honoring and validating and gravitating towards—the misogyny, the objectification, the things that I think that they are loving—it's not. It's the power. And while that power seems to be manifesting as things like misogyny or objectification, it's really about young people needing that [power] in their lives. For me, that was the turning point in the class.

Manny Faces: I think that's valuable for a lot of people who have a very surface level or cursory knowledge of Hip Hop in general. They look in and they see those things. They see misogyny, or how it glorifies violence. But I think the violence or the powerful drug dealers or the powerful people are like the powerful mafia bosses. It's the power. "Do you respect me or fear me?" It's that dynamic. And of course, who feels more powerless than young people? Especially young minorities or oppressed or marginalized communities. So, wouldn't that be the pinnacle of what they want out of life? Not necessarily a birthday cake shaped like a woman's posterior...

I'll have to cancel my order.

Dr. Lauren Leigh Kelly: [LAUGHS] Listen, if it's what you want, it's what you want.

Manny Faces: [LAUGHS] I have the power to do this! But that's a really interesting angle. I like to speak to people who have that very surface level of Hip Hop who will say, "Why do they like this?" And you have to go through this whole long thing. What you just said is very insightful in that it's that power that they really crave and look at.

I like how you freestyled your entire course because you basically had to flip it on the go, but you got to an interesting place. There were two things that stuck out to me that you also said made it difficult to get to the place where you wanted to go, maybe things that generally get in the way of bringing Hip Hop into a classroom as a way to connect to students.

One of the things you mentioned was the physical space. The other was the power dynamic. How do those things—in general and even specifically to your case—make it more difficult to get the advantages that Hip Hop-based education can bring?

Dr. Lauren Leigh Kelly: Really, what gets in the way is school. The structure of the school itself and the structures of power, as you mentioned. Part of the issue is that the students in this class were in 11th and 12th grade. They've already been through more than a decade of schooling that told them that they don't have power, that they weren't the center of schooling and learning. They're just the recipients of knowledge, and they're being assessed on how much they can regurgitate that knowledge. So, by the time they're 17, 18 years old, they understand that's what school is and what it looks like. I was entering with this very social justice oriented, learn from the youth, very democratic idea of education, where all I had to do was introduce this new curriculum, ask them to forget these roads, move our desks into circles so we can all see each other, and [accept] that the teacher is not the center of power at the front of the classroom.

But they had already been socialized for so many years to do school in a very particular way. At a certain point in time, it's just easier to do the thing that you know how to do where they can just sit back and receive. Once they're asked to come up with ideas to be a leader, it's more work! It's much more work to build curriculum as a student than to just receive the syllabus and keep it moving.

Manny Faces: . . .plus having never been in that position before.

Dr. Lauren Leigh Kelly: The very first time! And so, really, it wasn't them not wanting to take hold of that power. It just felt really new. It came out of nowhere. We only had one semester, so by the time they started to really learn how to wield it, we were done. We were in our last few weeks.

So what we realized is that this type of schooling has to start way earlier, when they are elementary school students, and I think that's something that's happening. It's just gonna take a few years for us to see what that looks like in high school, from those who are already starting to teach from that space in elementary school...

Manny Faces: ...there's radical teaching, but there's also radical learning.

Dr. Lauren Leigh Kelly: Absolutely. And it needs to be something you're accustomed to doing, so by the time you're in high school, you're like, "I am ready to go." Like, here it is. Here's what we need to learn. Here's how we need to learn it. Just get me the resources.

That's unfortunately not what we had in that structure because they were like, "You want me to what? No. Just tell me." Literally, they're saying, "This is gonna take forever. I don't wanna do the mental work of it. Just tell me what to do."

Manny Faces: So, for instance, when they say that civics education has been removed from high schools and middle schools, and we don't get a lot of civics training... What struck me once was the [Marjory Stoneman Douglas school shooting in] Parkland, Florida, and how the young people who responded to that went on TV and were protesting and they organized the March For Our Lives and did all these things. And everyone was like, "Wow. These students are so educated and they're so articulate and they're so motivated." It turns out that Florida, of all places, voted that certain schools have to have civics training.[5]

So not to take anything away from [the students], but part of that may be because they had that [type of] educational focus at a younger age, so when they were older, they were, like you said, ready for it.

Dr. Lauren Leigh Kelly: Absolutely. Again, it depends on the context and it depends on the place. Because we know there are plenty of school systems outside of the U.S. where it's even more rigid. Where students are accustomed to going through their entire day and not saying a word. I remember when I was teaching in Japan, when I would ask my students to be in conversation, they're like, "What?! I know the answer, and I can get one hundred. What is all this interaction that we're asked to do?"

It really does depend on the context. I do think that even the idea of cultural responsiveness and cultural relevance is so dependent on what the culture is, who's in the culture, and what feels organic to the space.

Another example from Japan. I remember watching breakdancers in the subway, way after we had breakdancers in the subway. This is early 2000s. There was something about the ways in which I saw them moving that just seemed very, very structured. Like, this is how one breakdances. And I felt like some of the soul of it wasn't there. It wasn't necessarily organic. It was this external thing that they had learned. [Similarly,] the ways in which there's been a reappropriation of Chola culture,[6] and L.A. Latinx culture. Again, there are a lot of subcultures in Asian countries, where you see them [adopting] aesthetics, but not being as connected to the heart of it. So again, we look at Hip Hop as a culturally relevant response to education, it is so context specific. It's not just gonna work anywhere, even if it is popular and cool.

Manny Faces: I think that's what I really enjoyed about this paper. You're coming from the culture, and you predicted things would happen, and you had to flip it and remix it, and you were able to do that and still get the desired results, because of your authenticity. But a lot of times, we see people who are not necessarily *of* Hip Hop culture, but they're attempting to incorporate it. And that's great. I think we welcome that. But I think what you want to protect against or warn against is educators stepping into this space and doing some of the wrong things that really erase some of the potential of these ideas. That's a worthy concern?

Dr. Lauren Leigh Kelly: It is. Yes. And I was warned, even before I taught the class. Dave Stovall,[7] who's in Chicago, had taught a Hip Hop based class. Bryonn Bain had taught Hip Hop based classes. . . And they both had warned me to not do that thing. They're like, "You will never be the expert on this thing more so than your students." So I still had some missteps there, but I came in knowing that I would really need to not act like I knew all the things about Hip Hop.

I think unless you're teaching a Hip Hop history class, that's the only context in which I think it is acceptable to be the expert and say, "I'm gonna teach you about this thing."

Manny Faces: . . .and even then, you better make sure that you're telling all different sides of those stories because even the *facts* aren't all the *facts*. There are *alternative facts* in Hip Hop history. . .

Dr. Lauren Leigh Kelly: Right. No one even agrees on what the first recorded rap song was. So I think what I have to learn and what I think is really important for educators to learn is that the expertise we're bringing in, is in teaching and facilitation. How do I cultivate a classroom environment that is safe and supportive where everyone's voice is heard? How do I choose some of the supplemental text that can help us develop critical theories and perspectives to bring in from Tricia Rose[8] or Elaine Richardson[9] or Britney Cooper.[10]

But outside of that, I think we need to step away from bringing in the Hip Hop knowledge, the text, the songs, the language, and really focus on facilitation. Don't come in saying, "I know the good Hip Hop... This is what you all should be listening to... This is who has value... This is important... We're gonna listen to Mos Def and J. Cole, and not Da Baby. What does *he* have to offer?"

I think we need to be really careful to recognize that's not our expertise. Our expertise is how you teach. How you facilitate. How you cultivate theories and perspectives in the classroom. And I think once we can enter from that framework, we're good.

Manny Faces: So that no matter what they choose, you could find a way to work it into the mix...

Dr. Lauren Leigh Kelly: Listen. Our primary text was 2 Chainz... [LAUGHS]

Afterthoughts

I purposefully placed my interview with Dr. Kelly toward the end of the book. Though it could have fit anywhere, I felt as if in as much as Dr. Bettina Love's interview set the tone for this book, Dr. Kelly's put an exclamation mark on it.

As one might have noticed, our conversation echoed several important themes we've heard from other educators. I did find value in how certain key throughlines appeared after speaking with so many teachers and teachers of teachers—almost like a set of Hip Hop-based education best practices. What strikes me most about speaking with, and in recent years, having the privilege of working with Dr. Kelly is how her work—and her demeanor—exemplifies *so many* of the qualities I've observed through dozens of interviews with innovators integrating Hip Hop into their disciplines—crucial aspects that anyone seeking to uplift society through Hip Hop should consider.

Dr. Kelly explains that though she learned from Hip Hop-based education pioneers, she is willing to experiment on her own. She is unafraid to check herself, echoing how even "the O.G." Dr. Gloria Ladson-Billings adjusted her own groundbreaking work over time. Dr. Kelly has reached outside of the university walls to explore how others are utilizing Hip Hop for youth development beyond academia. She came into academics having been a practitioner of one of the culture's artistic elements. She centers young people, honoring the knowledge and value they bring to educational spaces rather than imposing judgments or restrictions.

All of these lessons, I have come to believe, are foundational virtues and keys to success if Hip Hop is to be used as a force for social innovation, and Dr. Kelly personifies them all, with grace, professionalism, and a truly caring spirit.

When it comes to Hip Hop's role in the ongoing, ever-evolving battle for social justice and equity, the Hip Hop Youth Research and Activism (HHYRA) conference serves as a remarkable case study for young people to feel welcome as academics, researchers, and activists, showing them that their culture transcends mere entertainment. As a disclaimer, I have become a mentor in the program, but I have learned as much from Dr. Kelly as her students have. Her skill as a mentor is evident in how students emerge from the program as next-generation leaders, prepared to lead not only future iterations of HHYRA but other civic and community-minded initiatives. Through this, I believe Dr. Kelly and her team have created a valuable blueprint for other schools and organizations to follow.

The program further exemplifies how Hip Hop-influenced social justice has evolved beyond protest music or mainstream artists supporting politicians. As Dr. Bettina Love's "Get Free" program, the work of the late Daniel "Majesty" Sanchez, the activism of Tef Poe, political work of Rosa Clemente, and efforts by so many other Hip Hop-minded activists have shown, America is poised for a new generation of Hip Hop-flavored civic engagement in disciplines far removed from entertainment—something we'll explore further in the next chapter—and the HHYRA program is positioned to be part of that movement.

It is the synthesis of all of these ideas and ideals that Dr. Kelly represents to me. She wisely extracts the best of what legacy institutions can offer while guarding against their harmful traits. She merges radical teaching with radical learning, articulates her findings, self-corrects, mentors others with care, and documents all of these things—leaving thorough yet accessible receipts for others to build upon.

The story she shared about how we can so easily misjudge young people's perspectives is quite simply the best analogy for how Hip Hop—and by extension, those who engage in it—can be misconstrued that I've ever encountered. It offers such vital insight that every adult who interacts with young people—particularly those in positions of authority—must take to heart, and I cite it regularly as a foundational concept supporting the very idea that Hip Hop can help save America.

Since we first spoke, Dr. Kelly has authored numerous articles, papers, and books, including *Teaching with Hip Hop in the 7-12 Grade Classroom: A Guide to Supporting Students' Critical Development Through Popular Texts*.[11] She is co-editor with Dr. Daren Graves of *The Bloomsbury Handbook of Hip Hop Pedagogy*,[12] and she served as the 2023–2024 Nasir Jones HipHop Fellow at the Hutchins Center for African and African American Research at Harvard University.

Key Takeaways

1. Hip Hop education can be an effective tool for engaging students and fostering critical conversations about race, class, gender, and privilege.
2. The effectiveness of Hip Hop education is often context-specific and depends on factors such as student demographics, geographic location, and cultural background.
3. Hip Hop education should be flexible and adaptable, as the nature of Hip Hop itself is constantly evolving.
4. Educators should be prepared to learn from their students and adapt their curriculum based on student input and interests.
5. Traditional school structures and power dynamics can present challenges when implementing Hip Hop education approaches.
6. Students may need time to adjust to more democratic and participatory learning environments, especially if they've been conditioned to more traditional educational models.
7. Hip Hop education can reveal unexpected insights about students' motivations and perspectives, such as their desire for power rather than specific material gains.
8. Educators should focus on their expertise in teaching and facilitation rather than trying to be the authority on Hip Hop culture.

9. Starting Hip Hop education earlier in students' academic careers can help them become more comfortable with this approach by high school.

10. It's important to be critical and reflective about Hip Hop education practices, acknowledging both successes and challenges.

Discussion Questions

1. How can we create a balance between structured curriculum and student-led learning in Hip Hop education?

2. What strategies can be employed to help students transition from traditional learning models to more participatory, Hip Hop-based approaches?

3. How can educators and administrators address potential concerns from parents or community members about incorporating Hip Hop into educational settings?

4. In what ways can Hip Hop education be adapted to different age groups, from elementary to high school students?

5. How can we ensure that Hip Hop education remains culturally authentic while still meeting academic standards and goals?

6. What kind of professional development or training might educators need to effectively implement Hip Hop-based teaching methods?

7. How can Hip Hop education be used to address issues of equity and inclusivity in schools and youth organizations?

8. What are some potential challenges in implementing Hip Hop education, and how can they be addressed proactively?

9. How can we measure the effectiveness of Hip Hop education beyond traditional academic metrics?

10. In what ways can Hip Hop education be used to bridge generational gaps and foster better understanding between youth and adults in authority positions?

This podcast episode was originally released on February 11, 2020.

Notes

1 *Rutgers Graduate School of Education receives grant from National Endowment for the arts.* Rutgers University. (n.d.). https://www.rutgers.edu/news/rutgers-graduate-school-educat ion-receives-grant-national-endowment-arts

2 Kelly, L. L., & Sawyer, D. C. (2019). "When keeping it real goes wrong": Enacting critical pedagogies of hip-hop in mainstream schools. *IASPM Journal*, 9(2), 6–21. https://doi.org/ 10.5429/2079-3871(2019)v9i2.2en

3 The First Wave Hip Hop & Urban Arts Scholarship Program is a "is a full-tuition, four-year scholarship program for students that are seniors in high school or freshmen in college that are applying to the University of Wisconsin-Madison." *First Wave Hip Hop & Urban Arts Scholarship Program.* Office of Multicultural Arts Initiatives. https://omai.wisc.edu/progr ams/firstwave/

4 2 Chainz. (2012). Birthday Song [Song]. *On Based on a T.R.U. Story.* Def Jam Recordings.

5 Islam, F. (2018, March 5). Why are Parkland Students so Articulate? Because they were taught civics in Middle School. *Washington Monthly.* https://washingtonmonthly.com/ 2018/03/05/the-civic-education-program-that-trained-the-parkland-student-activists/

6 A Chicana/Mexican-American female identity and style movement from the 1960s–1970s, known for its distinct fashion and expression of cultural pride.

7 Dr. David Stovall is a professor of Black Studies and Criminology at the University of Illinois Chicago, known for his scholarship on critical race theory, education reform, and youth activism in urban communities.

8 Dr. Tricia Rose is a professor and leading Hip Hop scholar whose work "Black Noise: Rap Music and Black Culture in Contemporary America" (1994) helped establish hip-hop studies as an academic field.

9 Dr. Elaine Richardson is a professor whose scholarship focuses on African American literacy and language, particularly through the lens of Hip Hop culture.

10 Dr. Brittney Cooper is a professor and feminist scholar who examines race, gender, and power in Hip Hop culture through Black feminist theory.

11 Kelly, L. L. (2024). *Teaching with hip hop in the 7-12 grade classroom: A guide to supporting students' critical development through popular texts.* Routledge, Taylor & Francis Group.

12 Kelly, L. L., & Graves, D. (2024). *The Bloomsbury handbook of Hip Hop Pedagogy.* Bloomsbury Academic, Bloomsbury Publishing Plc.

· 1 2 ·

THE STORYTELLERS | CHRISTOPHER TWAROWSKI, RASHED MIAN, AND MANNY FACES

In keeping with the theme of unexpected intersections, I want to tell you about a news podcast that covers social justice issues using a particularly groundbreaking format. It consists of professional, in-depth journalism, often covering stories before mainstream outlets, and is very much focused on shining light on issues that affect marginalized, underserved, and under-resourced communities across the United States—and sometimes, globally.

In this podcast, listeners hear from experts, analysts, educators, journalists, activists, people on the ground doing grassroots work, and often, the very people directly affected by poverty, mass incarceration, wealth and education disparity, and more of society's most insidious racial and economic injustices.

This particular podcast has won many awards and accolades. The New York Press Club[1] named it "Best Podcast" twice, in 2018 and 2020, winning over other New York-based outlets like *The New York Times*, *The Wall Street Journal*, *Bloomberg*, and other major organizations with podcasts.

Oh! And each full episode also incorporates original lyrical contributions from an independent Hip Hop artist who crafts three 16-bar verses written specifically for each episode.

The team behind it likes to say it's as if *Democracy Now!* and Black Thought[2] from The Roots had a podcast baby.

That team includes founder and executive producer Jed Morey, editor-in-chief and co-producer Christopher Twarowski, managing editor and co-producer Rashed Mian, and co-producer, audio editor, sound designer, and host, Manny Faces. (That's me!)

As such, this interview was extremely important, personally. For me, the *News Beat* podcast is *the* culmination of my abilities, interests, priorities, and experiences, and sits alongside *Hip Hop Can Save America!*—the podcast and, now, the book—as what I consider to be the most meaningful work of my life.

Still, when you look at our canon and the troubling nature of the issues we've covered, we often lament that *News Beat* is work we wish we didn't have to do. Nonetheless, it is work that is urgently needed.

As readers now will have learned, I believe that nearly *anything* can be improved by incorporating some aspect of Hip Hop music, culture, or sensibilities. It is my belief, and that of many practitioners we've heard from in this book, that simply understanding this concept, and making room for it in the world is, in and of itself, an innovative and impactful form of *doing* social justice.

Throughout this book, I've attempted to demonstrate through the work of these brilliant innovators ways in which this is happening in traditional fields and legacy institutions, including education, healthcare, technology, and several others.

This chapter is here to represent the enormous potential value of what Hip Hop's revolutionary spirit of the remix can bring to yet another important, and for some, unexpected field: journalism.

The Interview

Manny Faces: I want to welcome two of the three others behind this podcast, my friends Rashed Mian, managing editor and Christopher Twarowski, editor in chief of the *News Beat* podcast. Gentlemen, start your engines.

Rashed Mian: How's it going?

Chris Twarowski: What's up?

Manny Faces: I'm really happy to have you guys here. Obviously, we work together all the time, and I wanted to bring some attention to the *News Beat* podcast [on this show]. Thanks for coming on and talking about it.

For those who haven't heard *News Beat*, it might be a foreign concept. "How can there be news and Hip Hop and rappers and music all inside a podcast?" "What is it like, *Hamilton*? Do you guys rap the news?"

It's not that. It's not Lin Manuel Miranda's news podcast.

It's a blend of interviews where Chris and Rashed are interviewing experts, activists, people doing the work in these social justice issues, interviewing them about their work. You then weave those interviews into a flowing narrative, and I weave in music so that it's like a score in a movie. It sets a mood. It crescendos. It's really kinda cool.

And then, we've invited an independent Hip Hop artist to craft an original, lyrical contribution written specifically for and about *that* episode. We usually have them do three 16-bar verses, interspersed throughout the episode. You gotta hear it to understand it, but it's freaking awesome.

Let's talk about the importance of this, how it came to be, and how we began this journey to award-winning stardom. And that starts with you guys as much as it does with me.

You two are award-winning journalists, having won dozens of awards for your journalism over the years. Chris, [we worked together] when you were the editor-in-chief of the *Long Island Press* for many years back when it was an alternative weekly in print, and then online, and you covered a lot of the news that wasn't being covered by the mainstream. It was rugged, underground, *I'm-gonna-get-to-the-bottom-of-this* kind of investigative journalism that we were doing on Long Island, New York. But then we started branching out into other areas.

Rashed, you jumped in the mix as well during those times, and [at some point] the two of you started covering things that were outside of Long Island's purview. National news, [particularly focusing on] civil liberties. Can you guys explain a little bit about your background as journalists and how you outgrew the *Long Island Press*?

Chris Twarowski: I mean, what a blessing. As you said, an alternative newsweekly. It was *us against them*, you know? We considered ourselves the voice of the voiceless. We went after Democrats. We went after Republicans. It didn't matter.

Manny Faces: A few crooked cops thrown in the mix...

Chris Twarowski: We were after the truth. We exposed a lot of bad, bad stuff from environmental crimes to political malfeasance to corporate corruption. The list goes on and on and it was a total blast. That's where we cut our teeth. I had started as an editorial assistant way back when, Rashed came in [later] as an intern, and eventually we started covering [issues like] discrimination against Muslims and Muslim Americans. We started covering perpetual war. The war on whistleblowers waged by our government against the truth, which should be celebrated as being for the public good. We covered Chelsea Manning's court martial at Fort Meade,[3] at NSA headquarters...

Manny Faces: ...I just want to interject... One of only a *few* journalists that were covering that monumentally important story...

Chris Twarowski: That's right. It's testament to our publisher's commitment to the truth—Jed Morey, who is also the executive producer of *News Beat*. That's the kind of journalism that we did. What I like to say is we translate that sort of ethos, that spirit, and continue it with *News Beat*, now in a sonic form.

We take that journalism and meld it with what I think is our other passion, music. We get to shine a light on these issues, on these people, through the written word, through interviews, and through music.

Rashed Mian: Yeah. You mentioned, Manny, how we outgrew Long Island. I think the turning point for us was probably the Occupy Wall Street movement.

You know, during that time, our publisher Jed went out of the office one day to [New York City] and started covering the protests, before a lot of the mainstream outlets went there. He realized that it was gonna be a significant movement. It's sort of crazy when you think about a lot of the issues that they were talking about then, people were criticizing them for, complaining that they were taking a spot in the city and just becoming a nuisance. But a lot of things that they were talking about, especially income inequality, are still going on today. And I think from that moment on, the other issues that Chris mentioned, civil liberties, perpetual war in this country, and the social justice topics that we cover a lot on *News Beat*, just speaks to the crisis that has been plaguing America for a long time. Nobody, I guess, felt comfortable just digging in and exposing what's really going on, how the little people are the ones being hurt, even as we see corporations and billionaires making money hand over fist during the Coronavirus pandemic for example. So, it's all something that's just continued on for the last 10 years. . .

Manny Faces: [IN BERNIE SANDERS VOICE] We are the 99%!

It's interesting that a lot of the progressive thought, a lot of the Bernie Sanders movement, a lot of the things that we're talking about today as rights and necessity and fueling the social justice movement... The racial justice issues, which I think are the priority, but underlying that is poverty, the 1%, the wealth gap... It all came to light. Occupy Wall Street really started bringing that to people's attention.

And we were out there. We covered it. We were there in the middle of Occupy Wall Street. And I think we caught that bug too, to be honest. I know I did. I'd always been active in issues, but when we were out there in Occupy and we saw what it meant to really push back against things, something changed for us. We said, "We gotta tell these stories too, and we could do it in a in a way that MSNBC might not."

Rashed Mian: Yeah. That's the thing. A lot of people obviously caught on to that movement, as well as others later on like Black Lives Matter. But it's also the way in which these protests and demonstrations and larger political movements are covered by the mainstream press. They'll show the titillating coverage, buildings on fire, confrontational moments with the police and things like that. But what you really want to do is get into the nitty gritty and talk to people. It's really just talking about the issues and I think that's what's critical about what we're doing. We're getting down to the issues that are really affecting people, especially mass incarceration, what lays underneath it, and why people are suffering so much. We want to get to the root causes. I think that's what we were good at, and that's something that continues on to today with News Beat.

Manny Faces: We started this in 2017, picking it up in earnest in 2018 and 2019, and continuing in 2020, even under COVID circumstances and restrictions that the pandemic has placed upon us. We don't have as many artists contributing now—we'll talk about that. . . But just to show people what we're talking about here, explain the inaugural episode, the MLK pilot episode, and why we felt that disseminating information the way we can was important when looking at someone as well documented, as well known, as written about as Martin Luther King. What could *we* bring to the Martin Luther King story, and then subsequently, the Rosa Parks story?

Chris Twarowski: I mentioned Jed earlier and it all starts with him. He had a vision for an audio amplification of social justice issues. MLK's [birthday] was coming up and he had this vision of telling a different side of that story through music, shining a light on campaigns that most people don't know about, The Poor People's Campaign in particular. That's what [King] wanted his legacy to be, not the "I have a dream. . ." speech.

Showing these lesser known sides of these stories, correcting the narrative, was very important to him.

Manny Faces: Right. And it makes a lot of sense once you listen to the episode. You don't [typically] hear about Martin Luther King's Poor People's Campaign movement as much as you hear about the, as we say, whitewashed or whittled down epitaph of "I have a dream. . ." That speech is great, and it's certainly a pivotal point in history that should be lauded and studied and appreciated, but it was not the end all when it came to what Dr. Martin Luther King Jr.'s overall legacy should be about.

We had on that episode Reverend Roger C. Williams from the First Baptist Church of Glen Cove, NY. Also, we had Larry Hamm on there, a long-time activist and leader of the People's Organization For Progress, based in Newark, New Jersey. They explained why we're doing a disservice to Dr. King if we don't advance these ideas of the *rest* of his legacy.

Rashed Mian: Something that we point out in the episode is that in school every year, kids will learn about the "I have a dream speech" when King himself admitted that his dream had "turned into a nightmare."[4] That's something that we also put in this episode because we can't just whitewash the life and legacy of MLK. We need to talk about him as a real human and as someone who was more radical than the mainstream media would like us to know.

We've seen so many educators reach out to us and tell us they played this episode for their students because they wanted them to learn about the life and history of MLK, and not just what's in the textbooks or what society wants us to believe.

I think that's what makes us most proud, and I don't wanna speak for you guys, but just the fact that people are using these episodes like MLK inside the classroom, speaks volumes about what we're doing and, like what Chris said, we're just trying to get to the truth. And the truth is important, especially when we're talking about a figure like MLK.

Chris Twarowski: On that note, a lot of the topics, events, people, and atrocities that we cover, [a typical] American student is, unfortunately, just not going to read in a history book. [So] it's part of that series we have, What You Didn't Learn in School...

Manny Faces: Right. And ironically, the schools and some progressive teachers are saying, "We *wanna* teach this in school," and they're reaching out to us to be able to use our material, which is just astounding.

That again ties into the nature of how we present the material. We have in-depth interviews. We've had Dr. Cornel West on our show. We've had Rosa Clemente, former Green Party vice presidential candidate, and a Hip Hop head for sure. We've had Chris Hedges on the show. We've had Barrett Brown on the show. These are luminaries in these fields that they're covering and issues that they're involved in. These aren't just online pontificators, randos from a basement somewhere. We get to the heart of the issue with a lot of the actual voices that are leading these efforts.

Chris Twarowski: I would like to mention as well, besides the academics, the authors, the case workers, the staff attorneys shining a light and giving them a voice, and all the people in the field trying to make a difference, on the musical side, [our rap artists-in-residence] Silent Knight and LiKWUiD.

Manny Faces: We had Silent Knight on [many episodes including] the pilot episode and one called "Exonerated and Broke," where he took on the persona of someone who had been falsely arrested, falsely accused, and in jail for decades, who gets released but gets no compensation. Silent Knight [raps] about how it feels to *be* that person...

Now, we had Alan Newton[5] on the show as well, who was an actual exoneree, and his story was incredibly compelling. We spoke to him in his apartment. You can hear his birds chirping in the background. We were right there. He gave us his heart and soul in that interview.

And then Silent Knight incorporated a few elements of what he talked about. . . And he's great because he does his own research about other people going through the same problem, and he molds that into his artistic impression, his interpretation of the issue, and then delivers it with incredible talent.

Rashed Mian: What Silent Knight did on that episode was so powerful that he now does work for the Innocence Project[6] alongside other celebrities and high-profile people who are trying to raise awareness about people who are wrongfully convicted.

Manny Faces: Absolutely. He was invited by the Innocence Project to work with them, he's met "The Exonerated Five,"[7] he's gone to events, and he's one of their artist ambassadors, all because of what we did at *News Beat*.

[Sarcastically] Now look. I'm not the type to brag. . .

[LAUGHTER]

Manny Faces: . . .but I'm super proud of what we do. We're not just *talking* about an issue. We could do a round table, and there's plenty of shows that do that. No disrespect.

"Exonerated and Broke" made me cry when I was putting it together. There are news clips in there of other people that were exonerated after decades in jail. Didn't get a dime, and then died before they could get any compensation. You gotta sue the city or sue the state. You gotta find a lawyer that's gonna take up your cause. You're just coming out of jail after 30 years. That's hard enough.

I know people that are locked up. They come out of jail. It's a whole different world. Alan Newton told me, "What's a MetroCard,[8] bro? Where the [subway] tokens at?" You know what I mean? How to navigate the world, how to get a job, how to come back to society. . . And then not have any compensation for being wrongly accused all those years.

So we told people, if this bothers you, [you should know] about The Innocence Project. And we send people there. We're always happy to make these connections, even if it's just letting people know what they can do to take action, to effect change. I think that's by far the most fulfilling part of doing this.

We could just put out articles and write. You guys are fantastic writers, and [people should also know that] every episode of *News Beat* has a complete article to go with it that goes into more detail about the issues that we just covered. We do that on purpose. We write about the people that we worked with on this episode and whatever organization they're with. We give their information again.

Rashed Mian: You're right. At the end of the day, we wanna report the facts as we know them. But also, as you're saying, give people resources so they can do something. That can mean just going to vote. That can mean supporting a local organization that does similar work as the group that we featured on the podcast. It could mean spreading the news as a teacher.

And again, I just wanna highlight the work of our artists. We step away. We come up with the script of the podcast, and we give it to Silent Knight or LiKWUiD or the other artists, and we let their creativity just burn. Because we view what they're doing as a form of journalism as well.

Manny Faces: Yes! I was talking about this with Ernie Paniccioli[9] yesterday, how the artists of our generation are the griots. They are the messengers. They're as capable, and in some cases, *more* capable, than other journalists or people who call themselves journalists. They see the world too. They participate in the world. And they have this incredible talent at translating that into a compelling poetical, music oriented, or linguistic way of catching people's attention. They're just as qualified as we are.

Rashed Mian: I'm still amazed at the ability to condense the content of a 2,500 word script into three short verses! It's just incredible what they're able to produce.

Chris Twarowski: And the music and the craftsmanship that the artists bring, in terms of storytelling... I mean, we've written 7,000 word stories, trying to incite a reaction, trying to inspire, which is another part of our mission...

But music... It melts into your blood. You know? It digs into your bones. It hits your soul. To inform and motivate you and get you off the couch.

Manny Faces: For me, and I'm a little biased, but Hip Hop is the best musical genre, artistic form, linguistic form to do spoken word. There's something magical about poetry and the way things rhyme and why that affects us as humans. That's why songs and music and poems are always so forceful to us...

I always get frustrated or discouraged when people lament the inability of Hip Hop to be *protest music* anymore, or of [not] being *substantive*. Hip Hop was very well known for artists like Public Enemy, KRS-One, Brand Nubian, Poor Righteous Teachers, and when they were on the radio and Hip Hop was in that Golden Era as it's called, you had these messengers speaking these things, and they were reaching the masses, through *Yo! MTV Raps* on TV, on radio stations across the country, and mixtapes throughout the world.

And while that stuff has moved away from the corporate controlled ways of disseminating music, it is by no means a dead or dying thing. There are underground artists or independent artists that have wild followings throughout the world. There are artist-activists that are putting in the work. We've had them on our show. Rebel Diaz is a great example. They contributed to two episodes. These brothers have started community centers. They're activists. They're sons of revolutionaries. They're out there doing the work and putting it in their music, but also in the streets organizing. There's only one Rebel Diaz, but there's a lot of Rebel Diazs in the world, using the power of music, Hip Hop specifically, to inform, engage, and incite people.

It happens all the time, every day, and *News Beat* is just a really polished way of putting it all together.

Rashed Mian: Yeah. Again, we're biased but I think *News Beat* speaks to a couple things for me. I think it speaks to the importance of independent media and independent Hip Hop. . .

Manny Faces: And you love independent media. And I love independent Hip Hop. So it's beautiful. . .

Rashed Mian: A perfect marriage. But also, in independent media you're not supposed to be biased, but you're able to empathize. We're able to empathize with people and the issues that they're suffering from.

We mentioned the verse from Silent Knight, but also the verse from our other artist-in-residence LiKWUiD in the *me too, behind bars* episode. People might not have had these experiences. But the artists are able to empathize and connect in a way that delivers a searing performance. It speaks to the power of the art form. It also speaks to the power of independent media. So marrying those two elements together, to us is a no-brainer. Some people might not understand it, but like you said, when people say, "Where's the protest music?" just take 20–25 minutes and listen [to one of our episodes] and you'll hear those sounds. It may not be *protest*, but they are explaining to people. They are portraying what's happening in the real world, what's happening in the streets.

Manny Faces: Yes, shouts to our other artist-in-residence, LiKWUiD. She is an artist educator, a fantastic artist in her own right. She's a DJ. She's done a lot of music over the years. South Carolina and New York City.

That episode is called Abused and Alone: Prison Rape in the #MeToo Era.[10] And a warning that this can be triggering with sexual abuse topics.

We heard about Mc Too all over the place, everywhere in the news. And we never heard about *this*. It was so eye-opening to go through this process of constructing this episode and realizing that of course there's a problem of sexual abuse with women behind bars. Positions of authority, the whole dynamic. And everyone's like, "Hey. We're taking it down... But not for them."

And you guys brought it to the forefront with this episode. You recognized this issue existed and needed to be delved into, and we put it together in an incredibly compelling manner.

We often talk about how we get coverage out ahead of the mainstream. But by the time we get to put something together with our little scrappy group, mainstream media [finally gets to it], either right around the same time as us, or sometimes after us, but they get all the acclaim. Like, *The New York Times* put out a thing on redlining and climate change, and we did that already!

But *this* topic, I have yet to hear it covered as strongly and as effectively and as compelling as we did, and that's in a very large part to LiKWUiD, who contributed to this.

I want to play a clip for the people. Again, a little bit of a triggering situation, but handled tastefully and incredibly.

[Audio clip from "Abused and Alone: Prison Rape in the #MeToo Era"]

LIKWUID: [RAPPING]
I called for the guard...
I called for the guard, he looked back...

Our eye contact
was confirmation I was going where I can't come back
Even after the scars heal, my mental often relapse
He looked away and said nothing while they circled to attack
The first punch was blatant
My first sight of blood I almost fainted
Ingested by fear, regurgitated
I protested. This was worse than being arrested
He orchestrated the attack to flex the domination
I'd rather die than have my body invaded
Rob my house, bank account, but not this type of invasion
God help me. . .
God left the room. . .
I see the devil in the corner handing her a broom
What would you do?
I'm fighting for dear life, taking one of them with me
And if I gotta die tonight I'll make sure she won't forget me
The screams are silencing
It's like the embodiment of suffocating and never dying
While they're breathing free oxygen
Why you lie to me?
I'm supposed to pay my debt to society
The crime and punishment have no equality
Uncle Sam's gavel. . . to Billy Club Bill,
'posed to be a badge of honor, it's a license to kill
I'm still alive though a part of me arguably died inside though
But I survived, yo, now I'm letting everybody know
I'ma tell it, I'ma belt it while there's breath in my lungs
'Til every peak and valley felt it
Every woman, boy and girl that had their innocence stolen
You're not invisible
You're invincible
And now you know it
If no one noticed
It's not your fault.
We gonna point these monsters out till they all get caught

Manny Faces: Once again, the great LiKWUiD.

Rashed Mian: Soul crushing. When you hear the verse. . . I can't believe how she pulled it off. I have no idea how, but it speaks to the entire issue that we were trying to publish on this episode. We were trying to tell people not only that these horrific atrocities occur in jails and prisons throughout this country, but what the people on that episode told us was that these women are saying "me too" behind bars too. They want the movement to recognize them, and they're suffering.

Manny Faces: Well, again, major shouts to LiKWUiD and Kathy Morse,[11] another voice in that episode...

Chris Twarowski: A survivor...

Manny Faces: Yeah. It's so compelling. I'm super proud of what we do. If it wasn't us, I'd be so proud to be talking to us. Again, not to pat ourselves, but I think we're doing it the right way. We're incorporating not only the voices of those who are going through the issues and those who know the issues really well, but our artists' diverse voices also.

[In fact,] half of our episodes [feature] only women [guests]. And [as for] our artists...

Look. We often joke, "Look at us. We're two and a half white guys..." We know we can't be the voices of this thing, and we don't wanna be. Listeners don't even hear your voices interviewing the people. It's about [the guests'] voices.

So when you hear people say, "We've got to raise up underrepresented voices"... We've been doing that since 2017.

This isn't always the most sexy or lucrative. This is down and dirty journalism. This is stuff that's not flashy, but it's flashy. You know what I mean? Like, it's not cable news. It's not *talking heads* news. It's real work here, and it's not easy to do.

We have a few pillar pages of content on our website, themed collections of some of the episodes that we've done. They include our mass incarceration series, our guide to civil unrest which culminates with the great, award-winning episode of "Why We Riot," which features Silent Knight and original *music*, not just beats, by The Band Called FUSE,[12] a real band with instruments and everything that created that soundtrack.

This [episode] showed that we not only could take on evergreen topics or wide systemic racism, mass incarceration, and political topics, but also tackle things of the moment.

Can you guys explain how we handled covering social justice issues during the time of [COVID-19]

Rashed Mian: I think it was just a natural fit for us. We were covering this already. We were covering poverty. We spoke to the United Nations' special rapporteur on an episode.[13] We obviously had been covering mass incarceration and the criminal justice system. And then [COVID-19] hits and unfortunately, as tragic as this sounds, it's not surprising that communities of color were hit disproportionately by the pandemic.

So we already had some of these sources lined up and we were able to cover this issue as it should be covered, that [COVID-19] was a threat to a lot of communities that are already suffering from poverty, from the scourge of mass incarceration, from all these other issues, from disenfranchisement, from being marginalized. We were able to cover it from that point of view.[14]

The first episode we did on COVID-19 spoke to that. We called it "When Epidemics Collide: Coronavirus, Criminal Justice, and Poverty."[15] All these issues just came to a head at once.

You could yell about your 401ks or the stock market all you want but that's not the real America. The majority of Americans don't have 401ks, or a significant savings. So it showed what's really happening in this country.

Chris Twarowski: Yeah, you had people complaining about not being able to get a freaking haircut. Meanwhile, let's look at COVID and prisoners. You know, the U.S. is the world's largest prison state, 2.3 million people are incarcerated. What's gonna happen in there? So that's where we turn the focus. We try to think of who's not being represented, who's being affected the most, who's not gonna make it to the mainstream ten o'clock news. And what you find, unfortunately, is this continuation of inequality and horrors.

Manny Faces: We released "When Epidemics Collide" on March 24, [2020]. Think about that. March 24th. When you look at the timeline of all the coverage, all the explosiveness of the COVID-19 coronavirus pandemic, its effects on United States, when did you start hearing about how it was affecting those already underserved communities? We were *early* on this. We have always been ahead of the curve, and I just wanted to point that out.

We followed that up in April with "Coronavirus Behind Bars: Crisis in New York,"[16] and then a follow-up two days later, "Coronavirus Behind Bars: Florida Jails and Effects of Visitation Bans."

We were talking about the explosive potential of [COVID-19] in jails and prisons back in March. Dr. Homer Venters was a guest, he's the former head of the New York City Health Department and the jail system in New York City, Rikers Island, etc. We had a bonus episode where Dr. Venters said, "This is gonna be a problem in jails and prisons. Nobody's doing anything about it, but it's gonna be a problem!"[17]

Rashed Mian: Yeah, he called it, "a looming and perilous threat."

Manny Faces: "A looming and perilous threat," according to Dr. Venters, who you could hear on the *News Beat* podcast—the podcast that won all these awards that got a bunch of rappers in it, I might remind you. A Hip Hop-oriented, social justice news podcast with rappers—rappity ass rappers too, rappers that can rap!

Dr. Homer Venters told us beware of this. And then what happens?

Rashed Mian: There were some jails and prisons that decided to release some prisoners who were extremely vulnerable or people we don't really need to lock up anymore. It took a pandemic for them to realize that people who are aging or seniors or who aren't a threat to the community, could be released. But unfortunately, as we reported, cases of coronavirus behind bars spiked over the summer. As we document from one of the researchers at the Prison Policy Initiative,[18] a lot of the laws that were being passed or things they were doing to limit people behind bars in March and April and May, a lot of these jails and prisons throughout the country neglected all that over the summer.

So during one week in August, according to The Marshall Project, cases spiked to 8,000 inside these facilities.[19] And *The New York Times* has consistently reported that among the top so-called "clusters" of coronavirus in the country, the far majority are jails and prisons.[20] I think that as of last week, 23 out of the top 25 were jails and prisons.

Manny Faces: I often say I wish we didn't have to do this podcast. I think we're great at it. It's an award-winning podcast for God's sake. But these are all issues we wish we didn't have to cover.

Silent Knight said it's heavy for him. It's heavy for artists, especially when you're an artist of color who's going through all of these things, and then having to write about them and contextualize them and put them in verse form.

Shouts to our other contributing artists, by the way, a plethora of geniuses in my estimation. Shouts to Napoleon Da Legend who's contributed to a couple of episodes, just an incredibly prolific brilliant artist. Shouts to Osyris Anthem, the End of the Weak[21] world champion, a brilliant freestyle artist, a brilliant mind. Shouts to Rabbi Darkside [now known as Sam Sellers] who's contributed. Shouts again to Rebel Diaz and Cruz Control from El Salvador. They combined on an episode about the origins of MS-13 and how the United States government created the gang that they want to make seem like the boogeyman.[22] So, we actually brought in a Salvadoran artist to make sure that that happened.

Chris Twarowski: We had Intikana...

Manny Faces: Intikana! You gotta listen to the [Puerto Rico: A U.S. Colony] episode.[23] Intikana did his thing, but the whole episode is so insightful about how the United States has treated Puerto Rico for all these years. One of our best episodes as well.

Rashed Mian: We also had Kayem...

Manny Faces: Kayem, one of our OGs. Kayem's "Hijacking Jihad" episode,[24] which is a fantastic look at how language is used to fearmonger. Another award-winning episode, the Religious News Association gave us an award for that episode. Just a ridiculous roster of artists.

My long time in journalism work and independent Hip Hop has put me in touch with so many brilliant people. I've been screaming it from the rooftops for years, there is brilliance in Hip Hop. I don't know what people are talking about when they say Hip Hop is only what you see on the radio. You ain't looking. You're not looking hard. But I know [who they are]. And we're gonna bring them in and get them paid and they're gonna make these incredible episodes.

Rashed Mian: I got infuriated the other day—not infuriated because it's good that these things are being covered—but I got my weekend edition of *The New York Times* last weekend, and I saw the splashy headline about redlining and how that's contributed to climate change and the horrific effects of heat, which kills more people than any other weather related event in this country. Nobody talks about it because, you know, you see a hurricane coming and you like to send reporters onto the beach so they could get waves crashing on them.

It's splashy coverage. But this is something that the *Times* is covering, I guess at that point it was late August. . .

We had covered it in March or April. . .

Manny Faces: . . .April 27th, "Redlining and Climate Change: A Deadly Combination."[25]

Rashed Mian: So, as you mentioned, we're trying to find these stories that are under the radar. And then eventually, they'll rise up, and you'll see some mainstream outlet cover it.

Manny Faces: Yeah. Look, I think the power of Hip Hop to affect change, to improve humanity and uplift society—which is what this show is all about—is *here*. It's here in the people that don't get the spotlight. I don't mind that Revolt TV[26] is having a political summit, and it has a lot of the important people involved on a celebrity tip, on an upper-level tip. That's important. Some of those messages get out to the masses, and that's important. Puffy's "Vote or Die" campaign, and Jay-Z and Meek Mill with the criminal justice Reform Alliance[27]. These things are important.

But just as powerful, just as important are the thousands, not millions, that listen to *News Beat*. The thousands, not millions, that follow artists like Tef Poe and Rebel Diaz and what Genesis Be is doing to change the state flag in Mississippi,[28] going on tour across the country to tell evangelicals that they shouldn't necessarily vote the way the rest of them are voting. That there's something wrong with that whole equation.

That right there, that grassroots stuff, is just as important because it's happening all over. It's just as important as what Lebron James is saying on his Twitter account. That's not unimportant, it's just different. So, I value the work we do, and that's why I love our artists because they are artist-activists.

Chris Twarowski: Rashed and I experienced this back in print. Many times, we would do a story and it would be crickets for a while, and then all of a sudden, *The New York Times* or *Newsday* [would print a story about it]. Same sources. Very similar, if not the *same* headline. And the way you gotta look at it is, that's great. Because the mission is to spark change. The mission is to get word out about these issues, to correct the problems, to hold people accountable. The fact that now, *The New York Times* finally got around to covering redlining a couple months after us, it's bittersweet. But you know what? It's actually a huge positive because in a way, maybe we forced them to. Who knows the genesis. . . But. . .

Manny Faces: Right, we put it out into the universe. . .

Chris Twarowski: Injecting this stuff into public discourse and into the eardrums of listeners, you never know what can happen. You never know what it could inspire.

Manny Faces: I wanna wrap up by saying that in the last couple of months since COVID, although we've been covering the crisis in a lot of really effective and compelling ways, we haven't necessarily been able to work with our artist friends as much. We're gonna try to start building that back up, but we have been able to still put out episodes. I want to call attention to one particular episode, "#SayHerName: Confronting 400 Years of State Violence Against Black Women."[29]

This was important to do even though we may not have had an artist at the ready. We are very cognizant of the communities that we are trying to represent or amplify the stories and narratives of. It had been a recurring theme that we weren't hearing as much about Breonna Taylor,[30] for example, as we were about George Floyd,[31] and some of that was chalked up to *social justice sexism.*[32] This has been a long-standing issue and because we pay attention to the people who are talking about these issues, we recognized it.

We put together some great voices who really broke down the historical tragedy of this long, long history of state violence against Black women. [Because] a lot of folks who weren't into this fight [for racial justice], who weren't part of these movements, rose up when they saw George Floyd—as well they should. [What we said was], "Don't sit back down. Stay up for Breonna Taylor!" And, unfortunately, the countless names of [other] women that have [also] been affected by state violence.

I'm very proud to say that when people weren't saying her name, we did.

So again, just informative, heart wrenching, and necessary to get into how history ties into the current day. And I'm conscious of all the talk about "Oh, you're capitalizing. You shouldn't be showing a lot of this stuff. You shouldn't be talking about this stuff. It's traumatic. . ." and I understand that. I think we all understand that. We talk to the people that deal with this a lot, for example, Andrea Ritchie[33] and Michelle Jacobs[34] on this particular episode, to make sure that we're talking about these issues in the right way.

So it is with extreme caution and extreme reverence that we cover these issues. We spread these messages, Chris as you said before, to try to incite change, to try to incite people doing something about it, not just feeling bad about it. Here are the organizations. Here are the legislators. Here's legislation that is being enacted to try and combat these things. That's our work. That's what we do.

Rashed Mian: And in a moment like this where we're screaming for racial justice and equality and to defund the police and other policies, we seem to underscore just how much the prison system has exploded over the last 40 years—500% since the 1970s. And during that time, from 1970 to 2014, women were the fastest growing population of incarcerated people in this country. It went from 8,000 women in jail in 1970 to almost a 110,000 four decades later.[35] These are the kind of things that we're bringing up in this podcast, that there's a reason for all this.

The punitive sentences that were enacted during the war on drugs.. Law and order policies, something that we're again seeing during President Trump's campaign. . . The need to quash dissent and to be tough on crime. . . The reason we keep bringing this stuff up is because history repeats itself. We want people to be informed and understand the machinations and what creates these frameworks.

Chris Twarowski: Yeah. Rashed brings up numbness. Here's a time where, for months, everyone is stuck inside and watching the news or listening to the TV, and it can be numbing. This is another thing that we strive to remember here—these are living human beings behind these numbers. You hear a number like 2,300,000 people incarcerated. And you hear it again. You hear it 20, 40, 50 other times. But to both your points, in this particular episode, one of the things we did was look at the report that the African American Policy Forum created.[36] And what you'll find is a profile of, I think, 47 women and young girls whose lives were snuffed out.

You know, there's a point in the episode where Andrea Ritchie is sitting there and she looks up on a poster on her wall and says "I'm looking up at the names of over 100 black women and girls who have been slain, and they range in age from 5 years old to 94."

So, to both your points, listen to the episode and then do your best to learn more about these issues. Become involved, or just tell someone else.

We talked about the wrongfully convicted. You know, there's an estimate that 2–10% of that 2.3 million people behind bars never committed a crime. At the beginning of the "Exonerated and Broke" episode, we asked Alan Newton to try to convey what it was like being locked up in a cage for 21 years.

And his voice breaks. . .

There's so much emotion and so much torture and so much anguish and pain that he can't actually vocalize it.

Manny Faces: But you don't normally get that from an AP news story, let's just say. . .

Chris Twarowski: 100%. You know, we mentioned Andrea Ritchie when she's looking up at that wall. Well, Kathy Morse in the prison rape story was talking about how she would just lay in her bed and pray for death. Therein lies the truth in the words of the people who are experiencing it, and then amplified by the artists.

That's what we do.

I just wanna quote James Baldwin. He said something along the lines of the artist's role being to disrupt the peace.[37] So, thank you to everyone helping us and the artists that we feature on the episodes disrupt the peace.

Afterthoughts

Dangerous forces are reshaping the information age: Rampant misinformation spreads unchecked while people continue to lose the ability to distinguish fact from fiction. Traditional journalism has crumbled under funding cuts, replaced by a flood of unqualified voices posing as news sources. Meanwhile, digital platforms amplify false narratives at unprecedented speed and scale. Influencers, high-profile celebrities, and other elevated presences have the power to sway the general public in new and powerful ways.

Efforts to counter these seismic shifts in the information landscape face constant attack from shadowy operatives and organizations, puppeteers of an insidious, well-planned assault on the fourth estate, backed by billionaires, foreign states, and other dark money sources. The rapid growth of artificial intelligence technology and the empowerment of political forces who use these and other troubling tactics to their advantage will no doubt add to the discrediting, squelching, or undermining of efforts to correct, improve, or add balance to this new journalism reality.

Despite all my bias and pride, *News Beat* in and of itself is not a remedy. I do believe, however, that it represents the type of radical thinking that must be applied when seeking to design quality, informative, educational, and inspirational news gathering and delivery outlets.

In our case, it's more than just incorporating original rap lyrics. It's everything else as well: the musical underbelly, the absence of reporters' voices, the subject matter, the nod to solutions journalism.[38] We're not just sprinkling Hip Hop into an existing format; we see this as just one example of what a reinvention of news can look and sound like. The entirety of the format is the real innovation.

While we do incorporate Hip Hop elements, it's the Hip Hop way of thinking which truly powers this project. Taking heed to what Dr. Ladson-Billings implored us about education, we don't want the news to *use* Hip Hop; we want the news to *be* Hip Hop,[39] and as with everything else we've touched on, that often has very little to do with the music business or celebrity. It has to do with Dr. Anthony Kwame Harrison and Craig E. Arthur describe as a "Hip Hop ethos,"[40] or what Dr. Toby Jenkins refers to as a "Hip Hop mindset"[41]—a way of thinking that can be applied to any field or discipline, without necessarily including actual elements of Hip Hop arts.

Small businesses can find advertising inspiration from guerrilla marketing tactics developed or perfected by creative Hip Hop entrepreneurs.[42]

A politician might learn from culturally relevant pedagogical approaches championed by Hip Hop-based education advocates to better relate to constituents from diverse demographic backgrounds. Organizations across sectors can benefit from creative, Hip Hop-inspired approaches to cross-cultural understanding and conflict transformation. News outlets can be inspired to experiment with compelling format mashups that can reach and impact audiences in powerful ways, in a rapidly changing information ecosystem that tends to favor short-form content and social media.

These applications need not directly incorporate Hip Hop itself; rather, it is that Hip Hop mindset that can uniquely catalyze compelling reimaginations to provide newfound innovation to nearly any business, organization, movement, or discipline—provided they are open to the concept and willing to hire and empower individuals who inherently understand these principles.

And therein lies the ultimate promise of the thesis of this book, and the inspiration for the next steps if Hip Hop is indeed going to help "save" America: The catalyst to improving society through Hip Hop isn't about the output, it's about the approach. The vehicle could very well include rap music. But it doesn't have to. It could be gaming. It could be sports. It could be religion. It could be other genres of music. It goes back to Grandmaster Caz's foundational quote, that Hip Hop didn't invent anything, but it reinvented everything.[43]

This includes reinvention itself.

First, it was the music, the dance, and the visual arts. Then it was the distribution of those elements. Then it became fashion. Then it was language. Advertising and marketing. The music business as a whole. TV. Movies. Broadway. Education. Healthcare. Technology. Diplomacy. Politics. Journalism. All of these fields and disciplines expanded in some way by the direct incorporation of Hip Hop music and culture. Opportunities for economic advancement and the improvement of lives, livelihoods, and communities have emerged from these reinventions, like the ones we've been exploring in this book. They need to be advocated for, strengthened, expanded, and be prepared for the fight when certain powers that be realize their effectiveness at equaling historically unequal playing fields.

For Hip Hop to combat that, it will need to do more than just innovate in the ways we've examined so far; creatively and authentically incorporating its artistic output into existing systems to create new outcomes.

Hip Hop needs to fuel the invention of new systems.

With this in mind, it's fitting to end this initial exploration about Hip Hop as a catalyst for change in America on a chapter about media, perhaps the most influential system of the modern age.

Over the past decade or so, the 24-hour cable news cycle, celebrity and gossip outlets, reality TV, and internet technology have all helped transform our media landscape into a chaotic hybrid of information mixed with entertainment. Hip Hop journalism, as with any subgenre of journalism, was largely insular. But in ways that are just starting to be noticed by mainstream America, Hip Hop journalism has started taking on a more prominent role in what is largely a clickbait and shock-led media ecosystem. From celebrity voices to news-wrapped-in-entertainment aesthetics, Hip Hop culture has attempted to bring its own unique voice and perspective into the public media zeitgeist, though many would argue it leaves as much, if not more to be desired than the rest of modern media.

A deeper look suggests an even more insidious side effect of Hip Hop not having entered into the field with a plan. I have argued, for example, that proponents of right-wing extremist ideologies have done a better job than others at recognizing the power of Hip Hop culture to inform and inspire, and are using that power in purposefully deceptive ways, seeding Hip Hop's cultural hubs with custom-tailored forms of misinformation and artificially built-up influence, much as they have across traditional and social media, creating digital pathways directly to Hip Hop's multicultural and multigenerational audiences in coordinated efforts to push divisive and conflicting propaganda.[44]

We live in a world where "truth" has become amorphous. Though perhaps it always has been. While some lament the loss of a time when "the news could be trusted," it never really could. Sure, there are outlets that endeavored to be truly fair and balanced, and those still exist. But no one source can ever be fully unbiased. Even within those outlets, implicit bias, fear of a loss of funding, or simply having to omit some stories from being covered despite good intentions means that no single entity can be a journalistic paragon.

Remember NPR's Hip Hop transgressions I outlined in the introduction to this book?

But quality reporting, solutions-based journalism, and yes, the truth—as much as it can be so—and an informed society remain vitally important to prevent further devolution into full-blown idiocracy.

News Beat isn't a savior. It is, however, just one of the many ways that Hip Hop can inspire a new way to flip the page, turn the channel, or click away from an ineffective and corrupted status quo, and encourage new innovations, new inventions, new solutions, and new disruptions of systems to help counter a rapidly (d)evolving age of (dis)information and all of the ill effects on society that come with it.

Key Takeaways

1. *News Beat* uniquely combines in-depth journalism on social justice issues with original Hip Hop musical and lyrical contributions.
2. The podcast often covers stories ahead of mainstream media outlets, providing early insight into important social issues.
3. *News Beat* aims to amplify underrepresented voices and perspectives, including those of activists, experts, and people directly affected by injustices.
4. The podcast demonstrates how Hip Hop artists can contribute to journalism through their lyrical storytelling and ability to empathize with subjects.
5. *News Beat* has won several awards for journalism, winning over major media outlets.
6. The podcast covers a wide range of social justice topics, including mass incarceration, racial inequality, and the impact of COVID-19 on marginalized communities.
7. *News Beat* provides resources and information for listeners to take action on the issues covered.
8. The podcast showcases how independent media and independent Hip Hop can work together to create impactful content.
9. *News Beat* often presents lesser-known aspects of historical figures and events, providing a more comprehensive understanding.
10. The podcast demonstrates the power of combining factual reporting with artistic expression to create emotionally resonant and informative content.

Discussion Questions

1. How might traditional news organizations incorporate elements of artistic expression, like Hip Hop, to enhance their reporting on complex social issues?

2. In what ways could the *News Beat* model of combining journalism and music be adapted for other forms of media, such as video or interactive digital content?

3. How can educators use podcasts like *News Beat* to teach students about current events and social justice issues in a more engaging way?

4. What potential benefits and challenges might arise from incorporating artists into the journalistic process in other fields, such as science communication or business reporting?

5. How could the *News Beat* approach of amplifying underrepresented voices be applied to other forms of storytelling or content creation in various industries?

6. In what ways might other non-media organizations, such as non-profits or government agencies, use a similar model to communicate their messages more effectively?

7. How can journalists and artists collaborate more effectively to create content that is both informative and emotionally impactful?

8. What ethical considerations should be taken into account when blending journalism with artistic expression?

9. How might the *News Beat* model be adapted for local news coverage to increase community engagement and understanding of local issues?

10. In what ways could other creative disciplines, beyond Hip Hop, be integrated into journalism to reach different audiences or cover different types of stories?

This podcast episode was originally released on September 11, 2020.

Notes

1 A professional organization founded in 1948 that promotes journalistic excellence and connects media professionals in New York City.

2 Tariq Trotter (Black Thought) is the lead MC of The Roots, renowned for his sophisticated lyricism.

3 A 2013 military trial at Fort Meade where Army analyst Chelsea Manning was sentenced to 35 years (later commuted) for leaking classified documents to WikiLeaks.

4 As Dr. King told news correspondent Sander Vanocur during a 1967 television interview on NBC.

5 Wrongfully convicted in New York in 1984, Alan Newton spent 22 years imprisoned before DNA evidence led to his 2006 exoneration.

6 A nonprofit legal organization founded in 1992 that advocates for the use of DNA evidence to exonerate wrongfully convicted people and advocates for criminal justice reform.

7 Five men who were wrongfully convicted as teenagers in the 1989 Central Park jogger case, imprisoned for years before being exonerated by DNA evidence in 2002.

8 A reloadable fare card used to access New York City's subway and bus system, replacing metallic coin tokens in 1993.

9 A pioneering Native American photographer who has documented Hip Hop culture and its artists since the 1970s, creating one of the genre's most important visual archives.

10 Beat, N. (2014). *Abused & alone: Prison rape in the #MeToo Era | News Beat Podcast.* Usnewsbeat.com. https://www.usnewsbeat.com/abused-and-alone

11 Kathy Morse was featured in Bill Moyers' Emmy Award-winning 2016 documentary *Rikers: An American Jail,"* which exposed conditions at New York's notorious Rikers Island prison complex.

12 The musical group Fuse occasionally composes music for the *News Beat* podcast. One of their collaborations, the episode titled "Why We Riot," earned the New York Press Club 2018 Best Podcast Award.

13 Beat, N. (2018). *Land of the rich, home of the poor | News Beat Podcast Episode.* Usnewsbeat. com. https://www.usnewsbeat.com/land-of-the-rich-home-of-the-poor

14 Beat, N. (2024). *COVID-19: Coronavirus through a social justice lens.* Usnewsbeat.com. https://www.usnewsbeat.com/covid19

15 Beat, N. (2016). *When epidemics collide: Coronavirus, criminal justice & poverty.* Usnewsbeat. com. https://www.usnewsbeat.com/epidemics-collide-coronavirus-criminal-justice-poverty

16 Beat, N. (2019). *Coronavirus behind bars: Crisis in New York.* Usnewsbeat.com. https://www. usnewsbeat.com/coronavirus-behind-bars-crisis-in-new-york

17 Beat, N. (2020). *Expert warns of "Perilous" Coronavirus threat in jails & prisons [Podcast].* Usnewsbeat.com. https://www.usnewsbeat.com/blog/expert-warns-of-perilous-coronavirus-threat-in-jails-prisons-podcast

18 A research organization that produces data and analysis about mass incarceration and prison policy in the United States to inform reform efforts.

19 Beat, N. (2020). *Death Sentence: COVID-19 Cases are soaring in jails & prisons.* Usnewsbeat. com. https://www.usnewsbeat.com/death-sentence-covid-19-cases-are-soaring-in-jails-prisons

20 Williams, T., Seline, L., & Griesbach, R. (2020, June 16). *Coronavirus cases rise sharply in prisons even as they plateau nationwide.* Nytimes.com; *The New York Times.* https://www.nyti mes.com/2020/06/16/us/coronavirus-inmates-prisons-jails.html

21 A long-running Hip Hop event series which began in New York City and spawned several iterations throughout the world.

22 Beat, N. (2018). *MS-13: Made in the USA | News Beat Podcast Episode.* Usnewsbeat.com. https://www.usnewsbeat.com/ms-13

23 Beat, N. (2017). *The truth about Puerto Rico: A US Colony | News Beat Podcast Episode.* Usnewsbeat.com. https://www.usnewsbeat.com/the-truth-about-puerto-rico

24 Beat, N. (2014). *Hijacking Jihad | News Beat Podcast Episode.* Usnewsbeat.com. https:// www.usnewsbeat.com/hijacking-jihad

25 Beat, N. (2017). *Redlining & climate change: A deadly combination.* Usnewsbeat.com. https://www.usnewsbeat.com/redlining-climate-change-a-deadly-combination

26 A media network that produces Hip Hop and urban culture content across TV and digital platforms.

27 A criminal justice reform organization launched in 2019 that focuses on transforming probation and parole systems.

28 *Rapper Genesis Be's long battle versus the Confederate flag.* (2020, September 8). AP News. https://apnews.com/article/us-news-ap-top-news-mississippi-ms-state-wire-weekend-reads-7f3ddc1a40c02f6e4c58c78b9ef641ea

29 Beat, N. (2020). *SayHerName: Confronting 400 years of state violence against Black Women.* Usnewsbeat.com. https://www.usnewsbeat.com/police-violence-black-women

30 A 26-year-old Black emergency medical technician killed by Louisville, Kentucky police during a botched raid on her apartment in March 2020.

31 A Black man murdered by Minneapolis, Minnesota police in May 2020, whose death sparked worldwide protests against racial injustice and police violence.

32 Kemmerer, L. (2023). The "Why" of sexism in social justice movements. In: *Oppressive liberation.* Cham: Palgrave Macmillan. https://doi.org/10.1007/978-3-031-15363-1_4

33 A lawyer-activist and author whose research and advocacy address police violence against women of color and LGBTQ+ people.

34 A University of Florida law professor whose scholarship examines racial and gender bias in criminal law and justice system responses.

35 *Overlooked: Women and Jails in an Era of Reform.* (2018, July 7). Vera Institute of Justice. https://www.vera.org/publications/overlooked-women-and-jails-report

36 *SAY HER NAME | AAPF.* (2015). AAPF. https://www.aapf.org/sayhername

37 *James Baldwin discusses his book, "Nobody knows my name: More notes of a native son".* The WFMT Studs Terkel Radio Archive. https://studsterkel.wfmt.com/programs/james-baldwin-discusses-his-book-nobody-knows-my-name-more-notes-native-son

38 A news reporting practice that investigates and explains effective responses to social problems rather than solely focusing on issues and conflicts.

39 As Dr. Gloria Ladson-Billings explained in Chapter Six.

40 Harrison, A. K., & Arthur, C. E. (2019). Hip-Hop Ethos. *Humanities,* 8(1), 39. https://doi.org/10.3390/h8010039

41 Jenkins, T. S., & Kimbrough, W. M. (2023). *The hip-hop mindset: Success strategies for educators and other professionals.* Teachers College Press.

42 Ideas that have been outlined in books such as *The Big Payback: The history of the business of Hip-Hop* (Charnas, D., & Free, K. R. (2015), and *The Tanning of America: How Hip-Hop Created a Culture That Rewrote the Rules of the New Economy* (Stoute, S. (2011).

43 Curtis "Grandmaster Caz" Brown is a pioneering South Bronx Hip Hop artist from the 1970s, known for his innovative rhyming style, role in the Cold Crush Brothers, and for writing lyrics used in "Rapper's Delight."

44 Manny Faces. (2023, April 13). *The far right infiltration of Hip Hop.* Substack.com; Hip Hop Can Save America! https://mannyfaces.substack.com/p/the-far-right-infiltration-of-hip

· 1 3 ·

(OUTRODUCTION)
THE ADVOCATE | MANNY FACES

I almost decided against an epilogue of any sort. What more could be said than what the guests we've heard from have already said so eloquently? If there was a case to be made, I would hope that their collective voices—and perhaps some of my added commentary—would be all we need to inspire us to take whatever next steps we each personally feel we need to take to apply what we now know to the greater good.

I did, however, think it would be interesting—as this is essentially a book full of interviews—to be interviewed as to why this book even exists. It felt like a Hip Hop, flip it, remix it thing to do.

So, in lieu of anything overly crafted, I asked my *News Beat* colleagues to turn the tables on me, and hit me with their best journalistic shot, to help me wrap up this leg of my journey.

For readers, I thank you for the time and attention that you have given this book, and, if you remain interested, this last interview. It has been an honor to share these stories, ideas, and hopes with you all, and I look forward to what I'll be able to share about the next chapters of my journey.

Pun intended.

The Interview

Manny Faces: This is funny, like, you having to take me seriously. Like, I'm a real person.

Rashed Mian: Well, I'm gonna take you seriously, but, like. . .

Manny Faces: No. That's fine. Like I said, it follows the *News Beat* chapter, so it's obvious we know each other.

Chris Twarowski: We'll just roll with it. I put in a couple little zingers in here.

Manny Faces: Whatever happens, happens. I'm not afraid of y'all.

Chris Twarowski: You ready?

Manny Faces: Let's go.

Chris Twarowski: Alright. So here we are at the back of the book. . . I just wanted to start with that because I think it'd be cool to see that in print at the back of the book.

Manny Faces: It'll be at the back of the book. That's where it'll be.

Chris Twarowski: So, you've published a magazine about Hip Hop. You founded and you run a nonprofit about Hip Hop. You still perform Hip Hop. You participate in long-running cyphers and shows. You've mentored and championed Hip Hop artists. You do a podcast about Hip Hop, and it's, dare I say, transcendentalism. You host and produce *News Beat*[1] which features Hip Hop. Shameless plug for everybody to subscribe—go to usnewsbeat.com.

Manny Faces: Let's go!

Chris Twarowski: You literally travel the world preaching and sharing and championing all the incredible yet perhaps lesser known applications of Hip Hop. We can go on and on here, man. But, again, here we are in the final pages of this new project, your first book about Hip Hop. So let's start with that.

Tell us about your inspiration for this book, your hopes for it, and why you feel it's important specifically for folks who perhaps aren't as familiar with Hip

Hop or may not perceive it as anything more than a musical genre and one that, as you talk about in the book, gets smeared a lot.

Manny Faces: Yeah. And thank you guys for doing this. The inspiration for the book was to provide another outlet for the conversations that I've been having over the course of producing the podcast, but also to include some of the insights that I've gleaned after those conversations happened, and after conversation with other folks. There are 12 interviews in this book, but the podcast now has over 100 episodes. So there are some lessons that were gleaned from some of the foundational interviews that I included, that were expanded upon in the years since those interviews happened.

I wanted to take folks on the journey that I went on as I was discovering the work that these folks are doing and share my revelations as they came to me, really in the order of when I started talking to these folks for the show. I knew these types of things were happening, but once I started exploring them in detail, my eyes were opened even more to these ideas, these intersections and their effectiveness and, to be honest, the radical application of Hip Hop.

I find it fascinating. I also find it important to tell these stories because if you look at the media landscape—be it mainstream media, Hip Hop's own media, and hybrids of the two—you don't hear about these things. But these things are not new. They're not theoretical. Hip Hop-based education—one of the core elements explored in the book—has been around for years. There are publications. There are books. There's research. There are minor and major programs in universities. There are archives. So it's not like this is new, but it seems to be new information to many people I come across, even those attached to Hip Hop.

So for all of the reasons that storytellers tell stories or that journalists spread the word about important, untold stories—as we do with News Beat—I wanted to amplify the work of these amazing people.

You asked what I hope to get out of this entire process. It's very inspirational for people in these particular fields—education, mental health therapy, teaching artists, international diplomacy, journalism, all the things I touched upon in this book—but also every other possible field or discipline. If people look at their field of discipline the way that folks looked at these disciplines to create new, inspiring, innovative, and uplifting ways to integrate Hip Hop into them, then maybe we can expand into different areas and some of these positive results become reality across the board.

A lot of these folks are so busy doing the work. We learned this doing *News Beat*. We're so busy doing the work that we don't have the time, or very often, the resources or the bandwidth to market ourselves, to put our work out there. We just do good work, but it needs to be amplified.

And I learned that, as a journalist being tutored by you guys through the years, that's our job. We have to tell the stories and we have to let people know that these things are happening so that more of it can happen and more positive impact can be felt.

Chris Twarowski: Love it.

Rashed Mian: You talk about the limitless applications of Hip Hop throughout the book and these interviews. Anyone reading this book will now be familiar with Dr. Bettina Love. There was something sort of striking right there just in the first chapter where she said, "Hip Hop doesn't just come out of any-where." That sort of smacked me right there because it speaks to the core of everything that you've discussed over the course of your career covering Hip Hop, writing about it, and trying to, like you said, amplify the work and the meaning behind it. When she said those words, what was your reaction? And did that speak to everything that you've been accumulating in your head over the years about the way people can approach Hip Hop in terms of different applications, regardless of what platform, what industry, or what setting?

Manny Faces: Yeah. So, two things come out of that train of thought. You know, very often there's a mantra ascribed to Hip Hop that a lot of people, even casual observers might have heard that says Hip Hop "made something out of nothing." Right? You talk about the origins of Hip Hop, you look at the socioeconomic conditions of New York City in the early 1970s and where it all emerged from. But it wasn't a "big bang." It wasn't a spontaneous com-bustion. So when people say Hip Hop was "something out of nothing," I get what they mean because it was so rundown and under-resourced, with horrible conditions ongoing in that area. But the people were not *nothing*. [What came before them was not *nothing*.] So I always like to say that Hip Hop made some-thing out of *something*. Or that Hip Hop made something out of *everything*.

And I think that's what Dr. Love was getting at. Whereas, if you look at Hip Hop, it wasn't, again, a big bang, but a coalescing of decades—centuries—of influences that all kind of crashed together to make something new.

And from when all these elements started really coming together and then becoming mainstream, we're talking about less than 10 years. But it all came from what preceded it. And as Dr. Love says, Black and brown folk in the seventies in New York City, with these multicultural influences and musical influences from decades prior. You had James Brown. You had The Last Poets doing spoken word. You had the Black Power movement. You had the Civil Rights movement. You had a mixture of Latino culture in New York City. You had Black culture from down South, descendants of enslaved people, and also more recent immigrants from the Caribbean. What they would call a melting pot or what some might call a potluck, where everyone was bringing something to the table. [All under] conditions that helped sparked the creativity as we know it.

And what Hip Hop does really well is that it doesn't forget its core. And we're not talking about what commercialized bastardizations may have happened over time. But at the core of Hip Hop, it remembers it all. It's in its DNA. It's created a new timeline, but it's remembering all of the influences that that brought it to life.

As Grandmaster Caz, pioneering member of the Cold Crush Brothers says in *The Art of Rap* documentary, "Hip Hop didn't *invent* anything, but Hip Hop *reinvented* everything."[2] And that's where you see from that day forward, Hip Hop's influence taking everything that came before it and influencing everything that came after it. *Everything.*

I just gave a whole book full of examples, but I'll give one that I don't think that was touched upon—which someone pointed out to me and I wish I remembered who so I could attribute it, please reach out. But you know on Spotify, you can play a playlist and you can have it set so one song fades into the other so that it doesn't just end and you're left waiting for a new song to begin? Like... That [essentially evolved from] Hip Hop! The crossfader. Bringing one song into the next. The mixing of music together. The blending of songs. That's Hip Hop. But it's now the standard, most basic function of a media product that we consume every day. And you don't think of those connections. There are thousands of those connections. And that's because Hip Hop really did remix everything.

Chris Twarowski: You mentioned influences. On a personal level, you mention your late father in this book. You cited him. And you saw this almost like a reconnection, right, or like a wraparound back to your pops. If you could just talk a little bit about that. I thought that was really important.

Manny Faces: Yeah. Thanks for that. I mentioned in the book, being the son of a sociology professor, you learn things and you see things a different way. He would talk to me about his work, and I was an inquisitive, loudmouth little boy that wanted to know things. I looked up to my dad. He had a big study with papers everywhere, and he was always typing and doing all the professor things. And so I would ask, "What are you working on?" And he would explain things to me. That's why I joke that I knew what gentrification meant when I was eight. You know? And it's funny because it's true.

And because he specialized in urban studies and sociology of minorities, he was looking at the ways that society is affected by or affects communities, largely communities of color. He also studied Italian immigrants and Korean neighborhoods, so he was very much a multicultural urban kind of guy. I guess I got a lot of knowledge by osmosis from him.

He was also a jazz and blues connoisseur, so he was a music head, and I got a lot of musical influences from him. So when I delved into the music world myself, we would have these spirited debates about the musicality of Hip Hop, like I talked about in the chapter with Jarritt Sheel. And at the time, it was just banter between me and my dad but he kinda knew where I was going with some of this, even though I hadn't yet gotten really deep into—essentially— the anthropological applications of Hip Hop.

So thinking of it now, I don't think that I would be doing any of this if it wasn't for an early understanding of how to look past surface level renditions or media coverage or opinions or perceptions. My dad was a scientist, and he said, "We're gonna look at the facts. We're gonna look at the data. We're gonna dig in. We're not gonna be misled by what you see on the surface." It's looking at Hip Hop in the same way that led me down this path. So I owe a lot to my dad, and I wish he was still around, obviously, to bounce these ideas off as I step into more academic spaces.

I'm not a traditional scholar. I didn't go to college. I don't have a degree. But I'm absolutely an independent scholar. I think it benefited me to have a little bit of foundational understanding from a professor dad, but also being immersed and engaged in the culture and the artforms associated with it... Then stumbling into journalism, finding y'all, working in that field for several years, and coalescing all of those experiences into what I do today.

I guess in a way, it all starts with my dad. The work I do and the book that I've written and anything that I'm gonna do until the day I die is to be like, "Hey, dad. What do you think?"

So, that's at the core of what I do. He was—I use the term *less familiar* with Hip Hop culture. He wasn't really close to it. He didn't understand it. He wouldn't have known it. There was there's no reason for him to know it. But he would've understood, he would have been open to it. And therefore, we could have had some kind of dialogue.

So that's what I'm doing. I'm having that dialogue in the work that I do. And I think that by doing that, I not only get it through to someone that was a sociologist and an anthropologist, but also makes it accessible to the general public because I don't always speak in academic speak. I don't speak in sociological jargon all the time. I don't rely on studies all the time. I also rely on oral histories and anecdotes and my own observations. So it's that combination, that hybrid of academic journalism that I'm using to, in my mind, basically explain what the hell I'm doing to my dad.

Rashed Mian: I bet there would be some good banter.

Manny Faces: I think so. I wish it was so.

Rashed Mian: That's beautiful. So now everybody who reads this is gonna have their own takeaway just as they had from listening to your podcast or anything else you've produced. What would you say to everyone who's picking this up in terms of how they themselves can weaponize these conversations that you've had.

Manny Faces: Well, there are a couple of ways. One is specific if you're an educator or are, generally speaking, a person that has authority or some form of control over young people. The big takeaway, the big throughline through this book which several guests and I alluded to in individual chapters, is that a big piece of this puzzle is respecting and connecting with young people and finding ways to do that through this evolving culture that we're now all old enough to have had some experience with. We may not totally understand how it's evolved with young people, but we should be better equipped to inter-act with young people if we want to use Hip Hop as common ground. And we've seen examples of that throughout this book.

When I say "Hip Hop can save America," what do we want that to mean? Is connecting with young people the way to save America? Well, you want younger people to have better education outcomes. You want young people to be better equipped in terms of their mental health and their wellness. You want young people to be innovative and inventive. And we've shown here that if you approach young people in an educational setting or in a mental health setting or in an after-school program setting like some of the examples in the book, you'll get better results. You'll just get better outcomes. Young people will be better prepared to face the world. They'll feel less shut down when they try to express their true selves. And as we talked about throughout, Hip Hop really does do some inventive and innovative stuff when given that opportunity.

And in *any* discipline, right? We talked about education and others in the book, but also business. I didn't get into business and entrepreneurship much in this book, but there are marketing tactics, advertising tactics, business development, sales... There are lessons to be learned from how Hip Hop would go against the grain and create new industries out of old industries or disrupt or circumvent systems to be able to create a new way of deliver-ing information or a new way of delivering products. The record company wouldn't give you an album deal, so you just made your own mixtapes. And then mixtapes become a multimillion-dollar industry. So we've seen examples of this across *all* of these industries. [The question is], can you apply this way of thinking to *your* field or discipline? And if you don't know how to do that, reach out to the people who do. There are people who will know how to make those connections.

The other thing is a little bit more abstract, although it's related. As I empha-sized since the introduction to the book, for most people hearing the concept for the first time, or seeing the title, *Hip Hop Can Save America!*, the first impulse is going to be to think of music. The genre. Hip Hop, rap music, the music business, whatever. Drake. Whatever your first thought is.

And as we've seen through this book and through our discussions, 95% of what we're talking about has nothing to do with the music business, or with celebrity. It has to do with two things: culture and mindset. What I think that Hip Hop really does, what I think Hip Hop's real power is, is not in its specific applications. Most of the innovations we've talked about in this book and examples I talk about are incorporations of Hip Hop with a thing, right? An existing industry, or an existing practice, and seeing if we can make that practice reach more people or be more accessible, or more enjoyable, or more effective by incorporating Hip Hop. And the answer is yes. Yes! A hundred times, yes!

But looking at society. . . You know that quote regarding insanity where you keep doing the same thing over and over again and expect a different result? What some of us are looking for are radical ideas. Radical thinkers and radical applications that haven't been explored as much. So when I really sit back and I say, "Yeah. We'll get better education results, and we'll get better employment opportunities because we've introduced young people to tech fields they might have been previously shut out of because their schools didn't have a computer science department, because they're under-resourced and undervalued, because they are communities of color. . ."

All of that is true. We can get better education results, better workforce results, better mental health. All those things, yes. But where this hasn't been fully explored yet is in public policy. In politics. In top level discussions at universities to change the *entire* way that they're approaching X, Y, and Z. And I just think that if you look at what Hip Hop has done to the industries that we've talked about [for inspiration], there's potential there that is still untapped and unexplored.

So my main goal here is to make it so that the first thing you think about when you hear "Hip Hop" isn't music. It's innovation. Inspiration. Communication. Collaboration. Revolution. To normalize the idea that if you are having a conversation about what can *really* be done to change something but you're not incorporating Hip Hop into that conversation, then you're not really trying.

Rashed Mian: Disruption.

Manny Faces: That's exactly right. Hip Hop is a world class disruptor. I quote KRS-One a couple of times, and one of his quotes regarding all the negative perception that Hip Hop gets essentially argues that if Hip Hop has the power to corrupt young minds, then it also has the power to uplift them. It's just how you apply that power. For good or for bad, it's powerful. It's global. You can't find a place in the world that Hip Hop doesn't exist and have some influence. So you see something so powerful—but also so misunderstood. The powers that be don't understand it. People trying to make real change in America don't always understand how to use the power of Hip Hop in this way. Celebrity endorsements are important, and that's fine. Or someone in a political camp says, "Let's get on *The Breakfast Club*—that's Hip Hop!"

Cool. All important. Also, not as impactful as one might think. But you know who's also Hip Hop? Rosa Clemente. Dr. Cornel West. You know what I mean? So, are you *really* incorporating "Hip Hop" into your mix? You're not. You're incorporating what you *think* Hip Hop is, and you're stuck on music, music business, and celebrity.

If you were to incorporate the wide-ranging breadth of what a Hip Hop inspired political movement looks like, well. . .

So, like I said, radical ideas. Radical thoughts. Application with this kind of intent that is often overlooked or misunderstood or misused.

Chris Twarowski: You're talking about the soul of it, basically.

Manny Faces: Right. The cautionary tale is that you can't do any of this willy nilly. You can't just say, "Oh, we're gonna bring Hip Hop to into the school and do a concert, and people are gonna wanna come to this school," and then you don't know what to do with it when you get it. I've talked about this with a few people in this book. That authenticity is important. The full understanding that this is a culture. This isn't a gimmick. Like Dr. Gloria Ladson-Billings says, she doesn't want teachers to *do* Hip Hop. She wants teachers to *be* Hip Hop. And the example of her professor friend who said, "I never played a Hip Hop song in all my life." And she told him, but you *are* Hip Hop because you're inventing courses that didn't exist before. You're remixing the curriculum. You're listening to your students and getting their input and giving a safe space. That's also Hip Hop. There are tenets within Hip Hop that if we follow in other areas of society, we're inviting open, radical, forward thinking.

That's what Hip Hop did. It was done out of necessity. It was done out of desperation. It was done for freedom. When you don't have anyone watching you in the streets of 1970s New York City, you just do whatever the hell you want. And out of that freedom came this wild creativity that's now become global. It has all these tenets that are interconnected and has inspired all of these innovations and inventions across multiple industries.

Why wouldn't we wanna tap into that?

Chris Twarowski: Love it. I wanna bring it back to you.

Manny Faces: I love talking about me!

Chris Twarowski: You mentioned it earlier, a "journey." So, as we were preparing for this, we started reflecting on you and your work, saw the book, in some ways, as a chronicling of your journey. Right? Professionally, but also personally. Can you talk about how these guests and all the different people you've met and interviewed and collaborated with, all your experiences, how they have served as guides for you and anyone interested in the multidimensional facets of Hip Hop.

Manny Faces: You know, the mark of a of a journalist is to be [objective], right? I learned a lot from the journalism aspect of my journey, again, a lot of credit to y'all. Hip Hop is filled with mythology and differing perspectives and differing histories and alternative facts along the way. It's a complex mixture of subcultures. It's a lot. And people generally have, if you're connected to it, a strong feeling about it.

My introduction to Hip Hop was like a lot of folks in the late 1980s. We were learning the music and then the fashion and the slang and the dance and we were trying to draw graffiti or do whatever was emerging. We got into the arts. We didn't think of it as a culture. Most people don't, right? Even those attached to it don't necessarily think about it until someone points it out to them. But the cultural aspect of it grew, the lifestyle, the ethos of Hip Hop, what it means to be Hip Hop. Again, as KRS-One said, "Rap is something you do, Hip Hop is something you live."[3] When that started becoming more

important, some of us would take heed to that and say, "You know, not everything is what it seems. What's the real story? What's the real background?
Who's really looking at it in this [objective] way?"

So, for me, the journey that I take in the book is very much the journey when
I started realizing, "Oh, there're educators!" "Oh, there're mental health professionals!" "Oh, there're teaching artists." "Oh, there're people that work at
legacy institutions." "Oh, there're people that are working in technology."
OK. Let me explore each one of these. But also understand that that even
in any one of those fields, there are differing opinions. There are differing
methodologies. There are different pedagogical approaches. There are a lot
of folks that do "Hip Hop therapy," but there are factions. There are people
who look at these things in different ways. So you have to look at it from this
journalistic point of view where there may not be one answer. Like Dr. Lauren
Kelly reminded us, people can't even agree on when the first recorded rap song
was. Was it Sugar Hill Gang, was it The Fatback Band? We can't even agree
on some of these interpretations. It's very interpretive.

So my journey, personally, played into that. I wanted to make sure that I'm not
making any assumptions. I'm walking into a space that—first of all, I occupy
a place of privilege. You have to take cultural care to make sure that you're
really respecting who you're dealing with—their histories, their perspectives.
And again, looking at it [objectively]. Understanding that and listening more
than I talk gave me the understanding that we're dealing with something
that is as complex as any other culture in America. We treat the study of any
nationality or any religion or any large group of people with respect and dignity and we honor their traditions and honor their backgrounds. If you speak
of Native Americans, you know that there's different tribes that have different
understandings, but they also have some commonality between them. And
few people outside of academics were looking at Hip Hop that way.

It started teaching me more about race and gender and what it means to be
a person of color in America, but also, like how Dr. Andrea Hunt and Mark
Katz's chapters point out, you don't have to necessarily be *from* those communities, but to properly understand them and have the right amount of empathy
and understanding and cultural awareness you have to step in with a certain
type of open-mindedness. And I arrived with that myself because, as far as I'm

concerned, Hip Hop is my culture. But there's that Venn diagram of cultures that affect Hip Hop, and so you have to do this dance.

And if you're doing that at every step, if you're always conscious of that and always being careful to apply those things... An academic lens... A journalism lens... And again, that cultural lens, knowing where I come from, where I fit into the mix personally, and looking through all those lenses at the same time, that became my guide.

And it was influenced by people like Dr. Love. Right out of the gate, I asked, "So, who are you?" And she goes, "Well, I'm a Black Queer woman in America." Like, that's the first thing that she says. I thought, "Oh, you're a professor. You do Hip Hop." No. Don't think that. Don't start with that. She doesn't start with that. And so it was, "OK. Heard."

You have to remember that the way people appear in the world, whether they want to or not, is part of their identity. What does that mean when Hip Hop enters the fold? What does that mean when Hip Hop is also part of your identity. So all of these machinations, these cultural, academic, and journalistic outcomes from these discussions, each one led me to the next to investigate a little bit further.

Like Dr. Ian Levy, second chapter. White guy. What's *his* relationship to Hip Hop? How does that differ from Dr. Love's? You know what I mean? Where are the similarities? Where are the cautionary tales? How does he approach things as a *practitioner* of Hip Hop culture? Then we go to Mikal Amin, who's a Black man and is *also* a practitioner. Now I'm starting to realize each one of these individuals, where they come from, their perspectives, their background, their histories, their way of seeing the world informs their Hip Hop identity.

And when you start looking at all of that, you see all these beautiful nuances and how Hip Hop is not monolithic. The application of Hip Hop is not monolithic. Just like people. Hip Hop can't have an identity. It can't have a politic. Right? It's an amalgamation. It's a remix. It's all of these things put together. And when you start realizing that people see Hip Hop differently and how they apply it in their lives is different and how some apply it in their industries is different, you start realizing that it's beautiful in its infiniteness. It's beautiful in its wide-ranging, mosaic of connectivity that is really worth following and studying and amplifying and uplifting.

The problem with people less familiar with Hip Hop as a cultural movement is that they make assumptions. It's prejudice and bias, like any other group of people might have to face. When you remove that or you really try to get to the nuances and the intricacies of it, then you start really showing what it's like to value people for their entire selves. Because being Black is hard enough to be in America. Then you throw some Hip Hop on top of that? You have to code switch. You have to put on a mask. You have to hide that part of you. And when you start realizing—even from the beginning of the book and in the first interview—that there is something majestic about being able to walk into a room as your true and complete self and not feel any kind of restrictions.

That's what Hip Hop gives people. That's why Hip Hop is universal across multiple cultures. That's why as a grown ass man I call myself Manny Faces. That's the persona that I have invented for myself. That's who I want to be.

Manny Faces is cooler than Michael Conforti. Mike's a great guy, a good dad. . . But Manny Faces? He's an artist. He's a creative. He's a radical thinker. He's an activist. Are they the same guy? Kinda. But I like having the ability to create a persona exactly how I want to appear to the world. It's not fake. It's not phony. I'm not being an actor. This is how I want you to see me, and Hip Hop gives everybody that.

Now, can everyone use Hip Hop like that in *the real world*? No. Because you're shunned for it.

This work shows that you shouldn't be.

Rashed Mian: So then, in your view, what's next for Hip Hop?

Manny Faces: I feel like Hip Hop has been desperately trying to outgrow its perception. We talk about Hip Hop being this genre and this music, this corporate controlled, vastly popular, influential, entertainment *product*, for lack of a better word. But we know that Hip Hop is being used in all these different ways. I'm a big proponent of changing how Hip Hop is perceived so that we don't just default to entertainment and music. Otherwise, we miss out on all of these innovations.

I'd love to see Hip Hop get elevated across the board. We see this in pockets. We see it in academic circles. We see it in some activism circles. So that's the work I do, to help get to those levels where these things are happening more often than not.

It's not new information. I laugh every time there's an article these days, decades after culturally relevant pedagogy and Hip Hop-based education came into the educational zeitgeist where some local news outlet will cover a teacher that's using Hip Hop in the classroom, and they'll say, "Students and parents are loving this *surprising* mix of Hip Hop and education." They're using the word "surprising" as if it's actually surprising. It's only surprising to people who have not been engulfed in this for the past 20 years. I'd love to see a day when it's not called "surprising." I'd love to see a day when it gets its due. It gets its respect for being an inventive, innovative, cultural, and social movement that can uplift humanity and improve society as much as it can entertain or as much as it does any of the things that you don't particularly like about it.

That's what movies do. Some movies are shitty, and people say they're terrible influence on society. But some movies are beautiful. And then there are documentaries! There are art house flicks. You don't say, "All movies suck." You recognize that, in its entirety, filmmaking is a powerful and worthy thing. I want Hip Hop to have that same level of respect. That would make it easier to do some of the things that these folks are trying to get done. It creates less friction, less hesitation.

I talked to Dr. Msia Kibona Clark and Dr. Roger Carruth on the podcast recently.[4] They're part of the team that pushed for and launched the Hip Hop minor program at Howard University. They said that because there are folks who really understand Hip Hop on the board of trustees, it was less of a challenge to get the program approved. Whereas five years ago, you might not have anybody from the Hip Hop generation or really connected to the culture on the board of trustees. I want it to be seen like Dr. A.D. Carson, professor of Hip Hop at The University of Virginia, whose dissertation was an album.[5] He gets a lot of accolades for that, and it made a lot of noise because it was "surprising." Well, it shouldn't be surprising anymore. There should be other people doing that. There's no reason why you can't transmit information through Hip Hop. Like we do at *News Beat*. It's journalism. It's not *a funky mix*... It's not like some gimmicky thing. It is viable journalism. We're talking about viable forms of education, viable forms of mental health therapy, viable forms of dissertation, viable forms of teaching all these trades, viable forms—which is really what I think is next for Hip Hop—viable forms of influencing political movements for the better. In ways that are of the people, by the people, for the people. Because if nothing else, in its core DNA, the tenants of Hip Hop are peace, unity, love, and having fun. If we could all just have peace, unity, love, and having fun, then we could be a great country. We'd *really* make America great. And there's only one social, cultural, and therefore potentially political movement that I know of that crosses all demographics and all borders, that welcomes in everybody regardless of race, creed, color, location, linguistics, and even ideology and says, "Yo. If you respect this thing we do, we can mess with you. Come in our world. Come and be here. We can do this together." There's only one thing that I know of—and I'm still waiting for someone to tell me another. The one I know about is Hip Hop.

So Hip Hop could save America. And I guess what's next would be that it can save the world. That would be the next logical step, wouldn't it?

Chris Twarowski: Boom.

Rashed Mian: So there you go. Let's save the world.

Manny Faces: Yeah. It's gonna start in America, just because that's where it has its roots. But I think that though we've exported Hip Hop to the world, you do see Hip Hop doing [different things globally]. It's influencing elections, there was a Hip Hop political party in Germany, [there are great cultural organizations around the world.] You see it happening a little bit differently. So just as we've exported Hip Hop to the world, we also need to reimport some of those things back here. That's some of the interplay that has to happen. But it'll start here.

Rashed Mian: Appreciate you, man.

Chris Twarowski: We appreciate you, and that was a mic drop, but I just wanna add one last thing. Your passion, your heart, your love for this shines through, in this book and the podcast and in all you do. So we give it up to you, man. We love you.

Manny Faces: I appreciate the appreciation.

Rashed Mian: Chris just wanted the last line in the transcript of the chapter.

[LAUGHTER]

Chris Twarowski: I just wanna go back to the beginning real quick. So here we are. . . At the back of the book.

Rashed Mian: Yeah.

Chris Twarowski: Boom.

Rashed Mian: That's it? You're just closing it out?

Chris Twarowski: That's it.

Notes

1 The award-winning social justice podcast that incorporates original lyrical contributions from Hip Hop artists, detailed in Chapter Twelve.
2 Feltrinelli. (2013). *Something from nothing: The art of rap*. Milano.
3 KRS-One. (1993). Hip Hop vs. Rap [Song]. On D.I.G.I.T.A.L. [Album]. Front Page Entertainment and X-Ray Records.
4 *Hip Hop at Howard: Hip Hop Studies Conference and Minor Program*. (2024, November 10). Hip Hop Podcast—Hip-Hop Can Save America: The World's Most Important Hip Hop Podcast. https://hiphopcansaveamerica.com/episode/hip-hop-at-howard-hip-hop-studies-conference-and-minor-program
5 *Hip Hop x The Black Voice x Academia with Dr. A.D. Carson*. (2023, June 26). Hip Hop Podcast—Hip-Hop Can Save America: The World's Most Important Hip Hop Podcast. https://hiphopcansaveamerica.com/episode/hip-hop-x-the-black-voice-x-academia-with-dr-ad-carson

Hip Hop Studies and Activism

Edited by
Dr. Anthony J. Nocella II
Dr. Daniel White Hodge
Dr. Don C. Sawyer
Dr. Ahmad R. Washington
Dr. Arash Daneschzadeh

Hip Hop Studies and Activism is the first book series dedicated to hip hop studies. This series is an intersectional, interdisciplinary, liberatory project that promotes justice, equity, and inclusion. *Hip Hop Studies and Activism* will connect with a broad range of disciplines such as feminism, globalization, economics, science, history, environmental studies, media studies, political science, sociology, religion, anthropology, philosophy, education, and cultural studies. Against apolitical scholarship, Hip Hop Studies argue for an engaged critical praxis that promotes a listening and defending space and place for marginalized and silenced communities, especially Communities of Color and Youth of Color. While other book series are more rooted in theory and apolitical analysis, this series is committed to social action, advocacy, and activism. We make a strong effort to publish work by and of People and Youth of Color.

To order other books in this series, please contact our Customer Service Department:
        peterlang@presswarehouse.com (within the U.S.)
        orders@peterlang.com (outside the U.S.)

Or browse online by series:
        www.peterlang.com